W9-ARE-901

WHEN THE TIME COMES

WHEN THE TIME COMES

Families with Aging Parents
Share Their Struggles and Solutions

PAULA SPAN

SPRINGBOARD

NEW YORK   BOSTON

Springboard Press
Hachette Book Group
237 Park Avenue, New York, NY 10017

Visit our Web site at www.HachetteBookGroup.com.

Springboard Press is an imprint of Grand Central Publishing. The Springboard name and logo are trademarks of Hachette Book Group, Inc.

Printed in the United States of America

First Edition: June 2009

10 9 8 7 6 5 4 3 2 1

Library of Congress Cataloging-in-Publication Data
Span, Paula.
    When the time comes : families with aging parents share their struggles and solutions / Paula Span. — 1st ed.
       p. cm.
    ISBN 978-0-446-58113-4
    1. Older people—Care. I. Title.
    HV1451.S653 2009
    362.61—dc22
                                        2008037827

Book Design by Charles Sutherland

For my parents, Ruth Kleban Span and
Murray Span, with gratitude

CONTENTS

WHEN
the TIME
COMES

INTRODUCTION

WAITING IN THE DIRECTOR'S OFFICE FOR OUR TOUR TO BEGIN, I noticed that my father had dressed for this occasion with some care. He'd added a sweater vest and bolo tie to his normal pants and polo shirt, and selected—from his sizable baseball cap collection—a blue one bearing the New York Mets insignia. He wore bifocals, and a hearing aid tucked into each ear, but with a recent haircut and this morning's close shave, he looked almost dapper.

Yet when I moved a bit nearer, I saw that his sweater was stained with food. "You might want to put that vest in the laundry after today, Dad," I suggested carefully.

He shrugged. "I didn't notice." He also didn't notice that his apartment, on the other side of town, was often dusty, the kitchen countertops spattered. A woman came to clean now and then, and he didn't see much point in paying her to come more often, because he couldn't see the dirt.

I admired the way he'd put together a life since my mother died seven years earlier. He lived alone in an apartment building in southern New Jersey. He had good friends. He played cards a couple of nights a week, faithfully attended services and discussions at his synagogue, shopped and cooked (or defrosted, mostly) for himself. He was the guy who went out and bought the newspapers each morning for his neighbors who no longer drove. With prescriptions to keep his cholesterol and blood sugar in line, he was relatively healthy.

My sister and I proudly complained about how hard it was to reach him on the phone. "Up and around!" he always said, when we finally did. "Keeping busy!"

Yet how long could we be this fortunate? How long could he keep driving to the supermarket, handling his checkbook, remembering to take three or four different medications each day? Already, he'd given up driving north to visit us; three hours via the Jersey Turnpike had become too tiring.

Sooner or later, we knew, he would need more help. He'd just turned 83 that fall. Something—eyesight, heart, memory—was increasingly likely to fail. My mother had seemed fine, too, slowing but still engaged with life, until suddenly an exploratory laparoscopy found metastasized cancer, and we had to learn a lot in a hurry about hospice care.

I'd been dreading the next phase ever since. Nobody wants to be facing these questions. We talk sometimes about a role reversal, the children becoming the parents, but it's a flawed analogy. Our elders are not children; they don't have to do what we think best. There's no t-shirt that proclaims, "Because I'm the Daughter, That's Why." And this passage, unlike child rearing, will not result in eventual independence.

Still, we want to do the very best we can for the people who did the best they could for us. Looking ahead, I felt afraid—but I also wanted to understand, to feel prepared, to find a way to give my father comfort, security, dignity. His life may have begun winding down, but there could still be years of good times, friendships, laughs, and love ahead.

Maybe this assisted living facility place was where Dad would want to go, when the time came.

Our tour led past an outdoor courtyard, past the shop where residents could buy toothpaste and greeting cards. "This sitting area's going to have a 45-inch television," the director announced with pride. "You can watch a game together."

"The Eagles have gotta do better this week," my father bantered back.

I was lucky, and unusual, in one respect: my parents had always been clear-eyed about their futures, willing to talk about care and costs and preferences.

"Timing is the key to the whole thing," my father had announced earlier that morning, when we met for breakfast at Denny's. "People wait too long to make these decisions, and then it's decided for them."

So we mulled over some of the key questions again. For the cost of assisted living, I reminded him, we could probably afford enough home care to keep him in his apartment, at least for a while. But that didn't appeal to him.

One of the women in his building—which gerontologists would call (I love this term) a NORC, a Naturally Occurring Retirement Community—had been ill for a long time; an aide came in to help her every day. "Once in a blue moon she gets out, but 90 percent of the time she's in the apartment," Dad reported.

"To me, it's like being in jail. To never see anyone or talk to anyone, it would drive me nuts." He'd rather be with people, having conversations, trading wisecracks. He provided a sample of his repartee: "Hey, how ya doin'? You don't feel good? You're lucky you feel anything at all!"

Yet however suitable an institution appears in glossy brochures, or sounds in abstract discussions, it's often jarring to actually look at the place. Other assisted living apartments I'd seen aimed for elegance. When my mother-in-law moved into a one-bedroom in Rhode Island, for instance, she arrayed her antique chairs and lamps around a spacious, carpeted living room, slept in her own four-poster, hung her favorite prints.

In this place, the furnished small room reminded me, instead, of a spartan college dorm—tiled floor, single hospital-style bed, unadorned desk and bureau, TV mounted on the wall opposite a recliner. The kitchen consisted of a microwave, sink, mini-fridge, and two cabinets. There was a bathroom with a walk-in shower, and a single clothes closet.

"That's the whole closet?" my father said, alarmed by its narrowness. He had sport coats and ties he wore to synagogue, plus winter coats and boots, summer shirts. "I'd have to get rid of a lot of stuff." He could store his out-of-season wardrobe, the director said, but something about the closet brought home to my father how big a change he was contemplating.

The room made me uneasy, too. This particular assisted living—state-supported and more affordable than many—didn't pursue the illusion of an upscale apartment building by substituting a "concierge" for a nurse's station. It didn't put a premium on hominess. It was more honest, perhaps too honest: *This is where you come when you are old and infirm,* the room said. *We'll take care of you, but we're not going to spend money on carpeting when there's a good possibility* (the director quietly pointed out) *of urine stains.*

Later, the tour concluded, we sat on a bench outside the building, taking in the late fall sun, talking over what we'd just seen. We were both chastened.

"The only thing is, the closet will drive me insane," my dad said. "I don't know how I'd manage."

Why was he so fixated on the closet? It seemed harsh to point out that most people who move into assisted living don't go out very often, thus have less need for suits and coats. He was picturing his current self in this new place, I realized, not a diminished man who could no longer live alone.

Of course, it could be years yet before he needed assisted living—but he could also have a health crisis and need a nursing home the following week. Uncertainty was built into the process.

As it happens, our luck holds. Nearly three years later, my father still lives in his NORC, still picks up the paper and drives to card games and goes to synagogue each Saturday morning, selecting a coat and tie from his ample closet. He volunteers to stuff envelopes at the Jewish Federation of Cumberland County. A bout of Bell's palsy has left him with a slightly drooping smile; it also took the hearing in one ear, which wasn't great anyway, and some of his balance. He uses a walker to steady himself now, and he's minus a gallbladder. Otherwise, he's doing well for almost-86.

Though he can make me crazy—we should probably never discuss Middle Eastern politics—he knows he's not immortal. Unlike a lot of adult children, I have my parent's health care proxy, allowing me to make medical decisions if he's incapacitated, and his power of attorney—two of the better gifts he's ever given me. But so far, I haven't had to use either.

So I don't yet call myself—that awkward term—a caregiver. Knowing that I'm nonetheless highly likely to become one is part of what led me to undertake this book.

Another is the conversations I have with friends and acquaintances I run into at the coffee shop, the movies, the supermarkets in the town where I've lived for 25 years. Baby boomers all, we raised our children here, so we used to regularly trade gossip about day care centers, recommend pediatricians, debate the best art classes and middle school teachers. For years, it seems, we talked about APs and SATs and college admissions.

When did that begin to change? Somewhere in my late 40s or early 50s, every other exchange seemed to concern parents. The disputes about giving up the car keys. The promises and realities of assisted living. Geriatricians instead of pediatricians. We've entered a new realm, and we have things to teach one another about it. The family stories I've collected here are intended as a step in that direction.

Our Parents' Keepers

It really is a new realm. "We are living in an age like no other, and everybody is trying to feel their way through it," says Suzanne Mintz, president of the National Family Caregivers Association. "We're learning as we go."

Families have always cared for their elders, but our parents in old age are different from their forebears, just as we boomers are unlike previous generations of adults.

For our parents, there's cause to celebrate. They live longer, in large part because deaths from heart disease and strokes have dropped sharply. In 1970, someone who reached age 65 could expect to live another 15 years, on average. Men who turn 65 now, however, can anticipate another 17 years, and women another 20.

Happily, disability rates in the older population also show a clear downward trend over the past two decades, in every age group. Even among those over 75, more than 80 percent report "no functional limitations requiring assistance from another person," an AARP study recently found. We can probably credit some of this good news to current seniors being wealthier, better educated, less likely to be widowed. Fewer of them are smokers (though too many don't exercise regularly or eat wisely). They're the beneficiaries of improved treatments for chronic diseases; they routinely opt for surgery to replace worn-out knees and hips. It's startling to learn that as recently as the 1970s, almost half the elderly had lost all their natural teeth; now, with better dental care and fluoridated water, that number, though still too high, is closer to 20 percent.

Less obvious changes are also at work. The biggest declines in disability come in what gerontologists call IADLs, instrumental activities of daily living. These are the tasks associated with operating a household: handling money, shopping for groceries and preparing meals, cleaning the house, doing laundry.

Contemporary life has simplified a number of these chores. Elders who might have trouble physically getting to a bank have been able, since the late 1980s, to instead have their Social Security checks directly deposited; they may pay bills online or have them automatically deducted from bank accounts. A wider array of take-out food, the near-universality of microwave ovens, amplifying devices for telephones, Internet shopping—all these can help an elderly person, even if she's not necessarily in better health, to be less restricted, better able to maintain her independence.

Yet disability eventually will come to most of our parents, even if it comes later in life, and when it does—the bad-news side of the equation—it can be more severe than in the past. About half the population aged 85 or older either has a disability or is in a nursing home. When it comes to what gerontologists label ADLs— activities of daily living such as being able to bathe, dress, and feed oneself, to get in and out of bed and use a toilet—seniors who need help need more of it. Both among those in institutions and those still living in the general community, the proportion who need help with more than three of those ADLs has increased. Only a few decades ago, these seniors may not have survived; now that more do, they need higher levels of assistance.

And we're elected.

We've all heard laments, no doubt, about the way people used to take care of their aging parents. In these nostalgic accounts, everybody lived nearby, families unquestioningly took in their elders, grandparents were available to mind the kids and teach them everything from fly fishing to pie baking, and multigenerational serenity somehow reigned. (I personally think this sepia-toned image owes a lot to repeated viewings of *The Waltons*.)

Nowadays, the laments continue, we've all scattered across the country. We're too busy, too distant, too careerist, and perhaps too selfish to take care of our seniors, so we turn them over to hired hands and to institutions. We are harsh critics of ourselves—undeservedly so.

It's true, for reasons I'll explore later, that many fewer parents live with their children compared to a century ago. But it's hardly true that we forsake them. We remain "a nation of caregivers," says Elinor Ginzler, an AARP expert on long-term care. "Family is important to us, and that hasn't changed."

Less than 5 percent of the elderly live in institutions, in fact. Nursing home use has been falling for 20 years, even among those over 85. Overwhelmingly, the people who take care of seniors are the people who always have: their families.

Outside of nursing homes, paid help actually remains quite rare. Among frail seniors living at home, only 18 percent of the assistance received came from paid helpers, Urban Institute researchers have found. Even among those with severe disabilities, nearly 80 percent received no paid help. "If families were not available," says Lynn Feinberg of the Family Caregiver Alliance, "the whole health care system would fall apart."

Assistance for frail elders comes, the majority of the time, from a single individual, one unpaid person. More specifically, it comes from a woman. Spouses are the first line of defense against disability, but when they die or become too fragile themselves for caregiving, daughters and daughters-in-law step in. Though the family stories that make up the bulk of this book include several devoted sons, they remain a minority in this sphere. Seven of every ten adult children who help frail parents are daughters. Among primary caregivers, five of six are daughters.

Fortunately, the notion that we've all fled Walton's Mountain for the Coast is also untrue. Some caregiving is carried on long-distance, but interstate mobility has not increased much in decades, and more than 60 percent of frail elders have at least one child living within ten miles.

Moreover, even when seniors do enter assisted living or nursing facilities, their families stay on the case; most visit at least weekly, continue to monitor their relatives' care, and handle chores from scheduling dentist visits to doing their laundry.

We are, still, our parents' keepers, a situation unlikely to change anytime soon.

Stepping Up

Sometimes, our baptism comes suddenly. We get the phone call we all dread—your dad's had a stroke, your mother fell and broke her hip—and life is not the same again, not for months or years, perhaps not ever. But we can slip gradually into the caretaking role, too. We shudder when Dad's behind the wheel, so our regular visits now include trips to the bank, the pharmacy, and the supermarket. Neither parent wants to inconvenience the doctor with too many questions, so if we want straight answers, we go along to their office visits; after a while, we're the ones making the appointments and following up on the lab work.

It's especially hard to recognize this transition when parents develop Alzheimer's disease or another form of dementia; they can sometimes conceal their lapses and losses for quite a while, and we may not recognize the problem (or want to) until it's inescapable. Perhaps that comes on the Thanksgiving that Mom, an acclaimed cook all her life, puts the turkey in the oven and forgets to turn it on. Maybe the once-immaculate home grows grimy and cluttered with junk mail, or collection agencies start calling because the retired accountant can't seem to balance his checkbook any longer.

One way or another, it becomes clear that our elders need help, or more help. And we step up.

We step up even though we're not terribly well prepared for the job. Boomers don't know much about long-term care, an AARP survey found a couple of years ago. Among those 45 or older, the majority thought Medicare would pay for extended nursing home stays or for assisted living; neither is true. Very few could come close to estimating the average cost of a nursing home or assisted living, or home visits from nurses or aides.

We're reluctant to even ask our parents about what they want should they become disabled or face a serious illness (and so, sadly, are many of their physicians). "Most Americans don't talk about those things and don't want to talk about those things," Feinberg says. "It's the exception, rather than the rule."

True. More than a third of Americans have either given no thought to end-of-life care or have considered it but haven't told anyone their preferences. My father is in a minority with his signed health care proxy and power of attorney documents; only a quarter of Americans have put anything in writing. Even when people are severely or terminally ill, most have no advance directives to tell their doctors and their families what they want done, or not done.

We step up though the work is harder. Hospital stays keep getting shorter, so patients are discharged "sicker and quicker," in need of much more attention. The same medical and technological advances that help keep people out of nursing homes mean that their helpers' responsibilities now extend well beyond household chores. "Families are being asked to take on tasks that would make nursing students tremble," says Feinberg.

Family caregivers are dressing wounds, performing peritoneal dialysis, monitoring symptoms, and overseeing complicated arsenals of medications. Even simple bathing, one of the most common activities seniors need help with, requires skill in order to avoid injuring both the older person and the helper. All these tasks get more difficult if a parent with dementia becomes bewildered, resistant, or hostile.

Increasingly, "caregiving at home has come to take on many of the aspects of a mini intensive-care unit," as one group of experts put it. It involves jobs that licensed nurses used to do, that aides in nursing homes are trained to do, though not trained enough. Sons and daughters are expected, in effect, to join the health care team, usually with no training at all.

We step up despite the fact that most of us have jobs. For years, economists and health care analysts warned that women, as they entered the workforce, would become unavailable to serve as unpaid caregivers for the elderly. A plausible argument—but it hasn't proved to be true. Family caregiving continues at high levels, though more than half of adult children who help their elderly parents also work full-time, and another 10 percent work part-time.

Having dual responsibilities can exact a steep toll. Most caregivers with jobs report sometimes having to go to work late or leave early; smaller proportions take leaves of absence, cut back from full-time to part-time schedules, or turn down promotions. A few even give up work altogether. How often they make these choices depends on how heavy their caregiving duties are. It may also depend on how much they like their jobs; rewarding work can act as a buffer against family stress and has been shown to benefit caregivers' mental health. Still, lost hours and wages can cost caregivers thousands of dollars a year, and make them less able to save for their own senior years.

Nevertheless, when it comes to caring for parents, "work doesn't seem to reduce caregiving much," Urban Institute researcher Richard Johnson told me, trying to explain why women aren't behaving the way forecasters predicted. "They just do it. They suck it up. They make the sacrifices."

We step up despite the considerable expense. The out-of-pocket costs of caring for someone over 50 average more than $5,500 a year, a recent national survey found, causing about a third of caregivers to dip into their savings, cut back on basic home maintenance, or reduce or stop saving for their own futures.

We step up even though we may have children at home. Boomers deferred childbearing, so they can have dependents at both ends of the age spectrum. It's not a large group—in one set of national studies, about 9 percent of the women who were primary caregivers for the elderly also had minor children. But it's large enough that it has spawned its own apt term: the Sandwich Generation.

We step up even if we qualify as elderly ourselves. The bulk of adult children caring for parents are in their 40s and 50s. But seniors' lengthening life spans and declining disability rates can mean that by the time they need our help, we may be close to or in retirement. About one-fifth of caregiving children are 60 or older.

It's a good thing that we do step up. Attempting to pay for the hours families voluntarily devote to eldercare, even at the low wages home health aides receive, would break the national treasury. AARP estimated the economic value of family caregiving in 2006, for disabled people of any age, at $350 billion, roughly equal to the total annual cost of Medicare. Even if families wanted and could afford to pay for assistance, there aren't nearly enough health care workers to begin to pick up the slack. "Family caregiving is essential," says Feinberg. "And undervalued and underrecognized."

When children take on this role, fueled by a complex mix of emotions and motives, by love and obligation, necessity and fear and pride, they're thinking primarily of their parents and parents-in-law. But all of us benefit.

Without Capes

It's this quiet, frequently unrecognized courage and devotion that I find—a curious word, perhaps, when discussing age and frailty—heartening.

For people who haven't yet faced this phase of life, either be-cause they're young or because they've been fortunate, the whole topic seems dismal. "What's your book about?" someone I've just met, or haven't seen in a while, will ask brightly.

"It's about adult children and how they care for aging parents," I say, knowing it's a quick way to kill a dinner party conversation.

The most common response, at least from people under 40: "Isn't that *depressing?*" Those closer to my own age, on the other hand, nod and promptly launch into detailed accounts of their own eldercare sagas—and almost everybody has one.

The truth is, though I've empathized with sons' and daugh-ters' struggles, though I've seen and felt loss, I haven't found this project depressing. To witness families facing painful decisions in demanding circumstances, and to see them take on those duties with patience and generosity, has been moving, uplifting. Spending time with older people grateful to celebrate a 95th birthday with friends, to attend a beloved daughter's bridal shower, to gaze at Edward Hopper's paintings even if walking the museum halls is an effort, has been a privilege.

"If you get depressed about the way things are going in the world, just look at the people caring for their family members, the lengths they go to; there's nothing they won't do," David Ekerdt, director of the gerontology center at the University of Kansas, told me when I first began my reporting. "It can pull you out of any funk about the state of humanity." At the time, I didn't quite understand why it would; now, I get it.

I don't think *heroic* too strong a word for the families who share their stories in this book, though theirs is an understated brand of valor, with no red cape attached. The adult children aren't saintly; at times they grow tired of the responsibility they carry, resentful and exasperated. They can, no question, simply lose it. They often wish they could say, "Here, you take over for a while"—but usually, there isn't anyone to say it to.

Their parents aren't candidates for canonization either. Gener-ally appreciative of their children's efforts, they can also, for rea-sons not always within their control, be demanding and difficult.

Wherever they are—in their own homes or a child's, in assisted living or a nursing home—caring for them is a taxing job.

Still, their children carry on, and if you ask on one of the not-so-bad days, they acknowledge feeling that they're doing something not only crucial for their parents but meaningful for themselves.

Happily, there's more assistance than there used to be. Take adult day programs, aka senior day care. The phrase bothers some people, who find it infantilizing, but it explains the concept: When a parent's being home alone causes anxiety, she can take a van to a bright, cheerful center where she can chat with friends, eat a nutritious lunch, join in a mix of programs—from gardening and crafts projects to exercise sessions—to keep her mind and body active. Trained staffers will monitor her health, help her with bathing or the toilet should she need it. It's expensive, but more affordable than home care and far cheaper than assisted living or a nursing home. Her children are free to go to work, or take a few hours' break from their obligations. And at the end of the day, the parent goes home—which, research shows over and over, is where most elders want to be.

(I've listed organizations, with phone numbers and Website addresses, that can help you find such services in the resources section at the back of the book.)

Because an aging population with purchasing power will always spark new services, even whole new professions, to meet its needs, there's another innovation: the geriatric care manager. Usually a licensed social worker or, less frequently, a nurse or gerontologist, this expert can assess a senior's condition, help a family agree on what kind of help he needs, recommend agencies or programs or facilities, and monitor the situation afterward. She becomes a concerned family's eyes, ears, and Rolodex.

I recently spent a day following geriatric care manager Suzanne Modigliani around suburban Boston as she visited with her elderly clients to see how they were doing, made calls to physicians' offices to follow up on tests and prescriptions, drove one good-natured woman with dementia to her dentist and took her out for lunch afterward. Modigliani, who's been involved in geriatric services in the area for 30 years, has coordinated home care schedules, helped mediate family disputes, recommended physical therapists and financial advisors, arranged for everything from private drivers to therapy dog visits. She and her fellow GCMs aren't cheap either, but she's the one I'd call if I had an ailing parent in her neighborhood—especially if I weren't in the neighborhood myself.

This is a profession on the rise: membership in the National Association of Professional Geriatric Care Managers has more than doubled in a decade, to about 2,100. Similarly, membership in the National Academy of Elder Law Attorneys—elder lawyers handle matter ranging from guardianship proceedings and Medicaid eligibility cases to estate planning—has climbed nearly 50 percent (to 5,000). As the population ages, companies arise to retrofit homes with grab bars and ramps and stair lifts; people hang out shingles as senior move managers and take on the complex task of emptying too-large houses and helping people downsize. You can now hire professional money managers to pay bills and claims specialists to handle insurance tangles.

Part of my purpose in assembling these stories is to spread the word that help of various forms does exist for seniors who need it, even if it's sometimes no picnic to locate or to pay for. But as we've seen, in most families caregiving remains a largely do-it-yourself endeavor, and not a simple one.

Ain't I Rough Enough? Ain't I Tough Enough? Ain't I Rich Enough?

The phrase gerontologists use to describe the difficulties of this role is *caregiver burden*, a catchall for the physical, psychological, and financial stresses of shouldering responsibility for a loved one's well-being. When a Pennsylvania woman grappling with whether or not to place her sickly father in a nursing home admits, "I feel like I'm in a vise," that's caregiver burden. When a New York State woman shuttling between her mother in her own home and her father in a nursing facility a half hour away wonders, "How much do you sacrifice to be a 'good person'?"—that is, too.

It's important to understand, though, that a vise-like sensation of being overwhelmed, of having to do and give too much, isn't universal or even typical. Lots of adult children cope with the demands quite well.

In a national survey of more than 1,200 caregivers, for example, most said they experienced little physical strain, emotional stress, or financial hardship as a result. (The study, undertaken by AARP and the National Alliance for Caregiving, involved people caring for adults of any age, not only parents.) When problems arose, they were related to a combination of how many hours people spent on caregiving and the number of tasks performed, plus the caregivers' own health status and their sense of a choice in assuming that role. The group with the highest "level of burden," devoting the greatest amount of time and performing the most demanding duties, who reported worsening health and felt caregiving wasn't voluntary, were most at risk for trouble; they represented 10 to 30 percent of the sample.

Similarly, a *USA Today*/ABC News poll of baby boomers found that of those providing assistance—personal or financial—to an elderly parent, about half said their help had caused no stress in their own lives and their sacrifices had been minor.

But when it's hard, it's really hard. "I sleep with the car keys in my hand," one daughter with two parents in facilities, her mother in assisted living and her father in an adjoining nursing home, told me. I think she was exaggerating, but perhaps not by much.

How much time it requires is tough to pin down, in part because research sometimes combines all kinds of caregivers, including spouses and friends, who care for any adult. Moreover, averages can conceal enormous differences between an adult child who does some grocery shopping and bill-paying and one who's on duty virtually around the clock.

But the Urban Institute, focusing on the frail elderly, calculated that daughters and daughters-in-law provided an average 98 hours of care a month, and sons and sons-in-law 71 hours; the median, meaning that half the children spent less time than this and half spent more, was 30 hours a month. The time involved rose sharply for elders with severe disabilities: Daughters spent an average 134 hours a month caring for them, nearly equivalent to a full-time job.

Daughters are more likely to provide high levels of hands-on care, too, while sons are more apt to handle tasks like financial management, one study found. This may help explain a finding that surfaced in 2007 when a research team measured how much men and women liked or disliked certain activities. For men, spending time with parents was unpleasant only 7 percent of the time; for women, spending time with their parents led to negative emotions more than a quarter of the time. Princeton economist Alan Krueger, who worked on the team with four psychologists, offered an intriguing explanation. For women, time with parents can come to feel more like work, a task. "For men, it tends to be sitting on the sofa and watching football with their dad," he told the *New York Times*, admitting that he and his dad enjoyed Giants games.

Reams of research underscores that intensive caregiving is associated with poorer health, including high blood pressure and reduced immune function. Caregivers report such chronic conditions as heart disease, arthritis, and diabetes at almost twice the rate of those who aren't caring for sick or disabled family members.

The emotional effects are also well documented: Caregivers have higher stress levels and higher rates of depression. Caregivers may experience feelings of isolation, of being overwhelmed; many say they've sacrificed vacations, hobbies, time for friends or other family members. As the tasks intensify, moving from lighter duties to heavier ones, caregivers report increased depression, worsening health, neglect of their own care. (Again, these studies aren't specific to caring for parents.)

What's particularly taxing and distressing is caring for an elderly person with Alzheimer's disease or another form of dementia. Stress levels are markedly higher in this group, studies consistently show, with greater risk to a caregiver's psychological and physical health because of the nature of the disease.

As dementia progresses, the parent may lose the ability to communicate much, to say thank you, even to recognize the child who is working so hard to keep her safe and comfortable and engaged with life. "Truly, it's the loss of an individual," says Elinor Ginzler of AARP. "I've heard Alzheimer's referred to as 'living death.' I've heard people say, 'I lost her long ago,' and I think it's an accurate statement."

Moreover, contributing to the strains of caregiving, in ways difficult for any statistician to measure, are the complications of family dynamics. This is not just any ailing, elderly person you're concerned about, and her illness may not be the only thing you're battling.

Mom Always Liked You Best

Probably it shouldn't surprise us that loyalties, rifts, and grievances from decades past surface when the time comes. "Some families truly are cohesive," says Barbara Moscowitz, senior social worker at the Massachusetts General Hospital Geriatric Medicine Unit. "But many have lived apart for 20 or 30 years, in different ways with different lifestyles. If you have difficulty coming together as a family on Christmas or Thanksgiving, and the old sibling rivalries rear their heads during a three-day vacation, then why should it be easy for you to suddenly coalesce and make decisions about your parent?"

Moscowitz spends much of each day refereeing, interpreting, and nudzhing as families try to cope with both the crises before them and the tangled histories behind them. She sees parents waving off help they quite evidently need because "we all want to hold on to our roles, whatever age we are. Parents want to be parents." The suggestion that a child take over bill-paying, for a parent who has competently written the monthly checks for 60 years, is unnerving. Independence is such a signal American value that accepting help, even in small increments, can feel threatening.

Conversely, Moscowitz adds, children grow accustomed to seeing their parents as wellsprings of assistance and encouragement, even as those children move into their 40s and 50s. "When suddenly the parent is no longer that source of support and strength upon whom they can lean, it's devastating. There's a lot of grieving."

When several siblings try to apportion responsibility for elder-care, all sorts of psychological underpinnings come into play. Perhaps the son or daughter who was always the Dutiful Child shoulders most of the workload once more, and resents it once more. Perhaps the one who was never the Dutiful Child sees a last chance to win parental approval and takes over, or tries to. It can be a reasonably harmonious process, or one that generates years of bitter discord.

I'm thinking of the Connecticut woman who sent me email, after reading an essay I wrote about my father in the *New York Times*, with the subject line: "I GOTTA STORY!!!"

It was a miserable tale. My correspondent, the oldest of four, had been the primary caretaker for her mother, who had a long history of mental illness. Even with around-the-clock aides, the mother was failing in her own home, so the daughter moved her into a nursing facility. There, with private aides, a psychiatric nurse, and a new drug, she stabilized and appeared content. "We should have been thrilled with what we were able to achieve," the daughter told me.

Instead, her younger sister, who disagreed with the decision to move their mother but wasn't actively involved in her daily care, "continued to throw jabs and second-guess and undermine . . . I just wanted to bop her." Perhaps, the older one speculates, she disliked seeing their mother's estate being drained.

In any case, months after their mother's funeral, my correspondent didn't talk to her sister very often and no longer even wanted to sit next to her at family events. "If you're not willing to step up, then in my book you step back and keep quiet and be supportive," she said, still fuming.

But you also hear stories that make you think the Waltons live. Consider the large family in Glen Ridge, New Jersey, whose widowed father had grown increasingly confused and disabled by Parkinson's disease.

His children called a summit meeting. "It was very democratic, everyone putting in his own thoughts," remembers Kate Waldron, the daughter who hosted the gathering in her living room. It probably helped that she was a nurse and a psychotherapist; it definitely helped that all eight sisters and a brother wanted to share the load. Looking at all the options—the siblings living in one-bedroom apartments, the one whose husband had lymphoma, the newly-wed—Kate and her husband, Jim, agreed that they were the likely candidates to bring Joseph Grady, known to all as Bumps, into their home. They had enough room. They also had jobs, however, and three children at home.

Luckily, Bumps had made enough money from the sale of his house to afford home care aides. He also had a family that figured out how to work together.

Someone handled the scheduling, who would visit when, and passed the word via phone or email. Someone came to spend time with Bumps each weekend, often picking up groceries or drugstore items en route, so Kate and Jim could have a break and a family life. Someone came to stay in the house when they took vacations. "No one ever said, count me out," Kate says. Instead, "I felt enormous gratitude from everybody that we were making it possible to keep him in a family home, not a nursing home."

Their annual meetings continued for seven years. Toward the end, as her father became unable to use a toilet or chew solid food, the bulk of the burden fell on Kate and her family and she wondered if caring for Bumps would become too much for them. She never felt it did. When Bumps died at home in 2004, everyone planned his funeral Mass together. She doesn't require such constant contact with her siblings anymore, Kate reflects, and she misses it.

To Transcend Self

It's easy to sound unforgivably Pollyanna-ish about the silver lining aspect of eldercare. No one could characterize a parent's intensifying illness, or the response it demands from children, as a positive development. Get too chirpy about spirituality or personal growth, and a son or daughter who's lying awake at night, fretting about a parent's health or medical bills, may indeed want to bop you.

But you can't get away from this: The phenomenon called *caregiver gain* doesn't appear nearly as often in academic journals or gerontology texts as caregiver burden, but it exists. And it helps explain why people shoulder this job. Obligation and guilt are hardly the only motivations, stress and fatigue hardly the only consequences.

Rewards also surface when caregivers talk about what they do: pride in being able to meet the challenges, feelings of competence and mastery, a sense of meaning and purpose. The role's enjoyable aspects can coexist with its pressures; they include closer family relationships, warmth and intimacy, feelings of satisfaction and even joy, a University of Wisconsin researcher reported after analyzing numerous studies.

There's a spiritual dimension, as well. Some caregivers told St. Louis University researchers, who'd asked them to describe the ways the experience affected them, that they relied on their faith and their churches; others cited inner strength and more personal spiritual connections. But almost all religions and traditions underscore the importance of serving others, and that's what happens when a parent needs help. In some cases, gerontologist Kenneth Doka has written, "the self-sacrifice that caregiving entails offers a deep sense of personal fulfillment. It demonstrates a persistent ability to transcend self—to sacrifice for another without regard to one's own needs."

Does that sound too grandiose? A daughter-in-law I spoke with not long ago couched her satisfaction in more modest terms. Beverly Lazar Davis and her husband turned the parlor of their home in Saratoga Springs, New York, into a bedroom/sitting room for his father, Herman Raymond Davis, a retired dentist and lifelong artist. "Papa" was 96 when he came to live with them, and "he was a jewel," said Beverly, a clinical social worker.

She spent countless hours with him, reading to him, listening to Johnny Cash albums, watching *60 Minutes* every Sunday. She particularly cherished their "adventures," when they set forth with no particular destination, Beverly pushing Papa's wheelchair down the street until they encountered an interesting art gallery or a Japanese maple worth pausing to appreciate, or settled on a bench outside a downtown coffee shop to watch the passing parade.

"Time with Papa helped me to slow down and breathe," she reflected, after his death. He'd wanted to live to celebrate his 100th birthday, and he did. "He helped me to take out my mandolin after dinner and play a few tunes. He helped me take a walk and smell the lilacs. He helped me sit and watch a cooking show on TV that I wouldn't have seen, or listen to part of an opera. The pace of my life since he has passed is going all too fast; he helped me get off the train."

About This Book

I think of *When the Time Comes* as a support group in print.

Even under the best of circumstances, taking on responsibility for a parent introduces some degree of worry and effort into a family's life. Among the things that help are money, information, and emotional support.

Money, I can't do much about.

But I've packed information—about everything from how much home care can cost to what's likely to get a parent discharged from assisted living—into each chapter. I haven't written a step-by-step eldercare manual; a number of those already exist, and I've included a couple in the resources section. But I do want the book to be useful, and I think it is. It draws on hundreds of studies and articles, plus interviews with some of the leading researchers, experts, and advocates in the field.

At the heart of the book, though, are the detailed stories of individual families grappling with how to help their aging parents, and reaching a variety of decisions for a variety of reasons. One family decides to keep their 86-year-old mother in her own apartment in the Bronx for as long as possible by hiring home aides; one moves their mother into a daughter's household in upstate New York. Two families in the Boston area consider assisted living. Two others place their elderly parents in a high-quality nursing home outside Trenton. And in Baltimore, two families whose parents face terminal illnesses seek the help of a hospice organization.

I spoke with both children and parents, in most cases before they reached these decisions, and followed them for up to a year afterward to see how things were going, what was working and what wasn't, how everyone felt about their transitions.

As a veteran journalist, and now a teacher of future journalists at Columbia University, I observed the same ethics and practices I used daily during 16 years as a *Washington Post* reporter. These are real people, not composites or inventions; except for one daughter who insisted on using only her first name and her father's, they're fully identified. (I have, where noted, changed the names of families' employees.)

I listened to these parents, sons, and daughters talk about their histories and fears and satisfactions for many hours. I went along as they looked at facilities; I watched parents move into them and, in one case, move out. I took notes as nurses and social workers and geriatric care managers visited. I went to church services with an 86-year-old parishioner. I helped a 96-year-old eat dinner when her hands grew too shaky to effectively wield a fork. I attended a birthday party and a funeral.

People welcomed me into their homes and their lives, and they were thoughtful and candid about their experiences—all during tense, even frantic times when having any stranger around, let alone a journalist with a tape recorder, could have felt intrusive and far too time-consuming. Why did they agree to participate?

I think, in part, it was sometimes helpful just to have someone listen, something reporters learn to do well. For the children, taking on the care of a father or mother, however and wherever, is a seismic event, a major turning point. It's work that often goes unnoticed, that may not draw much gratitude. For the parents, approaching a point in life when they were no longer able to live fully independently was also momentous. To be able to muse aloud about the whys and what-ifs, to express the inevitable doubt and conflicting impulses and apprehension, perhaps came as something of a relief to both parties.

But I think these families' cooperation mostly comes down to that overworked word: *support*.

What we usually mean by it is the sense that someone else has gone through a similar situation, understands what we're confronting, allows us to express ourselves, accepts our feelings without judgment, and perhaps in sharing her own experience leads us to ideas and solutions that can improve our own. Americans believe in support groups; they exist for people who overeat, who are infertile, who gamble compulsively. They exist for caregivers.

But support outside the traditional group setting can also be valuable. For instance, researchers at the State University of New York at Albany found that adult children caring for their frail parents suffered less burden and depression, and had greater knowledge and use of community services, when they participated in a weekly support group via telephone; other studies have also found "telesupport" helpful.

Talking with friends or relatives is already one of the most common ways caregivers cope with the demands they face, surveys show. (Topping the list: praying.) In interviews with primary caregivers for elderly relatives with dementia, most of them adult children, researchers found that those with "experientially similar" people in their social networks had less psychological distress. They felt understood and supported, even though their contacts with these people were informal, not part of any organized intervention.

Agreeing to have their stories published was one way for the families I visited to have contact with thousands of others in parallel predicaments, people they would never meet but wanted to help. Caring for elderly parents had set them on steep learning curves; they hoped that talking about what they were experiencing and discovering might be useful to somebody else. I hope so, too.

I sometimes hesitate to applaud too loudly for the way families care for their senior members, because I'm reluctant to reinforce the status quo. It shouldn't be so challenging for families to undertake this mission. A great many families need more help than they get, know where to find, or can afford. Support and information only take them so far; tax credits, flexible workplaces, and shifts in Medicaid policies might help more.

Still, I do applaud. Children wondering how on earth they're going to manage this job may not appreciate platitudes about God never giving them more than they can handle. In fact, I'm sure they wish that Commandment about honoring one's father and mother was a bit more specific. But when I see how they rise to the challenge, I'm awed.

A Great Woman

Let me show you a close-to-home example.

Marla Shachtman lives in my town, Montclair, New Jersey, in a small house that reflects the lively chaos of raising two young boys. What would have been the dining room has become a playroom instead, strewn with Legos and robot parts. "Don't trip over Buzz Lightyear," Marla cautioned, the first day I went to see her.

Framed family photographs filled the living room mantel: The annual July 4 reunion. Weddings. Newborns. And Marla's parents, Bob and Doris Levy, in a picture taken on a cruise a decade earlier. "They had a really happy marriage," Marla said with a sigh. "Years of good health and fun and good times."

Marla was 45, a warm, ample woman with wire-rim spectacles and flyaway hair tucked into a barrette. She had an MBA and had worked in marketing, but she'd been home with her kids for several years. And for the first few months I knew her, she wept during every conversation. She'd been through a dreadful time.

Marla's mother had been diagnosed, in her late 50s, with multiple sclerosis; over time, it had taken much of her mobility, and caused deepening dementia. But her husband, vigorous and buoyant after a successful kidney transplant, was taking excellent care of her.

So it came as a horrible shock, in the spring of 2006, when he developed pneumonia and then severe multiple infections. A supposedly brief hospital stay turned into weeks in intensive care. When doctors said there was nothing more they could do, it was up to Marla to direct them to turn off the ventilator. She sat holding her father's hand, telling him how deeply he was loved, as he died.

And now it fell to Marla—because her brother and his family lived overseas—to wade into a series of tasks she felt utterly unprepared for. As executor of her father's estate, she had to deal with insurance, trusts, investments, a host of things she barely understood. More urgently, she had to figure out how to care for her mother, only 71.

All the while, her grief at her father's death was so raw that she was seeing a therapist and looking for a bereavement group. "I'm blindsided by all of this," she told me, her eyes filling. I was distressed to have upset her, but she waved off my apology. "I cry all the time. I cry at the post office. I cried at Denny's the other day because I used to go there with my parents."

Early on, Marla had thought her mother might possibly live with her, and she brought Mrs. Levy to Montclair for a kind of trial run.

But with Mrs. Levy sleeping on a futon in the playroom, "there's no privacy," Marla found. The boys had to pick every toy up, lest her mother—who used a walker—trip and fall. Mrs. Levy was incontinent. And with her dementia, "at 7 o'clock, if she was tired, she'd get undressed and put her nightgown on, no matter what."

What particularly chilled Marla was the night she heard Mrs. Levy moving around downstairs at 5 a.m. "I came down—it was pitch black—and she had the front door wide open," Marla recounted. "She was dressed for the day, in her street clothes, sitting in a chair. I said, 'Mom, what's going on? It's the middle of the night.' She said, 'I'm waiting for my brother to come take me to see my husband.'

"This wasn't the right place for her," Marla concluded. "It wasn't right for my family, either."

So she was looking for an assisted living facility where Mrs. Levy would be comfortable, well cared for, and close by. I tagged along on her scouting expeditions, and so did five-year-old Teddy, because—the Sandwich Generation in spades—school was over for the summer and Marla had no child care.

The first place she checked out was a porticoed building surrounded by gardens that reminded her of a Palm Beach hotel. The marketing director asked about Mrs. Levy's condition. "She needs help bathing," Marla said, ticking off the ADLs. "She's incontinent. She has dementia."

But, she added quickly, "she has a sweet personality. She can carry on a conversation; she has a sense of humor." Some assisted living facilities, she'd learned, wouldn't accept applicants with behavioral problems. "She was a wonderful, competent woman"— Marla was weeping now. "It's an awful situation."

She toured perhaps half a dozen places, Teddy in tow, and she cried at each of them.

The facility she eventually selected served only residents with dementia. It was divided into four smaller "houses," each with its own dining room, living area, and bathing room, an approach thought to reduce the disorientation that could result from moving everyone around several times a day. Aides were assigned to a specific house, so that they'd get to know their residents and vice versa. Like most dementia facilities, it secured its front door so that residents couldn't wander away. But its rear doors opened onto a large fenced yard with paths and benches, so that they could wander safely.

"I was expecting the worst, but it was sort of pleasant," Marla said after her first visit. "I could see her here." Still, when she first moved her mother in, she made sure to be there daily.

Doris Levy was a plump, smiling redhead who liked to laugh. Greeting her daughter with silly jokes and kisses, she could hold a reasonable-sounding conversation. But she might also lose her way en route to the dining room or, heartbreakingly, wonder aloud where her husband had gone.

"I'm her whole connection to who she is and who she was," Marla said, explaining her attentiveness. "I remind her that she's an important person, that she has a family who loves her." The staff assured her that her mother was settling in, but Marla, still struggling with everything she had to do and everything she'd lost, couldn't relax.

The fall passed. Marla brought Mrs. Levy to the family's Thanksgiving dinner and took her out on her birthday. She took the boys to visit, and even though her mother couldn't recall their names, she was happy to see them.

Over the next six months, I saw Marla begin to regain her equilibrium. If life wasn't the way it had been, it was more manageable, less crisis-driven. She got a grip on the estate and the finances. The Shachtmans took a Disney World vacation. Marla wasn't crying much anymore.

"I think it's the right place, or as close as I can get," she said after one visit with her mother. She had fulfilled her father's expectations, she decided. She missed him daily, but "I don't have any guilt. I'm doing what I'm supposed to do, what he wanted me to do. He'd be pleased."

When a professor friend at a nearby state college needed a part-time administrator, Marla welcomed the prospect of working on a campus—a welcome counterpoint to spending so much time among the ailing and elderly. She took the job and liked it. The 15-hour-a-week schedule meant that she could ferry the kids to school and still visit her mother twice a week.

Mrs. Levy seemed stable, at ease. The day would come, Marla knew, when this period, demanding as it was, would seem like the good times. But for now, a year after her father's death, "I'm taking a breather from agonizing over whether I did the right thing."

Nothing about this was fair. Marla's contemporaries were taking vacations with their parents, or leaving the kids with their parents so they could vacation *à deux*. Marla was taking on obligations most of them wouldn't face for a decade. But she had stepped up, in the midst of her own grief, and she'd done a fine job.

The last time I went along on a visit, we found her mother in the community room; she beamed when Marla approached and held her arms out for an embrace.

"Where are you going?" Mrs. Levy asked.

"I'm coming here to see you," Marla said cheerily.

"I love you."

"I love you, too."

They sat in the lounge, Marla reporting on the boys' latest school triumphs. Mrs. Levy pointed out that every passing aide was "super nice." It was clear, when she clasped a tablemate's hand or had a little conversation with a neighbor, that she'd made some friends. There was a brief spasm of grief when she somehow remembered that her husband was gone, but Marla reminded her mother that they'd had a terrific life together, then quickly segued into a joke and got a laugh.

"Marla's such a super person," Mrs. Levy said, turning to me. "She's a great woman. A great, great woman."

And I was inclined to agree.

ONE

STAYING PUT

Home Care

ON A SPRING SUNDAY, SHIRLEY GRILL WAS STEERING HER BLACK Volvo toward the George Washington Bridge and her mother's house in the Bronx, plotting her strategy. Assuming everything went as planned, this would be a significant moment, a turning point.

As Shirley drove in from New Jersey, a young Polish woman was taking the subway from Queens, heading toward the same address off Pelham Parkway. If this candidate passed muster, if her references checked out, if she took the job, then months of cajoling, blustering, warning, and imploring by Shirley and her sister would pay off. After nearly 30 years of living alone, Dora Appel, their 86-year-old mother, would finally have a live-in companion and caregiver.

Shirley was ticking off her employment requirements as we drove; I'd come along to watch this new phase unfold. "I want this woman to be able to have a basic conversation with me," she began. Home care workers in New York City are frequently recent immigrants, and frequently Eastern European. That posed no problem—Shirley's mother had grown up in a small Polish town and spoke Polish, Russian, and a little German, plus Yiddish and Hebrew. But Shirley wanted the aide they hired to be able to communicate with *her*, too, which meant having a reasonable command of English. "I want her to be able to go to the pharmacy, which is within walking distance. And to be able to call for help and articulate what's needed."

She also wanted "someone incredibly careful about safety, hovering when my mother's walking, helping her," Shirley continued. "I don't want her going up and down the stairs alone, it makes me crazy."

The precipitating event in this years-long campaign for additional help was that a month earlier, Mrs. Appel had walked literally around the corner to her cousin's house and taken a very nasty fall. It sent her to the hospital for five days, and she'd yet to fully regain her strength. Now, Shirley didn't want to take any chances.

Most important, she hoped this helper would have a good heart and an easygoing disposition. *Feisty*, the word so often invoked to describe the spirited elderly, barely sufficed for Mrs. Appel. Unstoppably independent, she didn't really need much hands-on care; she could bathe and dress herself, still did some cooking, handled her own medications and maintained her checkbook, read the *New York Post* daily and then shared it with her next-door neighbor. Her live-in helper would mostly keep house while simultaneously keeping a watchful eye on her employer. In terms of duties, "it's actually an easy job," Shirley thought.

But Mrs. Appel was particular about many things, from the way meat loaf was seasoned to the way the towels in the linen closet were folded; she also kept a kosher kitchen, necessitating separate sets of dishes, utensils, even sponges, according to the Jewish dietary laws. This helper had to therefore grasp and accept myriad dos and don'ts—while maintaining affection toward the person issuing them. "My mother needs someone who will treasure her," Shirley said.

Shirley was 59, a droll, energetic redhead who kept her Black-Berry *and* her cell phone clipped to her waistband. A business consultant and a civic and religious leader in her town, she radiated extreme competence. "I want *myself* there," she recognized.

That wasn't in the cards: Shirley and her husband lived 40 minutes away in Montclair, New Jersey. Now that their two children were grown, she traveled frequently for her work. Her sister, Anita Appel, who lived in Manhattan, headed the New York City office of the state mental health department and was also often on the road. Anita called her mother every morning, Shirley every evening, and one or both came to see her each week, bringing groceries, prescriptions, a bunch of flowers, or some other small gift. Shirley took her to her cardiology appointments; Anita filled in when Shirley was away.

They were both, therefore, already functioning as caregivers; gerontologists would say they were assisting with IADLs, instrumental activities of daily living.

But since neither could be on the scene daily, "I want a surrogate," Shirley said. For the past month, "I've had no other thought in my head than, 'What are we going to do about my mother?'"

⚶

Mrs. Appel lived in a neighborhood of modest brick houses with tiny front yards filled with rosebushes and carefully tended flower beds. She and her husband, Morton, who'd owned a kosher butcher shop, had bought this two-family house, their first and only real estate venture, in 1968. He died in 1978—he was just 62—and since then, she'd lived there on her own.

She was enormously proud of her educated, successful daughters—on a previous visit, she'd shown me all their diplomas and awards, framed on her bedroom wall—and she greeted Shirley with a big hug and a wide grin. Mother and daughter had the same lively eyes.

"I love the haircut, it's adorable!" Shirley cooed. Mrs. Appel had acquired what used to be called a pixie cut; its silver bangs covered the scar on her forehead from her fall and the stitches it had required. Short and round, she was wearing a brown skirt, a striped sweater, and—significantly—a pendant that would summon help in case of emergencies. Anita had been paying the monthly charge for this device for five years, during which it had died from disuse.

Shirley had recently put it back in service and extracted a promise from her mother that she would wear it.

"I have two beautiful kids, God bless them," Mrs. Appel liked to say, bragging about how protective they were. "I can't complain."

The truth was, both beautiful kids wished she would sell this house and move already. The place needed extensive repair. The washer was down in the basement; using the clothesline—there was no dryer—required leaning precariously over the back porch railing. Their mother's apartment was on the second floor, so merely taking a daily walk involved a steep flight of cement steps. It struck them as an increasingly hazardous environment for a woman who'd had her first heart attack in 1982 and a pacemaker since 1988, who needed half a dozen prescriptions for congestive heart failure and hypertension, who could no longer shop for groceries or walk the two long blocks to the synagogue for Friday night services.

Several years ago, Shirley had taken her mother to look at a Jewish independent living community near her home in New Jersey. "I thought she'd have a better quality of life at one of these places," Shirley said. And last summer, Anita had found another possible residence in the Riverdale section of the Bronx, part of the Hebrew Home for the Aged. Both offered pleasant private apartments with kitchens, along with kosher meals, social and cultural activities, and housekeeping. They were expensive, but by selling the house, Mrs. Appel could afford them for years—as many years, Shirley thought, as she was likely to live with her chronic illnesses.

The first facility had alarmed her mother, who cried, "You're making me do this! You're taking my freedom! There's too many old people." Tears, fright, resistance—"I backed away," Shirley said. But the intervening years had brought increased frailty; maybe this time, the sisters thought last summer, she'd go for it, move to the Riverdale complex.

"I thought it was perfect," Anita told me. "My mother is incredibly social, loves to talk, loves to play games. I thought she'd get into it and have fun."

"It looked like we were close," Shirley said. Then they made a second visit, and a third. "We spent more time there and what we saw—I could feel it happening—was women bent over their walk-ers," Shirley recounted. "She said, 'I can't live here. I want to live in my own house.' So I backed away again."

Two matters nobody had to mention, because everyone was acutely aware of them, heightened her reluctance. Lots of seniors are uneasy about leaving their homes. But Mrs. Appel had also lost almost everyone—mother, sister, brother, an entire extended fam-ily—in the Nazi camps, escaping death herself only because her brother had paid a priest's family to hide her. After the war, she'd spent six years in a displaced persons' camp in Munich, where she married her husband and where Shirley was born. (Anita, the fam-ily joke went, was "the American.") Any sense of being corralled or pressured, therefore, could trigger reactions from that traumatic era, never far from her mind.

Then there was the Gertrude factor. Morton Appel's family had been decimated as well, but an uncle and aunt had survived and emigrated to New York; they took the Appels, who followed in 1951, into their own apartment. Gertrude was their daughter, technically Mrs. Appel's cousin by marriage, but always more like a younger sister. Their closeness, Anita said, "goes back so long and it's so deep."

They functioned like one family. Gertrude and her husband bought a brick house in the Bronx and the Appels soon moved as close as possible; their backyards adjoined. Mrs. Appel still spent every Friday night and Saturday with Gertrude and her husband; it was Gertrude's house she'd been walking to when she fell. They spoke multiple times each day. Gertrude, 15 years younger, did Mrs. Appel's grocery shopping. To Mrs. Appel, leaving her home meant leaving Gertrude, an unfathomable separation. Anything, even having a stranger move into the unused bedroom next to hers, was better.

So she would stay, even though "my preference is that she move to a facility," Shirley said. Home care seemed iffy to her. "The aides come and go. There are disruptions . . . It doesn't feel stable." Yet her mother's intransigence was somehow reassuring, as well as maddening. This was a woman who, however physically diminished, knew precisely what she wanted and wasn't afraid to insist on it. "I'm glad she has that will," Shirley admitted. "The minute she turns the decision over to me, she has no interest in living. Her will has kept her alive."

So someone named Alina was en route to the Bronx. Shirley had located her through an agency specializing in domestic workers from Poland. It wasn't a true home health agency (more about that later) that trains its employees and provides supervision; this business might more properly be called a registry. It charged Shirley a hundred bucks and supplied a few names, but took no responsibility for what happened once someone was hired.

Shirley was okay with that. She trusted her own interviewing skills, honed by years in corporate human resources, and she trusted her mother's ability to tell her if anything was wrong. (In fact, she was braced for a rash of complaints.) With Gertrude and Anita and herself often in and out of the house to monitor the situation, she thought she could do as good a hiring job as an agency.

As they awaited Alina, Mrs. Appel made a last stab at warding off live-in help. "You know, I was thinking," she said casually. "The woman who comes to clean on Thursday for four hours—if I can get her one more day for four hours . . ."

"I don't want you alone in the house," Shirley interrupted. "That was our agreement." There was some urgency: Gertrude spent two months in the Catskills each summer. Mrs. Appel hadn't been walking much, hadn't been strong enough to return to the cardio rehab program she used to attend. She still exhaled deeply, with a string of *oy*s, whenever she lifted herself out of her favorite recliner or sank into it. Someone had to be on the scene, her daughters thought, before Gertrude left for the mountains.

"I don't need steady help, Shirley. Thank God, I am walking and talking and doing everything."

Shirley wasn't about to cave. "The agreement is, we have someone in the house with you," she said. "We'll find somebody nice."

Alina turned out to be 27, a slender blonde in a white sweater. (I've changed her name and those of Mrs. Appel's other employees.) She lamented, in English, the cold spring weather. Mrs.

Appel told her, in Polish, all about her accident and how copiously she'd bled.

Alina was from Krakow, a onetime economics student. "I came in January last year," she said in accented but comprehensible English. "I came in Chicago and from Chicago, I came here. A friend in New York called and said she would find for me a job." She'd worked as a "houseworker companion" for an Italian woman who was "very sick, liver cancer," and then for an Italian man in his 90s, she said in response to Shirley's gentle interrogation. She was staying with friends in Queens "for now."

Shirley, watching her mother chatting comfortably and thinking *this could work*, asked about her previous duties, outlined the family's expectations, led a quick tour. Mrs. Appel drew Alina into the living room, with its array of family photographs, and she duly exclaimed over the children and grandchildren. "The room of memories," she said. As for her salary, she said she wanted $100 a day—fairly standard for live-ins in New York—with Sundays off.

"So, Alina, what do you think?" Shirley said after half an hour. Lots of times, supposed job candidates didn't even show up for interviews. "Do you want to try this?"

She did. They agreed that, pending Shirley's calls for references, Alina would move in Wednesday afternoon. Then Shirley drove her mother around the corner to Gertrude's house, carefully watching Alina help Mrs. Appel down the stairs, into the car, out of the car.

"This is someone who could be warm and supportive," was Shirley's conclusion as she drove home. "Very respectful of my mother. Offered information about herself in an appropriate way. She's got the skills I need. She's got the language. She has a cell phone and can call me. She could go to the doctor with my mother, if need be. She clearly has some level of education, she's overqualified for this job, but for the moment, this is what she can do. And, she needs a home."

Shirley suspected that Alina had overstayed a visa and was, therefore, illegal. "So I can never run for president." She shrugged, unperturbed.

"I didn't think it would go this fast," I said.

"It's not over till it's over," Shirley cautioned.

True enough.

Next

When I drove in with Shirley a few weeks later, a stocky, gray-haired Polish woman with spotty English—Magda—was setting the dining room table for lunch. "Hello thank you how are you?" Magda said, as Shirley toted in groceries. "Very hot today."

And what of Alina? When Shirley called her supposed previous employer, she got the troubling feeling that the woman wasn't really that elderly Italian man's granddaughter, but a friend of Alina's. Consulting a reverse phone directory online, Shirley found not the name Alina had provided, but a Polish one. On top of which, Alina was saying she had business at the consulate on her Wednesday start date, and couldn't begin work until Sunday.

"She has to understand that the most important value here is that I can trust her to tell me the truth," Shirley thought. A previous job that perhaps hadn't worked out, a young foreigner afraid to say so—that, Shirley could understand. But she couldn't put up with dishonesty. Alina maintained her story, however, and declined to come for an orientation session until Sunday. "At which point," Shirley said, "I knew we were done."

On to Aide Number Two. Magda, on the job for a couple of weeks now, had come recommended by her friend, Gertrude's longtime cleaning woman. That made her "a known quantity," in Shirley's mind and her mother's.

"The truth is, my mother hates having someone in the house," Shirley reported on the trek into the Bronx. "*Hates* it." She understood. "There's not a lot to do in my mother's apartment. How many times can you clean four rooms? So, imagine someone sitting around your house, reading the paper, doing nothing—and you're paying them."

Yet to Shirley's mind, Magda had already proved her worth in a crisis. The very day she arrived, a relentless rainstorm flooded the basement of the house, cutting off the heat, causing Mrs. Appel great anxiety. Having someone there to help mop up, and to steady the homeowner, had been very useful.

Worse, Shirley called her mother one evening and immediately realized that she'd had a stroke. "She was slurring her words. She was not responsive. I knew. I *knew*." Magda, also recognizing the twisted mouth and limp left arm as an urgent situation, had already called Gertrude, who had already taken Mrs. Appel to her doctor, who had indeed diagnosed a transient ischemic attack or TIA, sometimes called a "mini-stroke."

Although the visible symptoms had abated by the next morning, as often happens, Shirley thought her mother was continuing to deteriorate; she was less active, more forgetful, perhaps depressed. So having someone else in the house seemed even more crucial.

Mrs. Appel, sitting with me in the dining room as Magda heated the quiche Shirley had brought for lunch and Shirley washed the salad greens, had her own expectations. Yes, she was feeling awfully weak, she admitted. Still, "I always hope, in another week, another week, I'll be back to myself and I won't need help all the time." Maybe by the end of the summer.

Whereas Shirley, who'd been traveling a lot (and found, with mingled relief and dismay, that she got great cell phone reception all across Europe), wondered whether an independent living community would even accept her debilitated mother now. Magda, or someone like her, wasn't going away.

After lunch, after some of Mrs. Appel's famous sugar cookies—Shirley could instantly taste that she'd left out a key ingredient—we withdrew to the living room.

And the complaints began. "She upset me so this morning," Mrs. Appel reported, meaning Magda. She segued into Yiddish, telling Shirley that "it was like a wind blew over her. She woke up with a *dybbuk* "—a devil—"inside."

I asked what Magda did for her. The response was an eloquent shrug. "What does she do? Whatever she wants, she does. Look at this, look at this couch." Mrs. Appel gestured toward the long orange and green floral sofa. "We live here since 1968. I have friends come and I raise kids and the little ones you see"—in the clustered photos of her family and Gertrude's—"are here most of the time. Look how dirty it is."

I stared at the couch and confessed that it didn't look dirty at all.

Triumph! "So you see," Mrs. Appel declared, "what a big job she has."

It wasn't entirely clear to Shirley whether her mother disliked Magda in particular, or would dislike anyone in that role. "I don't think we have the right person," she mused, ferrying me to a farther-away subway station, so that I could return to New Jersey. At that moment, driving through the Bronx for a few additional minutes was soothing compared to returning and dealing with her mother.

By the time she got back, Mrs. Appel had walked, unassisted, to Gertrude's house, where she announced that Magda had left and wasn't coming back. She'd fired her.

Where the Heart Is

The AARP regularly polls seniors across the nation and asks, among many other questions, where they would like to live as they age. The consensus is overwhelming, says AARP's Elinor Ginzler: "People tell us again and again and again—they want to have the care they need brought to them in the setting of their choice. And the setting of their choice is not an institution."

It's home, "not just the house itself, but the community in which that house is placed," Ginzler goes on. "It's where their neighbors are. It's where they have not just their stuff but their memories. It's where they spent all their years. Those are enor-mously powerful."

Most people stay. They remain "in the community," as gerontolo-gists refer to the noninstitutionalized. They say things like, "The only way I'm leaving this house is feetfirst." Even among the very elderly, those 85 and older, more than 80 percent are *not* in nursing homes.

When they need help—and more than a third of those over 80 do report needing assistance because of a disability—they turn to their families. Paid help for the frail or disabled elderly is rare. "It's pretty much as it's always been," says Gail Hunt of the National Alliance for Caregiving. "Families take care of people at home."

Perhaps that's why introducing paid home care can cause apprehension; it hasn't been the norm. For the parent, the entrance of strangers into the household can feel intrusive, awkward, even frightening—an unwelcome sign of dependency. "I always wonder how I would feel," one social worker confessed, "if someone I'd barely met said, 'Okay, honey, it's time for your shower.'"

The children may also balk at paid home care, believing they should be able to handle their elders' needs in the traditional way. "Consciously or unconsciously, we have to make our peace if we're not doing it ourselves," says Donna Schempp of the Family Caregiver Alliance.

Moreover, to this generation of Depression-era seniors, home help often seems horrifyingly expensive, even if they can pay the tab. They want to leave the assets they've managed to accumulate to their families, I've often heard seniors say, not spend it on a succession of aides. (And of course, whether or not they say so, children sometimes share that sentiment.)

So home help can be a hard sell. In a telephone survey of California residents, the preference for help from family or friends was pronounced: about a third of respondents would ask a relative or friend to help, and another 30 percent would pay a relative or friend. A minority preferred to hire outsiders.

For the recipient, then, paid home care may have little appeal. But while there may not be much of a carrot, there is a stick: This sometimes represents the only way to remain in familiar surroundings. When health worsens or memory declines, when a family can't provide enough care, either because relatives have jobs, live too far away, or are beginning to endanger their own well-being, then the next step is home care. Or it's a move.

In theory, almost everyone could stay at home. Short of surgery, virtually any form of health care—kidney dialysis, physical therapy, wound care, intravenous medication—can be delivered in a private home. Companies have sprung up to modify homes for safety and accessibility; they install grab bars and toilet risers, ramps and stair lifts.

Since capitalism abhors a vacuum, the growth of a more affluent group of seniors, and other disabled people determined to remain independent, has fostered a raft of new businesses. Is your parent doing pretty well at home, except that she can't handle the bill-paying any longer? Or drive to the supermarket? Or manage small chores like changing lightbulbs? You can hire firms, or sometimes find social service agencies or volunteers, to do all those things.

Whether you should, whether a frail or ailing parent ought to stay at home, is another question. Home is so favored over any other alternative that staying put has become an aim in itself, regarded as the highest good, and families turn themselves inside out to make it possible.

"But there's no question that it's not the right answer for everybody," Gail Hunt points out. Figuring out who will do well at home is a complicated equation.

Seniors who live alone, for example, can find themselves increasingly isolated. Nearly a third of the elderly, and half of women over 75, live alone. That's not always a problem. For an older person who has maintained strong community ties—the weekly bridge group, fellow parishioners who visit regularly, neighbors and friends of long standing—home probably still is where the heart is.

But a senior who has outlived friends, whose social relationships are disrupted by her confusion or immobility, can find home a bleak place. Possibly the house has six or seven rooms, but the occupant's world has shrunk to an armchair in front of the TV, a bed, and a bathroom, with occasional forays to the kitchen. "Introverts are going to be fine being more isolated, home alone," says Schempp. "Extroverts are going to be depressed."

Health also matters. Many illnesses can be managed successfully at home, including the early to middle stages of Alzheimer's disease and other forms of dementia. But if dementia causes agitation, problem behaviors, a need for constant supervision, then keeping someone at home becomes markedly more difficult. It will be hard to hold on to aides for a senior who hits or uses abusive language, or wanders the neighborhood, or doesn't sleep well and therefore needs supervision both day and night. It will similarly be hard to care at home for someone large enough to be a "two-person transfer," meaning that a single caregiver, paid or unpaid, can't physically move her from bed to wheelchair to toilet seat.

Safety concerns come into play. In case of an emergency, is a parent at home capable of dialing 911 and giving her address? Will she remember to push the button on her emergency pendant?

"We should not always be so quick to make that commitment, 'I will never put you in a nursing home, Mom,' " says Hunt. "Sometimes, that's going to be the best option."

Moreover, even when paid help at home does seem a reasonable choice, it's not always easy to arrange. There's a shortage of good home care aides, who provide a variety of services and go by a number of titles, including "certified nursing assistant," "home health aide," "personal care attendant," or simply "homemaker" or "companion." Difficult to find, they can be even more difficult to keep; estimates of annual turnover rates range from 25 percent to 40 to 60 percent.

This is a paraprofessional workforce that's predominantly female, and heavily minority and immigrant; about a quarter speak a language other than English at home. Almost a third have some college education; a similar proportion lack a high school diploma. The median hourly wage of home care workers who are full-time agency employees, $11 in 2007, doesn't differ greatly from aides who work in hospitals or nursing homes. But home care aides are much less likely to land full-time jobs; many work part-time or part of the year. They're even more poorly paid than aides in facilities, therefore, and more than a third have no health insurance.

It's not surprising, given these conditions, that so many sooner or later leave their jobs—mostly, sooner. "People will be able to make more money flipping burgers at McDonald's than providing home care," says Lynn Feinberg of the Family Caregiver Alliance.

Still, more families might hire home aides for elderly parents, if they could afford to. Last year, an annual nationwide survey of home care costs found that consumers paid agencies an average $20 an hour for home health aides who provide hands-on assistance with activities of daily living, and $18 for homemakers and companions. So having a homemaker spend four hours a day in a senior's home each weekday, a modest level of help, can cost more than $1,400 a month.

You can pay much less if you live in Shreveport, Louisiana, or other places with lower living costs, or if you hire privately instead of through an agency. Live-in help also costs less, on an hourly basis. And even in more expensive cities like Seattle or Boston, several hours a day of home care through an agency looks reasonable compared to monthly fees in most assisted living facilities or nursing homes. It's a major expense for a senior or family to shoulder, nonetheless.

And that's usually who does shoulder it. It comes as a surprise when families discover that keeping an elderly parent at home is their financial responsibility. Government programs pay for hospitalization and for nursing home care. Why isn't there government support for home care? But neither Medicare nor Medicaid can be relied on for long-term care at home.

A brief primer:

Medicare is the federally funded health insurance program for those over 65 (and for younger people with permanent disabilities). It pays for doctors, hospitals, and prescription drugs. But it covers home care only briefly and under limited conditions.

The patient must be "homebound," able to leave his residence only with great difficulty or with assistance, and must require skilled care by an RN or LPN. During this period, a patient may also receive physical therapy or other therapy, social services, and home health aides to assist with activities of daily living like bathing, dressing, or using the toilet. But these home visits generally can't exceed 28 hours a week, and they conclude when a patient no longer needs skilled nursing. They're not intended to provide long-term care.

Typically, Medicare-provided home health aides care for people who've just been discharged from a hospital or rehab facility. Mrs. Appel, for instance, had aides for a few weeks when she came home after her fall (and didn't like them much). But Medicare doesn't pay for the kind of ongoing homemaking and monitoring that her daughters wanted now.

Medicaid provides health care for the poor. Since it's a federal-state partnership, its benefits and policies differ in each state, sometimes even within a state. To be eligible, seniors must have low income and must have exhausted ("spent down," in Medicaid lingo) their assets until they have only about $2,000 or so left, depending on the state. They can retain a house they own, however, if they're receiving Medicaid services at home.

It's quite easy, sadly, for people who've had a middle-class income all their lives to become impoverished in old age; all they have to do is enter a nursing home. At an average national cost, in 2008, of close to $70,000 a year for a semiprivate room, most seniors spend down within a few months, so Medicaid pays the tab for the majority of nursing home residents.

For years, advocates for the elderly have argued against this "institutional bias," lobbying for increased Medicaid-covered home care. Why, they reason, should government pay so much to keep seniors in the places they don't want to be—nursing homes—when it could pay much less to keep many seniors in the places they *do* want to be—their homes?

And they've had some success; Medicaid funding for "home and community based services" has increased significantly. In Oregon and New Mexico, for instance, more than two-thirds of Medicaid spending for long-term care goes to home and community services.

But change has come unevenly; the great majority of Medicaid long-term care money still goes to nursing homes. The kinds of home services available vary by location, and some states impose benefit caps or maintain long waiting lists. And most elderly people, if they're not in nursing homes, aren't Medicaid-eligible anyway.

In some locations, home care may be available from other sources—through state or county programs, local charities, or foundations. Veterans may be eligible for home care through the VA. Private long-term care insurance may also pay for home care, though few elderly people have bought such policies, just 10 percent in 2002.

So the bottom line is that the cost of keeping a parent at home falls largely on the individual and the family. "It's the most reasonable option," Lynn Feinberg says, "for people who have money."

⁂

Accordingly, families often stretch their dollars by assembling a package of services, hiring just enough help to supplement their own efforts. Perhaps a home aide comes only in the morning, to help the parent get up, bathed, and dressed, and to do the laundry and prepare lunch; family members take over when they come home from work. Perhaps, as with Mrs. Appel, a live-in helper is on the scene weekdays, while relatives handle weekend care.

Then they may arrange for Meals on Wheels deliveries, or a senior transit van so that an elder who's no longer driving can get to appointments or the supermarket. In many communities, Friendly Visitor volunteers come weekly to chat, play cards, or write letters. Local senior centers—there are 15,000 around the country—offer recreation, meals, outings; some are trendily reinventing themselves by adding fitness centers, yoga classes, and cafés.

Here's where adult day care can play a role. At an average national cost of $64 for a full day's care, which includes meals and snacks and sometimes transportation, it represents a reasonably affordable solution. Medicaid will often cover adult day care for low-income seniors, and other subsidies or sliding-scale rates may also reduce the financial sting.

I was impressed with the Spend-A-Day adult day center I visited in Summit, New Jersey, not long ago, operated by a nonprofit organization called SAGE Eldercare. The program drew about 35 seniors each day, who came by van or were dropped off by family members. They could choose to attend from two days a week to five, to arrive as early as 8 in the morning and stay as late as 5:30. A registered nurse was on hand to dispense medications, monitor blood pressures, check weights and blood glucose levels. Staff members helped with walking, feeding, or toilet use; they could even provide showers onsite.

But nursing care and ADLs weren't what I noticed most; what jumped out was that these folks, most in their 80s with some cognitive impairment, were having a good time.

It was after lunch and after a midday stroll along the corridors. An alert 88-year-old named Doris Bauer was proving a whiz at *Jeopardy*, calling out the name Elizabeth Barrett Browning when the emcee asked which poet had written, "How do I love thee? Let me count the ways." Her teammates patted Mrs. Bauer encouragingly on the arm as they cruised to victory.

Then it was time for Flex and Stretch, a seated exercise program. Mrs. Bauer went up front to help lead the group, and everyone raised knees and waved arms to a bouncy musical soundtrack. A casual observer couldn't discern the signs of Parkinson's disease and early dementia in Mrs. Bauer; I only knew about them because her daughter, with whom she lived, had told me.

"It was getting nerve-wracking to leave her alone," said her daughter, a teacher who felt herself beginning to fray. "You worried what you'd find when you came home. She'd leave candles lit." She was anxious, too, about her mother growing isolated and depressed. The adult day program had proved a godsend; Mrs. Bauer had friends, activities, good nutrition; she even used the center's beauty salon each week. Her daughter could work, and more. "I can breathe again," she said.

An estimated 4,500 of these centers—not nearly enough—

operate around the country, and researchers are discovering a variety of benefits. Participants with dementia showed modest increases in more positive, socially appropriate behaviors, for instance, and experienced fewer sleep problems at night. "We saw major decreases in the number of antidepressants and sleeping pills our clients were taking," recalls Peter Notarstefano, who for years headed a nonprofit adult day and home health agency in upstate New York; he now directs home- and community-based services for the American Association of Homes and Services for the Aging.

Family members benefit as well. Caregivers of dementia patients able to spend fewer hours coping with their relatives' memory problems report reduced "role overload"—the sense of feeling overwhelmed by their responsibilities. After three months of using adult day programs, family members showed significantly less stress and greater psychological well-being than dementia caregivers who didn't use them, Penn State researchers found in another study.

A good home care experience does more than give caregivers time off. In researchers' interviews, caregivers using paid home care at least weekly spoke of enhancing their relatives' independence and dignity. Having a professional perform intimate tasks like bathing and changing, which sometimes make both elders and families uncomfortable, helped in "preserving a traditional parent-child relationship." Caregivers learned new skills from trained aides, sometimes formed friendships with them.

Even a good match has built-in limitations, however: Seniors using home care—or any form of eldercare—will decline over time. The average enrollment in an adult day center, for example, lasts about two years. "If it's not just a broken leg, if it's multiple sclerosis, dementia, something that is chronic and progressive, what works today may not work in six months," says Barbara Moscowitz, senior social worker at the Massachusetts General Hospital Geriatric Medicine Unit. "It's a process of continually learning, continually trying, continually reevaluating." The most carefully assembled home care arrangements, unpredictably and for a variety of reasons, can fall apart.

"It's not over till it's over," Shirley Grill had warned. And then, sometimes, it's *still* not over.

Mrs. Appel, Continued

I missed Aide Number Three completely. That's because Betty, a 40-ish woman of Jamaican descent whose mother cared for one of Mrs. Appel's neighbors, came and went in eight days.

"Such a sick person!" Mrs. Appel declared dramatically, after her departure. "Extremely nervous! All day she was on the phone with her mother. Her mother used to come and see her ten times a day, she was so nervous! I was happy she left."

A minor oversimplification: Betty "left" because Mrs. Appel dismissed her. But Shirley, who had interviewed Betty and found her "really charming" but "not a low-maintenance person," confirmed the basic scenario: On her first day, the new helper had "a meltdown . . . She was crying. She was lonely. She didn't like her room, it didn't have cable TV. She was quite frantic." Matters didn't improve from there.

So now Jamila, a young woman with a husband and baby in Brooklyn, had moved into the spare room. Anita Appel had located her; Jamila, also Jamaican by birth, had cared for Anita's friend's mother and came well recommended.

"She is more relaxed," was Mrs. Appel's assessment, after Jamila—in her 30s, with a gentle smile and unaccented English— had gone out to pick up a prescription at Rite Aid. "What I tell her to do, she does . . . I have no patience for *mishegas* [craziness]."

We were chatting at the dining room table. The day was summery, but Mrs. Appel, who felt comfortable and hated big utility bills, wasn't using her window air conditioner. She asked me not to rat her out to Shirley, who called daily reminding her to turn it on.

Maybe her girls had a point, Mrs. Appel seemed to acknowledge for the first time; perhaps she did need "once or twice a week, some help. Too much, I cannot do. If I walk half a block, I get tired and I can't catch my breath . . . I can't pick up a vacuum cleaner. I can't do the floors."

She gave one of her what-can-you-do shrugs that seemed to involve her entire upper body: eyebrows, mouth, shoulders, hands. "What do they need their mother for?" she sighed. "What do I do for them? I used to help them, to sew, to fix things for the family. Now I give them only aggravation. But I told them, they can't divorce me. There's no divorce between mother and daughter."

The critical question, Shirley mused, was whether she and Anita could keep hiring people as quickly as her mother fired them. Shirley was feeling calmer now, able to see the absurdity in the situation. "I'm spending more on international cell phone calls than I'm earning by working," she lamented. Her husband, who pointed out that her mother "plays you like a fine violin," had even come up with a strategy: "You take your mother out to dinner, and I'll burn down the house."

Sometimes, Shirley still wistfully envisioned her mother moving into independent living. "I knew all along this was not a stable arrangement," she said—prophetically, because about three weeks after our conversation, Jamila's father-in-law died and she had to fly to Jamaica for two weeks. Luckily, her cousin could take her place, and Alicia—Aide Number Five—turned out to be even more competent and agreeable. "We're set for a while," Shirley said.

She couldn't help noticing that as the summer continued, her mother seemed stronger, less depressed—acting as CEO of her small household appeared to energize her. "She's a tough old bird," Shirley said, with mingled annoyance and admiration.

⁂

But Mrs. Appel wasn't as unconquerable as she sometimes seemed. In August, while Shirley was in Austria on business, she got the call every child of an ailing parent dreads: Her mother had suffered a serious stroke. Shirley flew home and went directly from the airport to Albert Einstein Medical Center; Anita cut short a long-planned vacation in Puerto Rico.

They found Mrs. Appel disoriented and frightened. "She's verbal," Shirley told me. "If you just have a short conversation with her, you might not know anything was wrong." But the stroke had affected her peripheral vision, and it made her unsteady on her feet, afraid to walk. It seemed to have taken some of her short-term memory, as well. Her doctors were advising physical and occupational therapy at a rehab center. "The question is," Shirley said, "has so much damage been done that she can't go home to her quiet life?" Nobody could really tell her.

It was a wrenching and exhausting time. For years, Shirley had kept her mother's advance directives, which appointed her to make health care decisions if her mother were incapacitated. But when the nurse at Einstein asked about a DNR (a Do Not Resuscitate order), Shirley found herself unable to broach the subject with her mother.

"I can't do it," she said. "*You* ask her." So the nurse walked into the room and asked the key questions: If your heart stops, if your breathing stops, what would you like us to do?

Mrs. Appel was unequivocal: "Nothing! Nothing! Where do I sign?"

At times, her daughters wondered if she would, in fact, prefer to die. "Emotionally, she's more ready than she's ever been," Shirley said. "She thinks there's no coming back from this." And if the alternative was a continuing series of debilitating strokes, Shirley thought, a swift death might indeed be preferable.

Congestive heart failure is unpredictable, however. In rehab at the Hebrew Home for the Aged, Mrs. Appel rallied. With physical therapy, she regained her mobility and was able to walk quite well with a walker. Her vision improved, too. To Shirley, she seemed flat, her vitality sapped. "There's a piece of her missing that I can't put my finger on," she said. "But she's been seen by psychiatrists and other doctors and they look at her and say, 'For an 86-year-old, she's fine. She's aware. She doesn't need diapers. What the hell is wrong with *you*?'"

In a curious reversal, Mrs. Appel finally seemed willing to move into some sort of facility; she was much more passive, no longer so insistent on returning home. But Shirley, seeing the unsettling psychological toll of institutionalization, had grown less eager to relocate her. "I think if we move her now, her will to live really goes away," she fretted. "I want her to get back into her life."

So in September, Anita took charge of her mother's checkbook and Shirley took over the mail, tasks that now seemed to confuse Mrs. Appel and that she seemed surprisingly willing to relinquish. They thanked Alicia and Jamila, who'd returned from Jamaica, and let them go with a week's pay. "They've been terrific," taking turns living in the house and staying with Mrs. Appel in the hospital and the rehab center, Shirley said. But Mrs. Appel needed someone with stronger health care skills now.

Aide Number Six, an older woman named Wira who'd been living with a daughter in Toronto, said she'd been trained in Poland as a nurse. Shirley had no way to verify that, she admitted as she prepared for still another interview, but there was, reassuringly, a Gertrude connection: At her summer home in the Catskills, Gertrude knew a man that a good friend of Wira's had worked for. The man vouched for the friend and the friend vouched for Wira.

"She comes highly recommended," Shirley said, again.

Hiring, Part One

There has to be a simpler way to find home care for a parent, you might think—and there is. Whether it brings better results is a matter of debate.

You can hire through an agency. There are close to 18,000 nationwide, says the National Association for Home Care and Hospice. More than half, usually called home health agencies, meet the federal standards required for Medicare reimbursement. The others may be licensed by states, whose regulations vary considerably; some states don't license at all.

You don't have to qualify for Medicare reimbursement to use a Medicare-certified home health agency; you can pay out of your own pocket. But it's usually a higher tab than a non-Medicare agency charges.

Either way, a quality home care agency should offer its customers certain assurances. Unlike the kind of registry that Shirley Grill first used, which offers little more than a list of names, it should screen its employees, check their education and employment histories, perform drug tests, and run criminal background checks. It should make sure its workers are adequately trained in the particular services your parent needs. (Home health aides in Medicare-certified agencies are required to either complete 75 hours of training or pass a competency test.) Good agencies supervise their people, including making unannounced visits to homes where aides are working.

An agency can alleviate one of the major problems with home care: an aide who gets sick, whose car breaks down, who simply doesn't show up one day. An agency can dispatch another worker to cover the absence. It also provides a fallback if you or your parent isn't happy with Aide Number One. "What if this person for some reason doesn't work out, you don't like them, they're not dependable?" says Donna Schempp of the Family Caregiver Alliance. Instead of starting the hiring process all over again, "you say, 'This person isn't working out. Send me someone else.'"

Further, an agency handles the paperwork, which can be burdensome. Families that hire privately take on all those tasks themselves. They may begin by putting a notice in the church bulletin or the community paper, or by asking friends and relatives for recommendations. "You've got to do the advertising, find the people, screen them, do the background checks, so you have all the hiring responsibilities," Schempp notes.

"Secondly, you have all of the legal responsibilities," Schempp adds. "You have to set up a payroll, have an employee identification number. Most people pay under the table, but in theory you should be taking out Social Security taxes, you have workman's comp, you should have liability insurance"—all things an agency will handle, along with insurance against theft.

Why would someone take on all that additional work? One big

reason is cost: hiring privately through the "gray market" is cheaper, allowing families to purchase more hours of care and perhaps keep a fragile parent at home longer. The gray market is simultaneously more remunerative for the aide. Nationally, remember, the median hourly rate for a home health aide was $19, and $17 for a less skilled home-maker/companion. Even among full-time agency employees—and many aides don't get full-time work—the median hourly wage was $11. These numbers come from separate surveys and don't reflect big regional variations, but they demonstrate that a hefty chunk of what consumers pay goes to the agency, not the worker. When Shirley pays her mother's live-in helpers $500 a week, they earn $500. Theoreti-cally, at least, higher wages should help reduce turnover.

The gray market may also permit greater flexibility. Agencies have rules and policies, some dictated by state regulations or by li-ability fears. Some agencies forbid their workers to drive clients, for instance. You may need a worker for two hours, the time between your father's return from senior day care and your return from work—but a home care agency might require a minimum four-hour shift. In some states, it's legal for aides to remind seniors of their medications, but not to actually administer them; an agency helper may be able to place a pill in your mother's hand, but not to squeeze drops into her eye.

The gray market allows you to develop your own job description, which could involve not only administering eyedrops but walking the dog. Private hiring through an immigrant network or ethnic newspaper may also help locate someone who literally speaks your parent's language.

The trade-off, though, is that "it's like running a small busi-ness," Schempp says. You have "the anxiety of being the boss," the one who makes the unannounced drop-ins, who explains and tact-fully reiterates what's expected, who may have to stealthily begin interviewing replacements before you can dismiss someone who's unsatisfactory.

Those who find these requirements onerous may feel more se-cure if they find helpers through an agency. Without one, "you can save quite a bit of money, but unless you really know this person well, you're putting your family member at risk," says Peter Notarstefano of the American Association of Homes and Services for the Aging. He remembers a day, at the agency he once directed, when five applicants came in for their background checks and drug and alcohol screenings—"and they all failed."

※

Agencies can have serious quality problems of their own, however. While Shirley and her mother were running through their series of privately hired aides, New York's attorney general, Andrew Cuomo, was investigating home health services and announcing a barrage of indictments and convictions.

The charges were appalling: Operators of schools that trained home health aides selling hundreds of state certifications to people who'd never enrolled, but nonetheless began caring for patients. Aides with phony credentials billing Medicaid for services they never provided, in one case including a 36-hour workday. Home health care, Cuomo said, was "a burgeoning industry that is ineffectively regulated, that is expensive for taxpayers, and can victimize consumers."

The Government Accountability Office, Congress's investigative arm, has also long been critical of home health agencies. Back in 1997, it reported "serious shortcomings" in the monitoring meant to assure that Medicare agencies met federal requirements. Five years later, the GAO found such inadequacies continuing, and warned that "situations endangering the health and well-being of home health patients may occur more often than documented." In a 2003 report, it called for stronger federal oversight of Medicaid's home- and community-based services for the elderly, where quality problems appeared widespread.

If consumers have reasons to be wary of Medicare-certified home health agencies and Medicaid programs, supposedly subject to federal supervision, they have grounds to be even more leery of other home agencies, which are less likely to be policed.

On the other hand, despite fears for vulnerable patients who lack the supposed safeguards of an agency, there's evidence that consumers hiring home care on their own don't do a bad job. Medicaid programs that attempt to give the elderly and disabled more control by letting them hire and supervise their own home care helpers—in effect, replicating the gray market—have been popular with both seniors and their families, and deemed largely successful.

A study of California's Medicaid home care program, for example, surveyed about 1,100 recipients, comparing the experiences of the "consumer-directed" clients who hired on their own with those who used a conventional agency. The researchers found little difference in the incidence of abuse or neglect. One reason may be that the California approach permitted clients to hire family members and friends, and most did. Still, the author wrote, the results "challenge the assumption that positive outcomes . . . can only be achieved with traditional agency and professional arrangements."

The decision may come down to personal comfort, to the specific strengths or vulnerability of the parent who needs help—even to the effects of geography.

I'm thinking of Elizabeth Wetzel, a writer and journalist who'd been living happily—with her terrier, Pixie—in the wood-and-glass house she and her late husband had built 30 years earlier in Bigfork, Montana. "It's the perfect house with the perfect view of Flathead Lake," she told me. The thought of leaving it was wrenching. Her four children had scattered—none lived within a day's drive, though two daughters kept summer homes nearby. But she had a coterie of women friends who dropped in for frequent visits, took her to an occasional movie (she'd stopped driving), and convened for Thursday morning breakfasts at the village bakery. "We gossip a lot," she reported, "but we call it 'character analysis.'"

When an episode of congestive heart failure toppled Mrs. Wetzel at 90, the youngest of her four children took charge. Becky Wetzel, a marketing consultant in Massachusetts, spent six weeks in Bigfork, working to help her debilitated and depressed mother regain her vitality and to put local caregivers in place. "We all knew how important being at home was to her, how much home influenced her sense of well-being," Becky recalled. "We knew it was the goal to strive for—if we could do it."

In a close-knit town with fewer than 1,500 residents, who needed an agency? "I didn't want any rigid organization deciding my living arrangements," Mrs. Wetzel said. Her longtime weekly housekeeper became the "household manager," who cleaned, shopped, brought the mail, drove her to doctors' appointments, and coordinated payroll paperwork with a local accountant. With crossed fingers, Becky approached a family friend. Pam (I've changed the names of these employees) had been the Wetzels' housesitter when they traveled. She agreed, while keeping her day job managing a store, to move into Mrs. Wetzel's house and be there from evening till morning and on Sundays.

"It's become Pam's home," Becky said. Pam ate dinner and breakfast with Mrs. Wetzel. When she needed a catheter, a visiting nurse taught Becky, who taught Pam, what to do.

That arrangement functioned smoothly for seven months, until Mrs. Wetzel fell and broke her hip. With physical therapy, she regained her mobility, but her children were afraid of her spending her days alone. So Becky hired local women to come in two shifts, morning and afternoon, to accompany her mother on walks, play cribbage, prepare meals, and keep an eye on things. "It's almost like a commune," she said.

Part of what kept the commune operating was money. Even at Bigfork wages, it required about $5,000 a month, more than assisted living or nursing homes in that part of the country. But what also helped, Becky pointed out, was that "we weren't all strangers. We knew people in common. My oldest sister in California said we had to run background checks, and I said, 'I don't think we'd learn anything we can't find out just by asking around.'"

The commune has passed two years and counting. "I've lucked out with everything," Mrs. Wetzel said. "I'm surrounded by very nice, independent women that I know." And her youngest could say, "I feel an enormous sense that I've done something important. It's hard work and it takes more of an emotional toll than I'd imagined. But knowing that my mom's in a good place, that's huge. If it falls apart tomorrow, I'll still be glad that I was the one to do it."

❧

It was different in midtown Manhattan, where Sally Eisenberg had spent 30 years in a moderate-income co-op complex called Penn South, a collection of brick buildings that housed several times more residents than all of Bigfork, Montana. She stayed in her apartment after she retired as an insurance statistician; she stayed after her husband died in 2003. She spent her days visiting children and grandchildren, going to the movies, window-shopping at Macy's, reading magazines and newspapers, watching TV.

But she suffered several episodes of heart failure as she rounded 90, the most recent involving surgery to install a stent in a blocked artery and eight days in the hospital. Two months of Medicare-reimbursed home health services came and went, and still, "I felt very weak," Mrs. Eisenberg recalled. "As soon as I did anything, even walk to the bathroom, I'd start to breathe heavy."

"We convinced her that she had to have someone here every day," said her daughter Judith Eisenberg, who lived in the same complex and dropped by every couple of days. "My mother is not a person who would automatically call a doctor. She'd say, 'I don't want to bother him.'"

Judith couldn't picture hiring on her own. "To find someone and take care of all the paperwork—it would be very time-consuming," she said. "I'd be concerned about the quality. Is this person really good? Can she be trusted? What about all the legal aspects? And I work—a lot" as a freelance art conservator.

Following advice from people in the complex, she called Partners in Care, the private-pay home health subsidiary of the Visiting Nurse Service of New York. It charged more than Mrs. Eisenberg would or could have paid on the gray market. But because she and her husband had taken out liberal long-term care insurance policies years earlier, the care she needed each day—at first four hours, then eight—was covered.

Partners in Care required more training, including ongoing workshops, for its certified home health aides than the state mandated. It verified personal and work references, ran background checks, and sent its aides' fingerprints to the FBI. It checked on workers' health, including immunizations, and screened for drug use. And it sent Martha (I've changed her name), "a wonderful lady," Judith said. "Respectful. Considerate. We were very lucky."

Martha arrived at 10 each morning and helped Mrs. Eisenberg shower and dress. "She does my shopping, my laundry, my light housecleaning. I don't have to tell her anything anymore; it's like she lives here," Mrs. Eisenberg reported. Martha changed the dressings on her infected toe, reminded her to take her medications, made lunch, and set out the dinner brought daily by Meals on Wheels. She accompanied Mrs. Eisenberg to the market, to the park in fair weather, to the beauty parlor on Thursday mornings because "when I look in the mirror, I have to see someone presentable."

Not everyone from Partners in Care pleased her as well. At first, the agency sent substitutes on weekends, different aides each time. Aside from having to instruct each newcomer on what she needed, Mrs. Eisenberg disliked their passivity. "They never bothered to ask if I wanted anything," she said. "All they did was make meals, and in between they sat in a chair or took a nap or they were on the cell phone. They never volunteered, and I'm not the kind to really insist on their doing something." Before long, Mrs. Eisenberg jettisoned her weekend staff; Martha now worked 12-day stints and took every other weekend off.

She served another function as well, Mrs. Eisenberg acknowledged. She had once known and visited with her neighbors; now they'd died or moved, replaced by newcomers away at work all day. "They're all strangers," Mrs. Eisenberg said. "It's a different atmosphere." So Martha, who knew Mrs. Eisenberg's whole family and attended her 92nd birthday party at a granddaughter's house in Brooklyn, was more than a caregiver. Mrs. Eisenberg looked forward to her coming each day, to talking about their families and watching *The View* together. "She's my companion," she said.

Hiring, Part Two

Arranging for paid home care—intended to lighten the load families face—can begin to feel like a full-time job. Or a second job. "The people who are actually doing the work themselves, for a family member, have one set of stressors," is Donna Schempp's conclusion. "And the people who are supervising *other* people who do it have a different set."

The first step, before a family responds to an ad or interviews a candidate, is a realistic appraisal of what a parent needs. Perhaps she can handle her personal care, like Mrs. Appel, but has trouble with the tasks of managing a household: shopping, cooking, cleaning. In that case, her aide doesn't need the health care skills required to assist someone who can't get out of bed on her own. A diabetic with a failing memory, on the other hand, might need a more highly trained helper who not only can remind her to take medications but can test her blood glucose levels.

Perhaps the family can collectively come up with a list of needs and tasks—but sometimes it's helpful to bring in a geriatric care manager, or a social worker with a local senior health program, for a professional assessment. Nobody likes to acknowledge dependency, so parents have been known to underestimate the help they need, to shrug off hazards, to put on a brave front for visitors but struggle when they're alone. Perhaps, like Marla Shachtman's mother, they've functioned well because a spouse has guided them; their families are surprised at the deficits that emerge when that support is gone.

Anxious adult children, on the other hand, may be too quick to hand over to professionals the chores a parent still can manage on her own. Assessing a parent's needs can be particularly tricky when children don't live nearby—and about 15 percent of caregivers live at least an hour away, one national survey found. A daughter who's juggling her own household tasks, her job, and her kids may think she's doing her mother a favor when she declares, "You won't have to cook or wash dishes; you can just take it easy." But not everyone will welcome such a change in her routines or challenge to her competence.

An experienced outsider can be more dispassionate, and mediate between wrangling relatives. She can also guide them through the dizzying array of programs and services, many with their own eligibility requirements and application processes, that can help keep a senior in his home.

Armed with an assessment, you're better able to figure out what sort of agency to approach—a home health agency that provides RNs and physical therapists? A home care agency whose aides are primarily companions and homemakers? A company able to retrofit your parent's home with ramps and grab bars?

You'll want to ask a home care agency very specific questions. Does it run background checks and require drug testing? What kind of training does it require? Do supervisors meet regularly with workers and drop in when they're on the job? Will your parent get the same aide each day? What sort of backup is available if an aide gets sick or quits? Is the aide an agency employee, or a contract worker not covered by workman's comp or liability insurance? Will aides be able to administer meds or drive your parent's car? Can you call previous clients as references? Whom do you talk to if you're unsatisfied; how are complaints addressed?

If it's a Medicare-certified home health agency, you can find the results of its most recent quality survey on the www.medicare.gov Website. The findings are primarily geared to the kinds of improvements you'd want to see after an illness or hospitalization, more than to long-term supportive care, but they're one indicator of an agency's quality.

If you're hiring on your own, long-term care experts advise starting with a written job description. How often do you and your parent want the aide to help with a shower? Do you want her to do grocery shopping? How far ahead does she need to call if she's sick and can't come?

You'll want references, of course. If an applicant doesn't come through someone you know and trust, you may also want to run your own background check. Investigators advertise online or in phone books; local police departments or sheriff's offices can also be helpful.

When you've found a promising prospect, suggest a month's trial. It's not unusual for an employer to go through two or three people before finding a good match. A probationary period lets the worker know she has to meet certain expectations, and sets up a mechanism for frank conversations about how things are going.

You'll need your own contract or written employment agreement, specifying tasks, hours, payment schedules; several caregiving Websites offer samples.

However you've found a helper, let her know that family members and friends will be dropping by at all hours—then make sure that's true, especially if your parent can't be a reliable reporter. "Don't call and say, 'I will be over in 45 minutes,'" cautions AARP's Elinor Ginzler. "You're not going to have the same opportunity to see what's going on as if you just walk in."

Elder abuse, an elastic term that encompasses everything from neglect and financial scams to verbal threats and physical assault, is a fear that nags at both seniors and their families. It remains a poorly understood phenomenon, with little reliable data on its prevalence, but it's believed to be substantially underreported. We know it occurs in institutions, yet a survey of state Adult Protective Services administrators in 2000 found that more than 60 percent of tracked reports, and 43 percent of substantiated reports, involved "domestic settings."

We also know that, as with child abuse, fears often don't jibe with facts. Families worry about hiring home care aides—but abusers are most often family members, not employees or strangers, the research to date shows.

This is unlikely to quell fears about abuse by paid helpers, just as statistics about child abduction (which overwhelmingly involves noncustodial parents or runaway teenagers) don't prevent parents from issuing warnings about talking to strangers. There's a growth industry in surveillance equipment, the so-called grannycams.

Most families, however, rely on their own watchfulness. It's smart not to leave valuables or cash around, and to arrange for direct deposit of Social Security and pension checks, but it also becomes necessary, at some point, to trust one's own skills and instincts.

Often an aide's personal attributes, her ability to form a friendly relationship with both the older person and his or her family, contributes more to family caregivers' satisfaction than her training or specific skills. As with Mrs. Wetzel's commune and Mrs. Eisenberg's companion, close friendships, even familial feelings, do develop between aides and clients.

One thing that helps foster them, however, is continuity—having the same helper week after week, so that both parties get to know and trust each other.

In the Bronx, this was proving difficult.

Mrs. Appel

In November, Shirley Grill turned 60 and threw herself a celebration, a Sunday afternoon open house featuring tons of good food and wine, a steady stream of friends and relatives, a nostalgic photo album her husband had assembled—and her mother, looking remarkably well. Gertrude and her husband had driven Mrs. Appel over to New Jersey.

She was holding court on the living room sofa when I arrived, chatting with her girls' childhood friends from the Bronx. She'd dressed for the occasion and when I complimented her on her elegant appliquéd blouse, she gave one of her substantial shrugs. "This blouse," she said, "is older than you."

Shirley swept in and helped her mother up from the couch. "Ma, c'mon, you have to help me blow out the candles." Everyone sang, Anita took photos, Shirley and her mother together extinguished the six candles—one for each decade—on the big chocolate cake, and then hugged and smooched. On any number of occasions, Shirley had doubted her mother would be around for her 60th—but here she was, and in great spirits. "She had a good day today," Shirley said happily, after the Bronx contingent left for home.

Initially, when Mrs. Appel came home from rehab, Shirley found her cranky and irritable, and less mentally sharp than normal. She was also less than pleased with Wira. "They irritate each other," Shirley said. But her mother tolerated Wira, and Wira wasn't overly sensitive, so "we're muddling along."

Mrs. Appel was in a philosophical mood when I had gone to see her the week before Shirley's party. Her Borscht Belt timing was intact:

Me: "I haven't seen you in a while."

Mrs. A: "You're better off."

But she was no longer talking about getting well enough to let her helpers go; that battle was over. "I manage okay, I read the paper, I am cooking, not always but sometimes. I'm a fighter," she reported with some pride. But when she took a walk, "I don't go by myself. God forbid if I take another flop, ay yi yi."

Wira, who looked to be in her 60s despite shoe-polish-black hair, passed through, toting the laundry. Mrs. Appel, it's fair to say, did not light up at her presence.

"I would love to do everything myself, that's the problem," she said. Now that she couldn't, "it's sad, but I can't help it. That's life."

Wira lasted another three weeks. Then Shirley, in Munich on business, got email from Wira's daughter in Toronto: She needed her mother at home. "Perhaps this was the plan all along," Shirley mused. "Work a few months in the United States, save some money, return to Canada." Back to the drawing board.

It was Wira who proposed that the family hire her friend Tekla. By my calculation, Tekla was Aide Number Eight, counting people who'd been provisionally hired but never actually started work. Shirley didn't include the no-shows, so considered her Aide Number Five.

She liked Tekla. "A very gentle, quiet soul, just lovely all around," Shirley emailed after her first week. What was more important, "My mom seems to like her quite well and even gave her a Christmas bonus!"

When I next drove into the Bronx with Shirley, Tekla had been on the job for ten weeks, close to a record. "My mother likes her the best," said Shirley. She was bringing a load of groceries and a battery for the carbon monoxide detector. "Would she be my ideal? No. She's not independent enough; her English isn't great . . . She's not someone who could take my mother to the doctor, for instance.

"But she's a loving caretaker. They cook together. We went to a bat mitzvah and Tekla did my mother's nails." If her mother was content, she was content.

It had been nearly a year since I'd first taken this ride with Shirley, during which, I suggested, she and her sister hadn't known much peace of mind.

"It was horrible," she agreed. "When it snows, you worry. When a pipe bursts, you worry . . . That's why people say, 'Go to a home.' It's much more efficient, and we convince ourselves that it's better."

Sometimes, she added, it probably *was* better. She had a friend whose father, living in his own apartment, kept falling even with aides around to help. The daughter found the situation dangerous and moved him into a nursing home near her in Connecticut. "And guess what—he's doing fabulously!" Shirley said—with perhaps a touch of envy. She hadn't completely given up on the possibility of her mother's moving.

Yet she'd seen how disruptive and confusing a few weeks in the hospital and in rehab had been. "In the house, she still manages her day. She gets out of bed when she wants to, she eats when she wants to, she still has a sense of owning her own space," Shirley said. For all her frustration, "I think this has been the right choice for my mother's sense of dignity."

When she pulled into the driveway, Tekla came out to help unload the groceries. She was perhaps 50, short and sturdy-looking, and she greeted Shirley with a kiss.

"Did my mother take a walk today?" Shirley asked.

"Mom going 15 minutes," Tekla reported. "She likes."

Mrs. Appel was feeling upbeat. "I love my two girls!" she exclaimed, enveloping Shirley in a hug.

Shirley could still see subtle signs of decline. Her mother sometimes now spoke to her in Polish, a language she didn't understand, before recognizing her mistake and switching to English or Yiddish. And she showed Shirley a check that had come in the mail. "What do I do with this?"

"We have to deposit it," Shirley said, slipping it into her bag. A year earlier, her mother would have known what to do with it.

But Mrs. Appel had good things to say about her new aide. "She's very good to me," she told me. "She tries to help. She likes me; she comes in and gives me a kiss. She watches me, I shouldn't fall, I shouldn't get hurt." Unprecedented praise.

We chatted a while, and then I left for the subway stop. Shirley walked me out and lingered out on the front steps for a moment. The air still felt chilly, but the stronger sun promised spring, and yards full of rosebushes.

"So we bought a year," she mused. "I wouldn't have thought we could.

"And I only had to make two emergency trips home from Europe. That's a good year."

SOME QUESTIONS TO CONSIDER ABOUT HOME CARE:

What tasks does your parent need help with in order to remain in her home? How many of the ADLs—activities of daily living like bathing, dressing, and eating—will she need assistance with? What about the IADLs—instrumental activities of daily living, meaning household chores like preparing meals, housecleaning, and money management?

Does your parent have a social network and community connections that remain important? Is she engaged with friends and neighbors, a religious congregation, volunteer projects, or civic groups? Those ties can be a strong impetus to stay put.

Can she move about her community for shopping, medical appointments, and recreation? Can friends, volunteers, local agencies, or paid helpers provide enough transportation to prevent isolation?

Is your parent's home safe and functional for a senior with health problems or disabilities? Can it be adapted by installing a shower bench, grab bars, toilet risers? Is it practical to build a wheelchair ramp if one's required, to widen doorways or put in a stair lift?

How much paid home care will be sufficient to allow her to age in place? A few hours of homemaker assistance daily? Home health aides day and night? Skilled nursing care?

Can she or the family put that much help in place, and pay for it privately? Can publicly funded programs—through Medicaid, city and state programs, or local charities—help make home care affordable?

Is your parent sociable and communicative enough to form relationships with paid caregivers? Does she have behavioral problems, such as those caused by dementia, that will make it difficult for them to help her, and difficult for her to retain them?

Will she be able to reliably report how her caregivers are working out, what problems have arisen, whether she's happy with the arrangement? Will you or other family members be able to drop in to monitor her care?

TWO

MOVING IN

The Shared Household

THE SOUP WAS STARTING TO SMELL GOOD. ILZE EARNER, MOVING around the kitchen in her stocking feet, had been chopping onions, carrots, and a turnip. She cubed some leftover chicken from the fridge and tossed that into the pot, along with sprigs of parsley.

Her mother, who'd just moved into the adjoining cottage, made her own breakfast and lunch. But Ilze, worried that she wasn't eating properly, stood firm about the evening meal. "Look, we make dinner every night," she told her mother early on. "It's at 7. I want you to eat with us." So dinner had become a trigenerational gathering: Ilze, her husband, Laurence; their nine-year-old daughter, Maize; and Ilze's mother, Milda Betins.

Mrs. Betins wasn't always so compliant. When she first arrived, for example, Ilze had cautioned her against going down into the basement to use the washer and dryer. The steep stairs seemed an unnecessary risk for an 88-year-old who'd recovered well from a broken hip but still walked with a cane. Besides, a part-time housekeeper took care of the laundry. But Mrs. Betins had strong feelings about doing things herself; she simply waited until Ilze headed off to work, then made her way downstairs with her cane and her washing.

"She completely ignored me!" Ilze groused, rummaging through her spice cabinet for paprika and dill. "It's frustrating! I feel responsible for her safety, for making sure she doesn't hurt herself. This house wasn't meant for an elderly person with limited mobility." So far, though, Mrs. Betins was winning the laundry skirmish.

"Pick your battles" was Ilze's mantra these days, she told me. She'd shifted into a campaign to install a stair lift in the cottage, where the kitchen was on the second floor and the stairs had no railing. Her mother, declaring that climbing stairs was good for her, was resisting that effort, too.

It was leafless November in Claverack, a hamlet in rural upstate New York; a series of multicolored turkeys, traced around Maize's hand and strung together with yarn, hung on the dining room wall. The house, a shingled Arts and Crafts bungalow built in 1929, was invitingly cozy, with a brick fireplace and maple woodwork. Ilze had painted the walls in warm colors, apricot and sage green. An old collie and a new corgi puppy, plus an ancient cat named Thistle, completed the household. (Ilze's son, Ziggy, from an earlier relationship, was a college student in nearby Albany.) Outside, on 16 acres of woodland and meadow, Ilze and Laurence had spent the warm months building a deck, putting in gardens, and tending Maize's pet bunny.

Now, with Ilze cooking in the kitchen, still in her riding pants after an exhilarating hour at the stables nearby, and Maize in the living room watching *It's a Wonderful Life* on her laptop (the Earners had banished television), life in the household appeared peaceful, settled. It was *The Waltons* updated, I thought, an urbanite's daydream of what it might be like to move one's extended family to the countryside.

The reality, though, was that almost everything about the past year had been a maddening ordeal.

❧

Ilze was 51, the younger child of Latvian refugees; she still usually spoke Latvian to her mother. Following the classic immigrant scenario, she had climbed into the professional class through education, earning a PhD in social work and joining the faculty at

Hunter College in New York City. Vibrant and outspoken, with a sleek blond bob and distinctive, craft-y jewelry, she had a certain urban flair.

No accident—until five months earlier, the Earners had lived in a gentrifying neighborhood in Brooklyn. The Claverack house was meant to be a summer and weekend getaway, financed in part by renting out the smaller cottage, attached by a breezeway, to skiers and vacationers. Instead, after a year of renovating, the Earners suddenly decided to rent out their Brooklyn brownstone and move upstate full-time.

The biggest reason was Maize (pronounced MAY-zee), whose learning disabilities necessitated a battle each school year with the New York City Board of Education; it took expensive lawyers to get her the classes and therapies she needed. The public schools here in Columbia County had been far more accommodating, and Maize was flourishing—"the country has been wonderful for her," Ilze said—but the move was disruptive nonetheless. Ilze hadn't yet had a chance to put down real roots, to find friends and community connections. She and Laurence, who sold industrial woodworking equipment, had adopted complex commuting patterns in order to work in the city while always keeping one parent at home.

Meanwhile, Ilze had also been preparing to move her parents, caught up in a chaotic situation as they entered their late 80s. They'd done well for most of 15 years in a retirement community, a Latvian enclave in Ocean County, New Jersey. "My mother was convinced this was it, the last place," Ilze told me. "She always said, 'When I leave here, it'll be horizontally.'" As often happens with such vows, "It worked fine, as long as they were able to take care of themselves."

For the past two years, however, "I'd been living on eggshells. Every time the phone rang and it was their number, I wondered what had gone wrong." Ilze drove two and a half hours from Brooklyn nearly every weekend to see her parents, but their problems were escalating.

Her father, Laimonias, a retired construction worker with heart disease and diabetes, was sinking into dementia, something clear to his family only in retrospect. He'd had four or five auto accidents, several of which Ilze and her brother, Hans, learned about months later. Mr. Betins had lost the ability to distinguish junk mail from bills and statements. He startled his wife one day by pulling the car over on the way home from a local shopping center and admitting that he didn't know where he was. He also decided, despite his children's pleas to reconsider, to undergo two simultaneous knee replacements at age 89—a move Ilze now attributed to his diminished cognitive ability. As they had feared, his legs had never fully healed after the surgery. He'd been in a wheelchair ever since, increasingly angry and antagonistic and suspicious.

Her mother, struggling to care for him despite painful arthritis, developed a hernia that required surgical repair, then fractured several vertebrae. Then last spring came "the tipping point," Ilze said—her mother fell in her bedroom and broke her hip.

It got worse: Ilze and her brother gradually became aware of the role of someone she called the Grifter Woman. The Grifter Woman, another Latvian immigrant, had befriended their parents, a relationship the children welcomed until her name and her families' names began showing up on thousands of dollars' worth of the Betins' personal checks. Mr. Betins said he was in love. Mrs. Betins was hospitalized with depression. The police weren't able to do much.

This couldn't go on, Ilze and her brother decided. She called the family lawyer and asked, "What do we do?"

They went to court to become their father's legal co-guardians, allowing them to make decisions for him because he lacked the capacity—as several gerontologists concluded in their evaluations—to make them himself. Their plan was to bring him to the best nursing home Ilze could find near Claverack, far from the Grifter Woman, and to move Mrs. Betins into the guest cottage. She could have privacy but be under Ilze's watchful gaze, and she could still see her husband regularly.

In late September, therefore, Ilze found herself painting the bedroom in the cottage at 1 in the morning. Mrs. Betins was coming to see the place the next day, "the big tryout," and Ilze wanted the place to look appealing, even though the renovations weren't completed. "I was bone-tired," Ilze remembered. "My daughter was hugely annoyed because I hadn't paid attention to her all day. My husband was away. I was still in boxes myself. But we had to convince my mother that this was going to work."

The cottage had a ski chalet–style interior, with some unvarnished board walls and a woodstove; would it strike her mother as too rustic? Ilze had made a last-minute dash to Wal-Mart, 20 miles away, to buy throw pillows and scented candles. "I was so nervous," she said. "I wanted it to be homey; I wanted her to like it. I was praying for a gorgeous Indian summer day."

They got one. "Beautiful sunshine, the leaves turning color—the timing was perfect," remembered Hans, who drove their mother up from New Jersey. She appreciated the rural setting. "It was sort of like where she'd grown up, the country and the hills."

Mrs. Betins walked through the cottage remarking on how spacious it was, and how beautiful. She saw the first-floor bedroom Ilze had just painted and announced, "This is it." Hans and Ilze cheered silently and within two weeks, "we moved her," Hans said. "Otherwise, she would start mulling it, finding things wrong, and she wouldn't do it." An ambulance brought their father to the nursing home Ilze had selected, about a 20-minute drive from the house.

When she described this extended saga to friends—the renovations, her move, dealing with school officials, the court proceedings, her parents' health problems, *their* moves—"They say, 'Oh my god!' But my life seems easier than it has in years," Ilze told me. She wasn't constantly dashing to New Jersey—a much farther distance now. She didn't fear every ring of the phone. Despite the upheaval, she sounded upbeat: "I think things are going wonderfully."

Life wasn't simple, exactly. Her workweek began with the alarm set for 4:30 on Monday mornings, so that she could drive to the Metro-North train stop, catch the 6:30 to New York, and be at her desk at Hunter before 9 a.m. She worked on campus Monday and Tuesday, spending Monday nights in a basement apartment in the house she and Laurence still owned in Brooklyn; he remained in Claverack with Maize, working from home. Tuesday evenings, as Ilze was heading back upstate and he was arriving in the city, they met for ships-passing-in-the-night cocktails in an atmospheric little bar at Grand Central. Then she got on the 5:59.

She spent Wednesday taking care of the house, the chores and errands, fitting in her sole indulgence, a horseback riding lesson. "It puts me into a different world," she explained. "It forces you to be in the moment, just you and the horse." Thursday and Friday were supposed to be devoted to her academic writing, crucial because she would come up for tenure the following year. Laurence returned Friday evening and they all spent the weekend together.

Friday afternoons were also when she visited her father; on Sundays, she took her mother to see him. He'd become so hostile and paranoid that Ilze couldn't eat before these trips; Mr. Betins routinely accused her of committing him to a mental hospital and stealing his money, called his wife horrible names, and sometimes literally shook with agitation and rage. Ilze spent hours each week trying to line up neurologist appointments, monitor his care at the nursing home, consult eldercare attorneys about Medicaid eligibility when his money ran out. She learned about the *dis*advantages of rural life when it took weeks simply to locate a new physician for her mother, one who would accept Medicare.

Plus, the guardianship she and Hans had been granted in New Jersey was being contested by their father's sister, who lived in the same retirement community and argued that Mr. Betins should live with her. Ilze and Hans strongly suspected the continued machinations of the Grifter Woman, who'd also befriended their 89-year-old aunt. Ilze glumly declared that the Year of the Hospital was being followed by the Year of the Lawyer.

Still, things seemed to be moving in the right direction. At least, the family was together, and Ilze felt she had greater control of her days and a better eye on her parents' well-being.

She tasted the soup, simmering fragrantly on the stove, declared it ready, and dispatched Maize to bring her mother in for dinner.

Mrs. Betins

Milda Betins was so tiny, not nearly five feet tall, that she sat at the dining room table atop a cushion, so that her chin wouldn't be in her plate. She was swathed in fleece clothing to ward off the chill. I could see why Ilze worried about her mother's diet—she was twig-thin, with the sharpened features and pared cheeks of a doll carved from an apple. But she walked quite briskly for someone who'd gone through rehab for a fractured hip.

And cognitively, she was all there, though not without her eccentricities. She told me, when I remarked on her recovery, that she still suffered from pain in her hip, plus crippling arthritis in her back.

"Why don't you take some medicine?" Maize wondered.

"Medicine is poison," Mrs. Betins said, holding forth on her theory that the human body could heal itself, that drugs were an impediment. It was an unlikely viewpoint for someone who'd trained and worked as a surgical nurse in Latvia, but it was the reason that, to her daughter's dismay, she wouldn't take medication for arthritis, or for the depression that sometimes dogged her. "Americans pamper too much the old people," Mrs. Betins declared.

After dinner, we walked across the breezeway to her cheerful cottage, its bright furniture and blond woods suggestive of an Ikea catalogue. She showed me her bedroom, with a Latvian talisman—white birch branches arranged on the wall above her bed. "They push out evil," she explained. "They protect you."

She'd mounted nature photos on another wall, and was delighted when Ilze installed a bird feeder just outside her window. "I feel that God is closer in the natural world," she said. "In the summer, when the autumn leaves were, and the mountains, it was like a picture. I feel very content here."

Mrs. Betins spoke slightly off-kilter English sprinkled with Latvian and occasional flecks of German or French, a rapid-fire mix I could understand but can't easily reproduce. It reflected her hard life, moving from a Latvian farm to a hospital job in Riga, to a German displaced persons camp when the Soviets invaded, to a French camp after the war, to Long Island USA, where her husband found construction work and landscaping jobs. They bought a house there, raised their children.

After they retired and found the house too troublesome, the Betins headed for the 55-plus community in New Jersey. "I was happy in this place—really, really happy," Mrs. Betins said wistfully, remembering Latvian-speaking neighbors that were like "an extended family" and the flower garden she tended lovingly. "When you live 15 years in a place you like, and then comes a change, sometimes you feel sad—why this happen?"

Her answer was that "my daughter worried, I was so far away. Four hours to drive." And that her husband was "not well in the mind. He cannot *versteh* [understand] that we cannot take care of him. He is a little bit mad." And that she couldn't manage alone— she'd never learned to drive—but also hated having home care aides ("torture") in her house.

So she could list the benefits of living here. And she insisted it didn't matter that she spent her days mostly alone, writing letters, doing word puzzles, exercising to stay limber, keeping house, taking walks when it wasn't too cold and icy—a condition not likely to recur upstate until at least April. "I'm really a solitary person," Mrs. Betins said. "I don't need people around." A keen reader, she was happily working her way through Alexander McCall Smith's *No. 1 Ladies' Detective Agency* series, which Ilze had bought her. "I am alone, but I'm not lonely."

She was also careful not to interfere with the way the household operated. "When you are old, sit in the corner and shut up," was her philosophy. "I see something a little different and think, 'That's not my way,' and I say nothing. This is not my life."

She told me again how much she liked her "nice surroundings." I had the sense she was trying to talk herself into it.

Under One Roof

How many families choose this option, when elders' health begins to falter, is hard to pinpoint. The 2000 Census, for the first time, counted the number of multigenerational households, defined as three or more generations of parents and their children. There were about four million, the Bureau announced—less than 4 percent of the nation's households. Factoring in population growth, and multigenerational families that might include other relatives besides parents and children, University of California, Irvine management professor John Graham estimated the number at about six million in 2008.

It's an arrangement more common among black, Asian, and Hispanic families, an AARP survey shows. They're also more likely to have grown up with grandparents and other relatives in their homes.

As for bigenerational households, consisting just of adult children and aging parents, Urban Institute researchers Richard W. Johnson and Joshua M. Wiener found that the proportions varied sharply according to disabilities. Sifting through the results of the large, nationwide 2002 Health and Retirement Study, they reported that among unmarried adults over 65 who weren't in institutions, fewer than 20 percent of those with no disabilities lived with a child. (Whether that child had children living at home wasn't measured in this survey.)

But among those who were frail, meaning they had "difficulty" with at least one of the activities or instrumental activities of daily living, more than a quarter lived with a child, a statistically significant increase. And close to a third of those with "severe disabilities," defined as needing help with three or more ADLs, shared a household with a child.

This was the way most families used to house elderly parents, of course, and it still sometimes seems the default, the expected solution; turning to some other option becomes something people feel a need to justify. I encountered this response myself, as I spoke with families about being part of this book: Sons or daughters whose parents needed help, but weren't living with them, invariably told me they'd contemplated moving them in, then explained why they couldn't manage it.

An AARP survey of women over 45 underscores how potent this picture remains, in thought if not in practice. Asked about various living arrangements, the highest percentage—43 percent—said they'd considered having a parent move in with them—"coresidence," researchers call it. Every other possibility—including the parent staying in her own home with paid help or moving into a facility—was less likely to be considered. Only 17 percent of the women said they'd contemplated a nursing home.

The Waltons remain our ideal, it seems. But there's good reason to think they're not our parents' ideal.

Coresidence was the tradition, not only in this country but around the world. Now, in the U.S. (and in much of Europe), it no longer is. What happened? Economists wondering about this shift in elderly living patterns since the early 1900s have been looking into various explanations. Did it have to do with seniors' improving health or women entering the workforce? With those unsettling charges that Americans became too individualistic and gave up on "traditional" values? Did parents simply change their minds?

None of the above was the main factor, several papers by Robert Schoeni and Kathleen McGarry have shown. Tracing Census data back to the late nineteenth century, they looked at the living arrangements of elderly widows, who are both more numerous and more economically vulnerable than unmarried older men. For 50 years the configuration changed very little: About 70 percent of widows lived with adult children. The proportion living alone was just 9 percent in 1880 and remained quite low until the 1940 Census.

"And then it takes off," Schoeni, a University of Michigan economics professor, told me in an interview. "You ask yourself, what happened around that time?"

What happened was the New Deal and Social Security, enacted in 1935. It was overwhelmingly this economic factor, Schoeni and McGarry calculated (and others have as well), that drove a steep increase in the number of widows living alone. As the program expanded, as the number of widows eligible for Social Security increased along with the generosity of benefits, living arrangements flip-flopped. By the 1990 Census, more than 60 percent of elderly widows lived alone, less than 20 percent with their children.

This was not a gradual shift. When Schoeni and McGarry plotted a graph showing the proportion of widows living with children, the line plummeted just after the first Social Security checks started to flow. "It looks very much like a ski slope, and a pretty steep one," Schoeni observed.

What does this tell us? Our society appears "to long for those golden days of the multigenerational family," he said. "But it's not the preferred outcome for a lot of people." Instead, the elderly have "an underlying desire for independence . . . and if you give them the income to do it, they do it."

It's still the case, a team of MIT and Syracuse economists reported in 2002. Applying their own econometrics to data from the national Current Population Survey, they concluded that living arrangements among the widowed or divorced elderly remain highly sensitive to Social Security benefit shifts. (Married couples, with more potential income sources, show less sensitivity.) "Our estimates imply that a 10 percent cut in Social Security benefits would lead more than 600,000 independent elderly households to move into shared living arrangements," the authors wrote.

In fact, multigenerational households were most common, Census Bureau demographers pointed out, in regions with housing shortages or high housing costs (like California) and with high rates of unmarried births (like Mississippi)—an indication that economic necessity, more than a desire for family closeness, was at work. Two-thirds of multigenerational households consisted of a householder taking in children and grandchildren, not parents or in-laws.

None of these findings means that a shared household is a bad idea for any individual family. Depending on its members' needs, histories, and tolerances, it can be a boon for both, or several, generations. That "underlying preference" probably does explain, however, why many of the people who think, write, and advise about eldercare urge caution.

Making Arrangements

"A family caregiver needs to be very thoughtful about bringing a person in to live with them," says Gail Hunt of the National Alliance for Caregiving, who thinks such commitments are sometimes made too quickly, "almost on the spur of the moment.

"You go down to visit your parents at Christmastime. You realize that they don't have a lot of food in the refrigerator and they seem to be a little forgetful. Your first inclination is to say, 'Let's bring Mom and Dad up here to live with us'—without considering the impact on you, the impact on your job, the impact on other family members—your kids, your husband or your wife, maybe your siblings.

"There's not necessarily a thoughtful family conversation about what's the best place for Mom and Dad. And let's let Mom and Dad have a say in that, too," she added. "Older people are very concerned about losing their independence. I think they worry about the adult child swooping in and saying, 'I can't put up with this anymore. You have to come and live in Paterson, New Jersey, with me.'"

The multigenerational household seems to work best when the parent has lived nearby and maintains some local connections, "his or her own sense of belonging to a community," says Barbara Moscowitz, senior social worker at the Massachusetts General Hospital Geriatric Medicine Unit. "I think it's hardest when parents move down to Florida in their 60s, and then in their 80s, they're not well and they move back up to be with their children."

By then, the elders may have to rely on their children for not only housing and care, but for company, outings, social relationships. Yet, "they're often moving into a nuclear family of two parents working all day and teenagers with blaring music," Moscowitz notes. "It's loving, but it's also chaos, because you have taken ill people out of their own habitat. They have expectations of being cared for, but there's also an active family life that's not theirs . . . Often, people need some help sorting it out and thinking it through."

Sharon Graham Niederhaus and her brother John Graham, co-authors of *Together Again: A Creative Guide to Successful Multigenerational Living,* are advocates of shared households ("the natural way for human beings to live," Graham says)—but they, too, advise careful planning.

Niederhaus, who wrote her master's thesis on this subject, interviewed 100 families that lived, by her very broad definition, multigenerationally: They occupied adjoining houses, "accessory apartments" added to houses, family compounds, or even separate condos in one building. "Fifty percent of the families already had a history of multigenerational living," she says. "Perhaps Grandma was with them when they grew up . . . The likelihood is, those families knew how to get along."

Niederhaus finds that "proximity and privacy are the two keys to success. Separate kitchens. Separate entrances. You have neatniks and messy people. You've got lifestyle differences, personality differences." With some separation, "there's less potential for conflict."

(In their very practical book, I should note, Niederhaus and Graham focus on parents able to care for themselves in their own quarters more than on the disabled; they also concentrate on families collectively able to afford the construction often required to create individual living spaces.)

Joining forces in this way can raise pragmatic questions. Some municipalities prohibit accessory apartments (aka "granny flats") or adopt zoning that makes it difficult to add units to existing houses, which can discourage multigenerational living.

Legal and financial issues crop up within families, too, points out Graham. "I recommend a family partnership agreement" drawn up by an attorney, he says, "particularly if there are a lot of assets floating around." If Dad sells his big house and uses part of the proceeds to build himself an addition to one daughter's home, how will that affect his other children's inheritances? How will the family balance the increased worth of that house versus the care the daughter may one day have to provide? What about wills, trusts, taxes?

"It's a time of friction and angst," Graham acknowledges. "We suggest getting everyone to talk about it: 'What am I contributing, what are you contributing, how do you value that, and what's fair?'"

Daily routines and responsibilities also require cooperation, Niederhaus says, along with understandings about what each generation needs or can provide. Adult children may see their parents as a source of high-quality child care, while seniors feel unable to lift babies or unwilling to plan their days around school schedules.

Who does which chores? Will the family eat dinner together every Sunday, or every day, or just now and then? Will seniors pay rent or utility bills or otherwise contribute to household expenses? Can the older generation tolerate the younger ones' noise, and vice versa?

Not every family is cut out for this. Elders who try to interfere with the way their children raise their own children, a history of crankiness or clashes, two parties dueling for household control—red flags, all. "When you discuss something ahead of time, you may cut off problems before they occur," Niederhaus says. "Get things established before you move in."

Graham is convinced that multigenerational households are the future, that Americans will get over their stubborn insistence on independence in their senior years, especially as the elderly population balloons and Social Security and Medicare come under greater pressure. "We're going to revert to the oldest system of taking care of each other," he believes, and personally, he's looking forward to it. "I've told my kids"—he has four—"that I'd be moving in with them. I'm just not sure which."

⁑

Maybe he's right. But 70 years of recent history argue otherwise: Most seniors still hold on to their own households for dear life, and decline to move in with children until poor health and other troubles loom. Then, if they do move in, utility bills and decibel levels may be the least of the tensions.

Old psychological patterns—conflicts and alliances, memories and wounds—arise whenever parents need help from their children. In most families, one child, usually a daughter, takes on the primary caregiver role—and when the parent is living in her house, *primary* may be an understatement. Along with the real-world situations that dictate who might share a home with a frail parent—who has too little space or too many stairs, who has a job with long hours and who's already retired—there are often subterranean emotional currents.

"I don't know any child who becomes a grown-up who doesn't carry with him wishes, dreams, disappointments," says Barbara Moscowitz. "I hear a lot, 'I've been waiting my whole life for Dad to be proud of me.' Or, 'I've been waiting my whole life for Mom to finally approve of my lifestyle.' There are many cases of waiting to get something, waiting for a parent to finally give something, wanting to give to a parent."

If those desires lead to consideration of a shared household, Moscowitz, too, urges discussions before the need arises, when a parent is still well. It's a complicated business. "Often there are tremendous misconceptions of what might happen," she says. "And there is a lot of unfinished business."

Unfinished Business

The Earners' Christmas tree was an aromatic Douglas fir that Ilze and Laurence brought home atop their station wagon.

"I hope it's tall," Maize commented as they toted it into the living room. "I don't like stumpy trees, you can't put as many ornaments on them."

This one was tall enough. Ilze and Maize pulled an assortment of years-old decorations out of boxes—carved wooden animals, a nutcracker, a circle of bells ("An angel is getting its wings!" Maize said)—while Laurence made lunch. A cheerful Irishman, he was at ease with multigenerational living; as a boy in Dublin, he'd shared a home with a succession of elderly relatives: three aunts, an uncle, his grandmother. "When you're a kid, you don't notice the difference," he said. "Taking care of old people, taking them to the bathroom, pouring food into a tube in their bellies . . . Everyone pitched in." So he had few qualms about having his mother-in-law around.

But this multigenerational household was under pressure; Ilze, untangling strands of Christmas tree lights, sounded less buoyant. "There is a honeymoon period; I expected it to be over at some point," she told me. But perhaps not this quickly.

Her mother was growing depressed. For the past three nights, she hadn't joined the family for dinner. Partly, Ilze thought, the season was affecting her: Her father used to drink during the holidays and her mother often felt low then. But partly, Mrs. Betins was responding to the reality of the situation.

The retirement community "was her home, it was familiar," Ilze recognized. "I think she had a sense of control there." Now Mrs. Betins, living almost like a widow, was telling Ilze she felt "shattered" and "lost."

"I don't know what to say to her," Ilze confessed. "She said to me the other day, 'This isn't my house.' And it's true, it's not. I said, 'This isn't your house, but it's your family.' I couldn't think of anything else to say to make her feel she belonged here . . .

"It's affecting me, too," Ilze went on. "I feel like I have to do something, I have to take care of it somehow, but I don't know what to do." Wearing her clinical hat—she was a social worker, after all—it seemed clear that her mother, diagnosed with depression in the past, should be taking medication. "But I can't make her take it," Ilze said.

Perhaps she had always experienced mood swings like this, but they'd been largely masked by distance. Ilze had seen her almost weekly, but she hadn't actually lived with her since leaving for college at 18. Weekend visits, she'd decided, presented "a phony snapshot of what's going on."

When I walked across the breezeway, I found Mrs. Betins upstairs at her kitchen table, drinking tea and feeling miserable. It was a sunny day, a bright room, "a very happy place to be," she said unconvincingly. "But I left my life behind. Not by my choice."

Maybe she'd made some mistakes, she thought. She'd hoped that her husband would be less angry here, but she'd seen no improvement. She wondered if she should have taken more time, visited for a couple of weeks, before deciding to move in. A woman who remembered shoveling snow and raking leaves at her own home, though she didn't acknowledge that it had been two years since she could, she now felt useless. She insisted on paying Ilze and Laurence $300 a month so that she wouldn't be "a burden"; understanding her need to contribute, they accepted her check. But she felt too weak to care for her granddaughter, or in some other way carry her weight in the household.

"I look like a healthy person," she said, growing weepy. "But I am not healthy. My back hurts so bad. When I wash and dress myself, I am exhausted." If she had an open wound, everyone would see that she was incapable of doing much more than caring for herself, she explained. But pain was invisible.

She also sometimes complained about her not-quite-finished bathroom and angrily fended off Ilze's continuing attempts to install a stair lift—yet she did acknowledge her efforts. "My daughter do everything to make me happy, to please me," she told me. "Better to say nice things, for my daughter's sake . . . I should pretend to be happy. When I have bitter feelings, I should swallow them."

But her daughter, of course, could clearly see the tailspin. Ilze empathized, but at the same time, she herself was suffering in her caretaker role. She was popping awake in the middle of the night, too anxious to fall asleep again. She was falling behind in her work, and had missed a deadline. The hours she spent each week dealing with the nursing home, the doctors and lawyers, the finances, practically constituted a part-time job. She let her horseback riding lessons go; there wasn't time.

She was "an immigrant kid" who'd always felt "overinvested" in family duties, who served as her parents' translator and advocate. Now, Latvian tradition dictated that a daughter take responsibility for elderly parents; any institution, like assisted living, was taboo. "How many obligations can you take on?" Ilze wondered.

One source of comfort was her brother. They hadn't been particularly close as children—he was 11 years older—but when their father's illness became apparent, "I called Hans and said, 'I can't do this on my own. I need you to help me,'" Ilze said. Now, they spoke almost daily, felt more allied than they had in decades. "Strength in numbers," Hans liked to say. But he couldn't help much with these daily ups and downs.

Things blew up a few days later. The trigger was trivial: Mrs. Betins had said she needed socks, the kind supposed to help diabetics' circulation, though she wasn't diabetic. Ilze ordered several pairs online.

"No, no. They're not good. They're not right," Mrs. Betins told her dismissively when Ilze presented them on Christmas Eve. "Send them back."

"Can you calm down and try them on?" Ilze asked.

They wrangled about socks until, Ilze said, "I lost it and said, 'Would you just stop it? You're making me feel like nothing I do for you is okay. I can't take it!'"

Mrs. Betins went back to her cottage in tears; Ilze, also weeping, withdrew to the library.

"This is old stuff," she realized after a few days had passed. "Because it's a parent and child, that old dynamic is still there; it doesn't go away." Even as a young girl, Ilze remembered her mother being "hypercritical" about a long list of things: her appearance, her reading habits, the occasional A-minus on a school test instead of an A.

There was a reason why, after getting her undergraduate degree, she headed for California and stayed for 13 years. "I made myself inaccessible," she said. Even when she returned to New York and loyally went to see her parents, she stuck to three-hour visits, "and sometimes we didn't last three hours."

This history was on her mind when she pressed her mother to come live with her. And yet, "I convinced myself I could manage it. I was wiser, I had defenses against it. I thought I could handle it."

By Christmas Day, the tension had eased; everyone genially ate a good dinner, opened gifts, sat by the fire afterward to reminisce.

But Ilze was wary. She clipped a notice from the local paper about an Alzheimer's support group that met nearby. It was an inexact fit, but it might help.

Just after New Year's, I rode along on a bright Sunday afternoon as Ilze and Mrs. Betins paid their weekly visit to the nursing home.

"I like snow so very much," Mrs. Betins declared, remembering the enormous drifts of her Baltic childhood. On their last drive to the home, "the trees were completely covered with snow, like a Christmas postcard. When you go for a ride and see nature, it lifts your spirits up." This trip, past farmhouses, barns, and John Deere dealerships, was lovely, too.

Mrs. Betins approved of the nursing home; she thought her husband was being well cared for. "So clean," she said. "When Ilze chose, she looked from place to place, not just the first one. But he complain and complain."

Today was no exception. They walked into Mr. Betins's semiprivate room, where his wife had arranged a montage of family photos on the wall to remind him of better days. Mrs. Betins trilled hello and sat down next to his wheelchair to chat; he didn't offer a smile or a greeting.

Ilze busied herself removing dead leaves from the plant she'd put on his windowsill, and quietly translated for me.

"He's complaining, 'Leave me alone.'"

"He's arguing with her about why he was brought here, saying he doesn't belong here. She's trying to calm him down, redirect him, change the subject.

"He just called her a whore."

Mr. Betins still had the barrel-chested brawn of a construction worker, a ruddy face, a forceful voice. Although multiple doctors, thanks to the ongoing court case, had testified to his mental incompetence, he could appear fairly lucid. "When you talk to him, he sounds okay," Ilze said. "He doesn't say he's Napoleon." But his "executive functioning," the ability to have insight and make judgments, was severely impaired, which was why he kept insisting that he could return to New Jersey and care for himself, though he depended on aides for virtually every function except eating.

Twice, Ilze had actually had a pleasant visit with him here, when he asked about the grandchildren and the new house. Perhaps, she thought, he was turning a corner. Instead, he resumed accusing her of theft and called her, in Latvian, a "bitch in heat." I once sat at the dining room table with her as she confessed her fantasy: "One day he'll snap out of this and he'll be my old dad," she said, sobbing. "And we'll sit and have a chat. He'll come to the house and see the garden and ask what vegetables I'm planting." The reality was that on a subsequent visit, he'd told her to fuck herself.

This visit seemed little better. His wife wheeled Mr. Betins into the hallway for a change of scenery. He furiously pulled the lever to lock his wheelchair. "My buddy," he growled in English to a passing aide, "throw those three ladies out."

"Okay, we go home," his wife said.

They stopped briefly at the nursing station. Ilze had been sparring with administrators because a nurse had canceled the neurology consult she'd set up for him weeks in advance. The reason: Mr. Betins refused to go. He also sometimes refused his medications. Ilze was calling and writing letters, reminding the staff that he had dementia and couldn't make such decisions, that it was the staff's job to ensure he got the medical attention she, his legal co-guardian, had arranged for. Discussions were continuing.

The ride home, in dimming afternoon light, was quiet. "Everyone reminds you that this is not your father talking, it's the disease," Ilze reflected. "But how do you separate the two when it *looks* like your dad and it sounds like him?" Their visits had gotten very short; this one had lasted barely half an hour.

"I think that is the right thing to do," Mrs. Betins said sadly. "Next time, if he is upset, bye-bye, honey, until next time."

"That's better for everybody," Ilze agreed.

Over the next few days, she looked for the support group announcement she'd clipped, but couldn't locate it. She called the county Office on Aging looking for a caregiver support program and came up empty. She looked into a geriatric care management practice at an Albany hospital, but learned she lived too far away to enroll. There was a geriatric care manager named Laura Murray in nearby Ghent, though, and Ilze arranged to see her as soon as possible.

She still felt it better to have her parents nearby, but tending to their needs while grappling with work, court, and her own family was so much more work than she'd anticipated, and so much more anguish. "I thought I could handle it and I still think I can," she told me on the phone. "I'm just feeling overwhelmed. I've realized, I can't do it alone. I need help."

Support

It's a point many caregivers reach, but don't like to concede. They want to be strong and capable, patient and nurturing; they're supposed to be the ones providing assistance, not the ones who need it. They try to shrug off problems—persistent sleep disruption, say—by telling themselves that other families have it worse. They don't want to acknowledge that they're struggling.

To recognize, however, when caring for a parent is injuring you physically, sapping you emotionally, or draining you financially is vital. Caregivers shouldering a high "level of burden," whose intensive duties consume many hours, whose own health suffers, who feel trapped in their roles, can endanger themselves as well as their loved ones. In a study by AARP and the National Alliance for

Caregiving, such people represented 10 to 30 percent of a national sample of caregivers.

At risk for a variety of problems with their physical health, caregivers develop chronic conditions like diabetes and hypertension at much higher rates than noncaregivers. They're also psychologically vulnerable, reporting elevated levels of stress, anxiety, and depression. The risks mount when a parent has dementia.

And having a coresiding parent appears particularly demanding. It's harder to evade conflict and tension when parent and child are under one roof. Sharing a household was one of the factors associated with caregivers' emotional stress, and with fair or poor health, in the AARP/National Alliance for Caregiving survey.

When another team of AARP researchers asked baby boomers aged 45 to 55 if they experienced stress from feeling "sandwiched between the needs of my immediate family and older relatives," 18 percent said they did. But among those who lived with a parent or in-law, the proportion nearly doubled, to 34 percent.

The experience can undermine relationships with the very people caregivers are working so hard to help. While only 16 percent of those boomers said caring for older relatives had caused "a lot of stress" or "some stress" in their relationship with parents or parents-in-law, that response was much more common (29 percent) among those who lived with their parents or in-laws.

The fact that the majority of the respondents who lived with their parents nevertheless portray the experience as positive, one that didn't cause much stress, shows that the multigenerational household can be a reasonable and rewarding possibility.

"Caregiver gain" is a real phenomenon: The great majority of baby boomers the AARP surveyed said they agreed with this statement: "Even if my parents could afford to hire help to do what I do for them, I would still want to do it myself." And the proportion who agreed was even higher—83 percent—among those who already were caregivers. Only a few said they felt resentful. More than 70 percent said helping their elders had drawn them closer.

Still, we know that for the most part, parents living independently who move into a child's household do so for serious reasons: Declining health and mounting disabilities, a spouse's death, depleted finances, a need for emotional and social support. Even more than other children caring for parents, those in shared households need to take support for themselves seriously—whether they turn to adult day programs, to geriatric care managers like Laura Murray, to siblings or other family members, to respite programs and other services.

More and more, geriatricians and senior agencies see both generations as their clients. At the Massachusetts General Hospital Geriatric Medicine Unit, "our philosophy and our approach is that the caregivers have to be as understood and cared for as the patients," says Barbara Moscowitz. "The most practical reason is, if the caregiver can't provide care, the patient won't survive." Caregivers resist such efforts at times, but "we tell them, 'We're talking about a chronic disease that could go on for years. You can't do it all.' "

I've seen even the most devoted children come to this realization when the months stretch on and a parent's presence in the household leaves them weary or besieged.

Louise Price, for instance, had been taking care of her mother, Mary Christiansen, for more than a year when we first began talking. Mrs. Christiansen had been a lively 84-year-old who volunteered at the senior center in Burlington, Massachusetts, kept up with a Thursday night bingo game, and so frequently walked around the nearby mall that store managers knew her by name. But after Mrs. Christiansen suffered a major stroke in February 2005, her doctor said she would need around-the-clock care.

"She's going to a nursing home," he told Louise. "She's not going home again."

"Yes, she is," Louise said. "She's coming to my house."

The nursing home where Mrs. Christiansen spent five weeks in rehab dismayed Louise and her brothers. When her mother soiled herself, it might take several hours before an aide changed her. Louise once discovered her mother's head wedged against the bars on the bed. At one point, Mrs. Christiansen became dehydrated and required intravenous fluids; she also developed a pressure sore on her heel—all indications of inadequate care. "I used to go to work at 4 a.m. and leave at 1 so I could be with my mom at lunchtime," Louise said. "I saw them set a tray in front of her and then walk away."

So Louise, then 56, left her accounting job and moved her mother into her spare bedroom in nearby Woburn. She learned to do everything trained nursing assistants do: She helped her mother transfer to a wheelchair and a commode, supervised physical therapy exercises, bathed her, gave her medications and nutrition through a feeding tube, did word puzzles with her to keep her alert.

And she didn't regret it. But as the months passed, even this energetic daughter began to falter. More than the physical toll of 24-hour caregiving, Louise suffered from isolation. Her husband, a truck driver, had gone to South Carolina to find work and came home only a few days a month. The cousin who visited regularly at first came less often, then not at all. Louise's brother in Pennsylvania called frequently, and the brother who lived closer visited twice a week. Still, "it's a very lonely job," Louise told me after the first year. "Like when someone dies and everyone's there—and then they go away. It's almost like you're forgotten."

Minuteman Senior Services, a nonprofit organization serving seniors in suburban Boston, came to the rescue in several ways. It helped enroll Mrs. Christiansen in a new program that paid family members to care for relatives receiving Medicaid. The paperwork was burdensome and the wages modest, but $1,700 a month was a big help to a daughter who'd lost her paycheck.

Minuteman also arranged for Mrs. Christiansen to spend two days a week at an adult day program. She wasn't crazy about it—she liked talking with the staff, participated in the sing-alongs and word games, but disliked the van ride to and from the center. Having five-and-a-half consecutive hours off the clock was a relief for Louise, however, who could run out to the post office, or visit family, or just relax at home.

"At first I thought I was Superwoman," Louise admitted. "But it takes a lot out of you. You can get burnt out." With adult day care, and with help from family and from Minuteman, Louise struggled but didn't burn out. She managed to keep her mother in her home until another stroke sent her back into a hospital and ended her life. "I'd do it again," Louise said, after her mother's death. "I wouldn't think twice."

※

Susan Yemin's father was in far better shape. Judah Tiktin didn't move from his own Brooklyn apartment into Susan's West-field, New Jersey, home until he was, astonishingly, 100 years old. He still took a daily neighborhood walk and could climb the short flight of stairs to what had been his grandson's bedroom. Though macular degeneration had left him unable to read much, he enjoyed a steady stream of free Talking Books from the National Library Service for the Blind and Physically Handicapped. (Mr. Tiktin's most recent shipment, when I drove down to meet him, included a biography of Dolly Madison, Lauren Bacall's latest memoir, and a book about Al Jazeera.)

Susan and her husband, Lowell, active retirees, had given Mr. Tiktin time to consider this move. With her father's eyesight, hearing, and stamina flagging, Susan was fearful of his living alone, though home aides came several hours a day. But he could also have decided to hire more help at home, Susan said, or to move into assisted living. "I'd never insist," she said. "It would be selfish to say, 'Do this for my peace of mind.'"

After her father agreed to move in, they kept his apartment for a few months, to leave open the option to return; he chose not to.

"It depends on the individual, naturally," Mr. Tiktin told me, listing his prerequisites for a shared household. "You have to be considerate, not too demanding, not too complaining. If you're rough, if you're tough, if you're loud and you like to fight, that's a different story.

"I'm satisfied," he concluded. "Of course, I'd like to be 20 years younger . . ."

Everything seemed to be working quite nicely. Mr. Tiktin took a van to the adult day program at the Jewish Community Center three days a week, so Susan and Lowell could go to the gym, volunteer at the Newark Museum, and continue their busy lives. He often went along to social evenings and synagogue events. "I think we're very fortunate. I wouldn't call it difficult at all," Susan said of the arrangement. "It's a privilege."

One day, a doctoral candidate will investigate whether there's some predictable wall children hit after their aged parents move in, and what factors contribute. For Susan and Lowell, much as they welcomed her father, the restrictions on their freedom began to chafe. "For the first six months, everything was coming up roses," she told me when I called to see how things were going. "Then, I started to feel the burden . . . It became more and more psychologically difficult, every single time we went anywhere and left him for a few hours, to have to stop and think, to leave food, to worry."

A couple that had cherished their travels, they hadn't been able to get away overnight for months. Even their once-frequent ventures into Manhattan for concerts and museums had stopped. Taking Mr. Tiktin away with them to visit family was difficult for everyone; he didn't do as well away from familiar environments. The shared household "can't change our lives to the extent that we can't do what we love to do," Susan fretted. They'd waited for their children to launch, then waited to retire. She was 66 and Lowell, 74; if they couldn't enjoy some autonomy now, when could they?

Their solution was to make use of respite care. Many assisted living communities offer apartments, meals, and personal care on a daily or weekly basis; Susan found facilities she liked nearby and arranged for Mr. Tiktin to stay while she and Lowell went to an Elderhostel program in Baltimore and camped in the Berkshires with their son's family. They also found, through a friend's recommendation, a woman willing to move into their home to care for Mr. Tiktin in their absence, which would allow them to make weekend getaways.

Reassured, they began planning a trip they'd always dreamed of—an 18-day Elderhostel island-hop through the Aegean. Mr. Tiktin would stay in assisted living while they were gone. Susan was looking forward immensely to the trip. It was possible, she thought, to take on responsibility for one's parent and still take care of oneself.

Let me share one more story. It wasn't one I expected to hear; I was interviewing Catherine Hawes, a Texas A&M professor, not because of her personal experience but because she's one of the nation's leading experts on long-term care. It turned out, though, that her mother had spent the last eight years of her life living with Catherine and her husband, Charles.

When Charlotte Roehl Hawes began to feel impeded by her arthritis at 71 and could no longer handle her finances, she asked to move in with her only child. Catherine and Charles, living then in North Carolina, added an apartment to their house so that her mother could have privacy.

Catherine also did something at least as important. Her mother was "demanding," she told me, and their relationship had long been complicated. "I'm going to have to go into therapy," Catherine told her husband. In fact, they both saw a therapist, trading off sessions according to who was more available and more in need, for two years.

"It was a wonderful thing," she told me. "You hardly ever have the experience that when your parent dies, there are no unresolved issues left." But when Mrs. Hawes died at 79, Catherine did feel that way. "Such a blessing," she said.

Therapy "was definitely worth it for me. Even if people don't have the sort of deeply ingrained issues we had, they could probably go for a few sessions and get some good pointers on how to live with your aging parent, if you're going to have them in the same household."

Ilze Earner, feeling increasingly buffeted, wound up doing something similar. The guardianship case was dragging on. She had work trips coming up that would take her on the road for days at a time, but she was afraid to leave her mother alone. And a new opportunity—and responsibility—loomed.

Two years earlier, before they'd thought of moving upstate and before her parents needed so much help, Ilze and Laurence had learned that a young cousin in Latvia, a child named Kristina, was in trouble. Abandoned by her teenaged mother, she'd been found emaciated and lice-ridden in an unheated hut. Ilze had met Kristina once on a visit, had been wiring money occasionally to the child's mother. Now suddenly alone, Kristina was available for adoption.

Ilze and Laurence had hoped for a second child, but after a miscarriage when Ilze was 43, they concluded the time had passed. But here was a member of her own family in desperate need. In Latvia, Ilze knew, Kristina would be an outcast; if the Earners didn't take her in, she would likely grow up in an orphanage. How could they turn away? "Go get her," Laurence said. They'd petitioned to adopt Kristina, and the adoption had recently been approved. In the spring, therefore, they'd have to spend a month in Latvia; then they could bring home their new five-year-old. It was both a happy occasion and an additional source of stress.

Laura Murray, whom Ilze had called, had been in practice as a geriatric care manager for more than a decade and was qualified to provide a number of services, from suggesting ways to make the cottage staircase safer to helping Ilze with nursing home conflicts. But Ilze decided that her most immediate need was psychotherapy for herself. As a licensed clinical social worker, Laura could offer that, too.

"This is primarily for me," Ilze said when she called for an appointment. "I'm the caregiver and I feel overwhelmed. *I'm* the patient. I need support. I need someone who'll listen to me, who'll let me cry and not feel like they have to fix it. And then, some practical advice."

Finding Oxygen

It's tough enough to care for two parents in different locations, harder still when one shares your home and the other's dementia causes heartache. And if you're also making long drives to court hearings in another state where the opposing lawyer portrays you as a heartless plunderer? "You tell people this story, they think you've been drinking," Laurence said.

The more Ilze thought about it, the more she thought a support group might not be sufficient, even if she could locate one in her rural county. Perhaps she wasn't yet ready to listen and help prop up someone else; what she needed was to talk and to be propped up herself. Aside from her husband and brother, whom could she confide in? Friends and colleagues in the city were sympathetic, "but they've never been caretakers," Ilze said. "They don't have children, nor do they care for parents. They politely listen and say, 'Oh wow, that must be hard. So—when can we get together?'"

Laura Murray, however, had spent years helping local families handle eldercare, and had cared for her own mother and mother-in-law. From the first session, Ilze said, "I had the sense of sitting with someone who *knew*. I didn't have to explain and explain. I was drowning, and having her feels like oxygen."

Laura initially spent a lot of time letting Ilze tell about her travails. "One of the biggest things you can give a caregiver is just compassionate listening," she said, after Ilze had given her permission to discuss their therapeutic sessions with me. But Laura also offered pragmatic counsel.

She suggested strategies for coping with stresses that couldn't be avoided, but might be managed more effectively—the mail, for instance. Ilze received a constant stream of bills, forms, legal documents, applications, all related to her parents' care and much of it distressing or frustrating.

Put everything in a box, Laura advised, and set aside a day and time to open mail and deal with it. "You have to contain it," she cautioned. "Otherwise, it takes over your life." Ilze liked the idea; she didn't set up an actual box, but developed a mental box and set this chore aside until Friday afternoons, from noon till two.

They spoke, too, about the distressing visits to her father, which made Ilze feel ineffective and guilty, the bad daughter who'd consigned her father to an institution. Children who care for parents could suddenly feel 12 years old again, Laura noted, as half-buried conflicts were retriggered and "a lot of old familyscapes get replayed."

Laura offered a mental image: a protective suit Ilze could put on and zip up before entering the nursing home. Ilze explained the technique: "I acknowledge that this is hard. I'm going into something that makes me feel vulnerable. I stop, have a look around at the world, take a deep breath, put on the armor, and go in." Afterward, whatever ugliness had transpired, she could unzip the hazmat suit and return to her own skin, to her hard-won sense of herself as a competent adult, a caring mother and daughter, a professional woman. "I like the visual image," Ilze said. "I'm going to try it."

Laura also began coming to see Mrs. Betins in her cottage twice a month. Ilze had introduced her, very neutrally, as a social worker she'd found helpful. Laura thought Mrs. Betins "a very strong-willed woman—she couldn't have survived what she has in her life, otherwise—who is able to articulate where she's at. She's a great counseling client. Even people in their 90s can benefit from counseling.

"She knows Ilze is doing the best she can in a difficult situation . . . She realizes that given the choices, Ilze had to bring her parents up here. But that doesn't negate her own losses."

Each woman was trying, out of love and concern, to protect the other from her sorrow; Laura's goal was to help heal the family by allowing them to grieve together, to support each other without having to pretend that everything was sunny. "There's a good foundation," Laura said. "Ilze's life will never be the same, and neither will her mother's. But do I hope and think things will be different, better for all of them? Absolutely."

꧁꧂

Already, as spring approached, there had been some improvements. Ilze thought her mother's emotional state had a lot to do with her diet and once more began insisting that she eat dinner with them; perhaps for that reason, Mrs. Betins rallied and appeared less depressed. "She's been easier," Ilze reported. "Easier to be around, easier to talk to."

On Ilze's 52nd birthday, her mother gave her a card and told her, "I really want to thank you for everything you've done. I know it's not easy."

"It's not easy for either of us," Ilze said truthfully.

They had a reasonably pleasant birthday celebration for Mr. Betins at the nursing home. Thanks to an antiseizure drug called Depakote, he was less hostile, less prone to name-calling. Ilze brought both her mother and her daughter, and a cake, flowers, and balloons; they opened a bottle of nonalcoholic champagne. "Let's toast your 90 years," his wife said. He blew out the candles and happily accepted kisses from the nurses. He was, Ilze said, "about as benign as he ever gets." With the new drug, "he still says hurtful things, but that aggressive edge is gone."

It had been prescribed after the latest neurological evaluation—his fifth. As part of the ongoing guardianship struggle, Ilze had been compelled to find a Latvian-speaking neurologist—and she'd actually located one ("I think I deserve a gold star") in Albany. She and her mother sat in as the doctor spent 90 minutes examining the obstreperous patient.

He had probably had a stroke after his knee surgery, the doctor explained in Latvian. She used the blunt colloquial phrase *caurums galva*—literally, holes in the head. "She told him, 'You're not going to walk again. You probably will need 24-hour skilled nursing care for the rest of your life. You're being well taken care of. Your family is doing the right thing,'" Ilze reported. Then the doctor took Mrs. Betins aside to privately assure her again: They'd done the right thing.

And even though they'd already known Laimonias Betins was mentally incompetent—he listened blankly to what the neurologist said, insisted that he could walk (but was unable to rise from his wheelchair when she asked him to demonstrate), and cursed his wife—Ilze and her mother drove home with a renewed sense of validation and relief. "Now, two doctors say he is in the right place," Mrs. Betins told me later. "The doctor tells us, 'Just visit him, say hello; when he gets angry, go home. You cannot change him. He doesn't know what he is doing.'"

As the encrusted ice finally receded after a tough winter, Ilze took to clearing scrub and digging out future flower beds, a favorite pastime and a good physical antidote to anxiety. She wanted to learn how to safely use a chain saw, she told me when I drove up in early spring; she thought it would be therapeutic.

A couple of business trips related to a research grant, which involved visiting detention centers where immigrant children were held, had left her feeling tired but affirmed. Work can be a strain for caregivers, but it can also be a source of satisfaction. "I felt competent," Ilze said. "Here were people who appreciated me, who thought I was helpful and knew what I was doing."

On the home front, she was planning some changes. With Laura Murray's full support, she intended to move her father from his current nursing home, where the staff had stopped administering Depakote when he refused to take it. Ilze had enough battles, she said, "the last thing I need is to fight with a nursing home." A smaller, county-owned nursing home with a good reputation was opening a dementia unit with specialized activities and a family support program. She sent in the paperwork.

She'd stopped visiting her father on Fridays. Going with her mother on Sundays allowed her to monitor his care, have a conversation if he was in the mood, while limiting her exposure to crude attacks.

"I felt very guilty," Ilze said, puttering around the kitchen as we spoke, preparing dinner. "But Laura"—concerned about her emotional well-being—"asked me, point blank, 'He's being taken care of. Why do you go?' I frankly didn't have a good answer."

She was stepping up the legal action, too, hiring a local attorney to move the guardianship case to New York State and retaining a more experienced litigator in New Jersey. "The truth will come out," Ilze kept telling herself.

She saw some benefits to her multigenerational household, along with the strains. She felt closer to her mother now, more empathetic. "I've taken to telling her how much I appreciate her support," she said. Mrs. Betins reciprocated, emphasizing that she knew how hard Ilze was working and that she was grateful. "Don't talk to your daughter that way," she scolded her husband when he assailed Ilze. Hans continued to check in regularly.

Slowly, not without pain, the family was beginning to coalesce. Perhaps the month Ilze and Laurence were about to spend in a beach house in Latvia—with Maize, Mrs. Betins, and five-year-old Kristina, their new child—could help strengthen those feelings.

Even the nightly dinner hour helped. Ilze was making salmon fillets tonight—protein was important for her mother—along with collard greens, and black rice from her favorite Asian food shop in Manhattan. Laurence was in Brooklyn, so it would be just the three generations of Betins/Earner women, plus an interloper—I'd invited myself.

The family meal had become something Ilze liked about this new life she'd undertaken. In her youth, her father came home from work and settled before the TV with his meal, leaving Ilze and her mother alone at the table. Eventually, they, too, started eating silently in the living room, staring at the screen. In their own busy, two-career household in Brooklyn, the Earners had often grabbed dinners at nearby restaurants or gone individually rummaging through the fridge.

It was different now. "I like the ritual of it," Ilze said, setting out place mats and candlesticks in the apricot dining room. "Five o'clock comes and I have to stop work if I want to get dinner ready. Seven o'clock comes and we're gathered around the table. Then we sit by the fire for a while, and sometimes my mother sits with us, and it closes the evening."

I saw what she meant. Summoned by Maize, Mrs. Betins walked in carefully with her cane. She'd brought her pill-pack, though all she took were vitamins and Tylenol. "I tell the doctor, if everyone was like me, the pharmacists go to the poorhouse," she declared proudly. Ilze, probably still thinking that antidepressants and arthritis drugs might be a fine idea, smiled and passed the salmon.

They talked of this and that, not always simple because Mrs. Betins didn't hear well but refused a hearing aid. Maize's rabbit had pneumonia, the vet said, but would recover. Mr. Betins had undergone an MRI, but with a sedative he'd remained calm during the procedure.

"Looking for the holes in the head," his wife said.

"Like Swiss cheese," Ilze agreed. They shared a quiet chuckle.

She couldn't say, Ilze told me afterward, that such interludes compensated for the pressures that sometimes still threatened to swamp her. But they mattered, nonetheless; they offered a vision of a more harmonious future.

"My mother appreciates this," she said. "One night, we were having dinner and she said, 'Look at this. This is really nice. Everyone sits down together and the table is beautifully set and you always light the candles. You didn't have this as a child, but growing up, Maize will have good memories of this.'"

Ilze allowed herself a moment's satisfaction. Things could seem bleak, but not always. Not tonight. "There are nice, peaceful parts of this that will remain," she said, "after the storm has passed."

~⌇~

_____

SOME QUESTIONS TO CONSIDER ABOUT
SHARING A HOUSEHOLD:

Can your parent function independently in your home? Will he be able to manage most of his personal care? Pitch in with some household duties? Or will he need not only a room, meals, and transportation but also help with ADLs—activities of daily living like bathing or dressing?

Can you retrofit your home, or sections of it, to make it safe for an elderly person with health problems or disabilities? Will your parent be secure on the stairs and in the bathroom?

How important is privacy, and can you adapt your home to provide it? Will sharing a bathroom, or a single television set or phone line, be problematic? Will household noises disturb your parent? Will his waking up at night or watching TV at high volume disturb you?

If you're working, will your parent spend his days alone? Will that be risky, or isolating? Are there local senior centers or adult day programs that can provide him with companionship, meals, perhaps health monitoring, during the day?

Have you discussed with other family members the changes your parent's move into your household will bring? The ways it may impact your schedules and routines, your work and school and social lives? Your finances?

If your parent is unable to be home alone for more than a few hours, can you arrange for occasional respite care, so that you can take a business trip, have a weekend away, plan a vacation?

Do you and your parent have a history of enjoying time together, discussing problems openly, reaching compromises? Will your personalities fit amicably under one roof?

Can siblings or other family members share the responsibilities, even if your parent is living in your household? Can they stay in your home while you're away, take your parent on regular outings, or help pay out-of-pocket costs?

THREE

MOVING ON

Assisted Living

THE HOUSE JOHN DUTTON HAD LIVED IN FOR CLOSE TO 40 YEARS was a classic. A kindergartner asked to draw a house would probably come up with something that looked like this, a white clapboard colonial with a green door, green window shutters, a brick chimney. The trees along the curved street were mostly bare when I first drove up, the buds still furled on the rhododendron that the Duttons and all their neighbors seem to have planted decades ago. But in a few more weeks, spring would engulf Newton, Massachusetts. And before long, it would be warm enough for Mr. Dutton to have dinner on the screened porch off the living room.

Mr. Dutton and his wife, Mary, had raised their two boys here, in a cultured household where everyone played a musical instrument, where the Metropolitan Opera wafted from the radio every Saturday afternoon. In many respects, the house had hardly changed since they'd moved in. "Same furniture," in the Scandinavian style popular in the '60s, said Steve Dutton, the younger son. "Same rugs. It's like a time machine."

It had grown a bit frayed, true, in need of new windows, a new kitchen, new lots of things. But it was spacious, with a spare bedroom where Mr. Dutton used his computer (an IBM retiree, he was the only senior with an email address I met while researching this book), and ample room for his older son Paul, a freelance accountant who was often on the road but lived here when he wasn't. It was full of things Mr. Dutton enjoyed having around him, like the still lifes his mother had painted and an extensive collection of old phonograph records. His goal, he told me, was "staying as long as I can."

But how long, exactly, would that be? Mary had died in 2000 after an extended struggle with cancer. Since then, trying to cope with that grave loss and also with his own multiplying health problems, Mr. Dutton had been giving some thought to assisted living. He'd looked at several facilities in and around Boston, had even put down a deposit at a well-regarded place called Goddard House, in nearby Brookline. But then a few months passed, and then a year, and he didn't move. Yet he hadn't ruled it out, either; Goddard House still had his $1,500.

The word Mr. Dutton used to describe this state of mind was "ambivalent."

"I'm ambivalent about the whole process," he'd say, or slip in a reference to "my ambivalent nature." He could see, with admirable clarity, the advantages and disadvantages to both moving out and staying put. Which set outweighed the other seemed to shift with his energy, his mood, the state of his investment portfolio.

We sat in the sunroom that spring morning, talking about ambivalence. Mr. Dutton, walking slowly with his cane, carefully carried in a tray of tea biscuits, then glasses of juice. Elegant-looking at 86, he was trim and elongated. He still had lots of hair, now frosty, and bushy silver eyebrows presiding over a sculptured face, and wore a hearing aid behind each ear. His navy sweater, twill trousers, and lace-up shoes could have come out of the L.L. Bean catalogue. "I guess I could call myself a WASP," he mused. He'd grown up in the small village of Hartford, Vermont, and retained the spare speech and thrifty ways that old-time Vermonters are known for.

This meant, among other things, that he'd saved old postage stamps, worth eight cents or 20, and still combined them on outgoing envelopes. And it meant that after Steve discovered a leak below his 30-year-old dishwasher, Mr. Dutton began washing dishes by hand rather than replace it.

The idea of spending $4,390 a month for a one-bedroom apartment at Goddard House felt, therefore, like a stab in the chest. (Assisted living costs in Boston were among the highest in the country.) Mr. Dutton could pay that sum, thanks to his IBM pension—he'd retired as a sales systems engineer—and his lifetime of careful investing, but not without true angst.

He wanted to pass on more to his children than his father, a rural mail carrier, had been able to give him. "I've accumulated a little bit and I'd like to leave it behind when I shuffle off," he explained, "instead of using it up myself."

"That's what you have it *for*," Paul said, joining the conversation in the sunroom. He was 49, single, and still a bit boyish in his jeans and sneakers and t-shirt. Steve, who was 47 and divorced, had a business in Manhattan. Both sons insisted that they didn't need their father's money (neither had children) and that a comfortable life in his later years was exactly what he should spend it on. But their protests didn't seem to have much impact, and neither wanted to push their father to leave his home. "I want *him* to make the choice," Paul said. "No one likes to feel pressured."

Yet they could all see the risks of waiting. Assisted living was for people who needed help with things like meals and housekeeping, bathing, or taking medications—but who could still function with some independence. A sudden health crisis could make someone too sick or frail for a place like Goddard House. "There's a point where they won't take people, in terms of mobility," Mr. Dutton pointed out. And he was already conscious of losing some ground.

"There are times it gets a little wearying, just to do simple things," he acknowledged. "Like changing a lightbulb—without Paul here, I'd be sunk . . . I used to rake the lawn and plant a few little things; now all that bending over is too much." He prepared meals—"nothing fancy, but I can broil a piece of meat and steam some vegetables"—but found the cooking and cleaning up increasingly arduous. "Sometimes, I take the easy way out and have a TV dinner."

Mealtimes could feel a bit solitary, too, since Paul was often out of town, seeing clients across New England. A neighbor sometimes invited them for dinner, and a cousin's son-in-law came on Tuesday nights with chili or pot roast in a Crock-Pot, generous acts that Mr. Dutton appreciated.

Yet he was still often on his own. He and his wife used to eat at the kitchen table and observed a strict rule: no television during meals. "But since I've been alone, I don't want to look at the kitchen walls while I eat," Mr. Dutton confessed. "I've been taking a tray into the living room," to have dinner with Jim Lehrer on PBS and Alex Trebek on *Jeopardy*.

Meanwhile, Paul worried. His father took half a dozen medications, most related to heart disease, and his days often revolved around doctor's appointments. In the past 16 months, he'd been hospitalized with pneumonia, hospitalized again after a fall in downtown Boston, had a defibrillator implanted in his chest to regulate his heart rate.

"His balance is significantly worse and his walk has slowed down," Paul said. Sometimes, just watching his father hover precariously as he tried to rise from a chair could give him an anxious moment. "Nobody's here if he falls," he said. "At Goddard House, there are people around; if something happens, there's help."

I saw what he meant when, a few days later, Mr. Dutton and I set out for an afternoon stroll around the block. We ambled along comfortably, talking about his Navy service on the USS *Alaska* during World War II, for perhaps ten minutes. After that, I tried not to be frightened about how long and hilly the block turned out to be, how hazardous the uneven sidewalks could become, or the way Mr. Dutton had to stop two or three times to rest on his cane. It was a relief to make our way back to the house.

He'd made some accommodations. For a long time, he'd staved off his children's concern about his driving. Then, a few months earlier, he'd suddenly decided it was time to stop, and sold his Honda back to the dealer. (On the way home from negotiating the sale, he edged too close to a parked car on a narrow street and knocked off its side mirror, confirming his judgment.) Now he phoned greater Boston's convenient door-to-door transit service for the elderly and disabled, called The Ride, to take him to doctors' offices and to Sunday services at historic Old South Church, where he'd been a member for nearly 50 years.

But he hadn't made as many adaptations as Steve and Paul argued for. If he wanted to stay in the house, Steve thought, "he needs to ramp up a notch" and hire more help. The estimable Donna, formerly his wife's home care aide, came twice a week for just two hours—barely long enough for a little housecleaning, laundry, some errands, and shopping. She could come more often, but Mr. Dutton hadn't asked her to.

So the status remained quo. Steve had suggested that his father move into Goddard House for a year's trial; since he didn't have to sell the house to finance the stay, he'd retain the option of moving back if he was unhappy. The idea met with little enthusiasm.

"His waffling is the thing that makes me crazy," Steve lamented after one visit. "I don't know what he really wants, and I'm not sure he does either." Sometimes he wished the family had "an independent third party to sit down and talk with my dad" and help reach some resolution.

Actually, such a person already existed—a geriatric care manager Mr. Dutton had consulted, several years earlier, on the advice of his neurologist.

Suzanne Modigliani, like most people in this emerging specialty, was trained as a social worker; she'd had years of experience with local seniors and was very knowledgeable about aging, family dynamics, and the array of Boston-area facilities, programs, and services for the elderly. She'd set Mr. Dutton up with a professional organizer who came regularly to help him sort through his many boxes of memorabilia. He also had an upcoming appointment with a financial consultant Modigliani had referred him to, to help answer the question of how long he could afford assisted living, should he decide to move. Modigliani had accompanied Mr. Dutton on one of his visits to Goddard House, which she thought would be a good fit.

But Modigliani charged $125 an hour at the time, and while lots of families found that a reasonable investment ("Cheaper than getting on the shuttle," one out-of-state daughter said), Mr. Dutton couldn't stomach such fees. He hadn't contacted her in months. Instead of talking with him frequently, monitoring his situation, and helping him and his sons work through their quandary, she'd been left out of the loop.

So they were on their own. Mr. Dutton thought Goddard House "a very nice place. The public rooms don't look institutional; they're small and cozy." It would be pleasant to have concerts just outside his door, he thought, and real people to eat dinner with. A friend from church who lived there seemed content.

When the marketing director had called a few weeks earlier about an available one-bedroom, "I was almost ready to take the plunge," he said. "Openings are rather scarce."

But when he and Paul went to see the apartment, Mr. Dutton decided it was too small—at least, that's what he said at the time.

"But the real reason," he confided now, "was that I was ambivalent."

Mrs. Wunderlich

Margaret Wunderlich had never met Mr. Dutton—she lived a half hour away, in senior housing in Arlington—but they had things in common. More than a year earlier, she, too, had put down a deposit at an assisted living facility, Providence House in Brighton, then subsequently wavered. She told her children she wasn't ready to move yet. That she was about to turn 95 didn't shake her resolve.

Moreover, she and Mr. Dutton had much the same sentiment about the cost of assisted living, and about money in general. On the face of it, this made little sense. Mr. Dutton had a private pension, investments, and a house in an affluent suburb that, should he decide to sell it, could pay for Goddard House for many years. Mrs. Wunderlich was living in a subsidized one-bedroom in a utilitarian brick building, for which she paid the Arlington Housing Authority $281 a month. ("With heat!" she pointed out. "*And* hot water.") The $1,000 a month, roughly, that Social Security sent was virtually her only income.

Yet to hear them speak about the monthly checks they'd have to write for assisted living—and Mrs. Wunderlich's would have been much smaller—you'd think they were equally bound for ruin. What underlay their anxieties, of course, was the Depression, along with the war the overarching event of their youths. "We were lucky if we could buy bread," Mrs. Wunderlich told me, when we first met in early spring. "People don't understand unless they lived through it."

I understood a little, because of my Depression-era parents. In fact, I told her about my father's latest money-saving scheme: When he and a friend realized they were sending their Discover Card payments to the same address, they started mailing them in a single envelope. And when the company understandably misapplied one's check to the other's account, did they stop? No, they merely began stapling the checks to their payment stubs, thus preserving annual savings of $2.52 each. It's a story that gets laughs from my peers, but Mrs. Wunderlich just said, "He and I talk the same language." She looked so approving and thoughtful that I wondered if she was mentally sorting through her friends in search of a potential accomplice.

She'd grown up in and around Yorkville, on Manhattan's then-scruffy Upper East Side. Hers was a tough saga: She'd lost her mother when she was 13, left school, trained as a baby nurse. Though she and her late husband, Rudy, an insurance underwriter and musician, had moved to Massachusetts more than 40 years ago, you could still hear New York in her voice. Stocky, with a fleshy face and bright blue eyes, she wore her hair so carefully styled that when we met, I asked if she'd just come from a beauty parlor. "Oh, this is a wig," she said, unembarrassed.

She was sitting in her recliner, knitting a pink afghan as she watched midday Mass on the Eternal Word Network, a Catholic cable channel. But she got up to show me around her place: the bathroom fitted with a handheld shower attachment, an extended shower chair that kept her from having to climb over the side of the tub, and a raised toilet seat ("I call it the throne"); the bedroom, where "I play my little radio all night and nobody bothers me"; the kitchen full of pots and pans. She was, still, the kind of skilled cook who'd throw together a pot of barley soup because "I had a lamb chop hanging around my freezer."

Friends in the building—after 18 years here, she had many—dropped by daily to gossip, pass around books and newspapers, talk about their children and their medications. Her best pal Mary had bought parsley and oregano and basil plants at a local nursery, and created the herb-garden-in-a-pot growing on the window ledge opposite Mrs. Wunderlich's front door.

Her daughter, Peg Sprague, an executive with the United Way of Massachusetts Bay, called daily, visited at least weekly, drove her to doctors' appointments, and took her on outings. She made sure that her pill-pack—Mrs. Wunderlich had multiple prescriptions for diabetes and heart disease—was filled for the week ahead.

So why should she move to Providence House, Mrs. Wunderlich reasoned, in order to have social contact, activities, meals, medication management—all the things she already had? Here in her little flat, "everything I get, I can pay for," she said. "That suits me just fine."

It was a perfectly rational perspective, except for what had happened two months earlier.

The incident came in March, while Peg was trying to enjoy a week in Florida with her husband—with some anxiety, because in her absence Mrs. Wunderlich was dealing with a nasty virus. Peg got the 6 a.m. cell phone call every adult child dreads, from an emergency operator saying that Mrs. Wunderlich had pushed the button on the pendant she wore and reported trouble breathing. Peg's call to her mother's apartment was answered by a paramedic: They were about to put Mrs. Wunderlich into an ambulance and race to the emergency room. "We believe your mother is having a heart attack," said the doctor Peg finally reached at the hospital. Within hours, the Spragues were on a plane headed north.

"Have you ever heard the term 'caregiver burden'?" I asked Peg when I learned what her winter had been like.

The previous fall, she and Stephen, a couple since her high school prom, had finally unloaded their big house in Arlington, now that their children were grown, and settled into this small, bright condo a block from the Harbor. The Spragues were both walking to work, enjoying downtown Boston together after decades in the suburbs, driving each weekend to the country retreat they'd recently bought in southern Maine.

"Was I just deluding myself that life could be that good?" Peg sighed. We were in her living room; she'd just gotten home from work, where she supervised a team of 12 and oversaw a more than $15 million budget. I could picture her on the cover of a business magazine, the stylish, authoritative 56-year-old with the blond bob and the briefcase. But she was also open, reflective—and tired.

Last fall, she explained, Stephen was at his office when he felt a rush of blood to his head, turned sweaty, had a seizure, and within minutes was at Mass General, diagnosed with a brain hemorrhage. "It was a horrific thing," Peg said, shuddering. His doctors, scheduling him for neurosurgery, couldn't tell her whether he'd survive or, if he did, how much permanent brain damage he might have sustained. She took a leave of absence from her job; their son and daughter rushed home to help.

Stephen was just 57, a regular at the gym. "He's a healthy guy, how could this be true?" Peg wondered. "I'll wake up tomorrow and it will be a bad dream."

Astonishingly, after the surgery, after two weeks in intensive care and three weeks in rehab, Stephen Sprague came home, "among the 5 to 10 percent who survived what he survived without major deficits," Peg recounted. He continued outpatient physical and occupational therapy, and though he still tired easily, went back to work in February.

In March, therefore, they decided they'd earned a week in the sun. "Let's go sit on the beach, reconnect, be a couple, not talk about doctors and hospitals, and just be grateful"—that was how Peg envisioned the vacation in St. Petersburg. And it *was* lovely, for three days. Then came the 6 a.m. phone call about her mother, and she went right back to doctors and hospitals.

She found the hospitalized Mrs. Wunderlich in bad shape. "She was dehydrated, she was disoriented, she hadn't eaten . . . She became delusional," apparently from a drug reaction. "It was really hard to experience my mother that way. I'd never seen her mentally confused." When Peg tried to get her to take medicine or prevent her from climbing out of bed, her mother railed at her—"Why the hell don't you just leave?"

"She didn't know what she was doing," Peg recalled. "I thought I'd lose my mind." Matters improved somewhat—and then, suddenly, a social worker with a clipboard was telling them that it was time for Mrs. Wunderlich, now weakened and unsteady, to be discharged.

Providence House was a place they'd visited a year earlier, after Mrs. Wunderlich saw its opening ceremony on TV and grew curious. Codeveloped by the Archdiocese of Boston—"the seal of approval, in her mind," Peg noted—it earmarked some of its assisted living apartments for low-income seniors who couldn't pay standard Boston-area rates. Mrs. Wunderlich could have a spacious studio for $2,100, a true bargain. "It has a very homelike feel. The people were very nice," Peg said. "She left with a good feeling—'I like it, I like it.'" More tellingly, her mother wrote a $1,500 check. "Then she came home and got cold feet"—and when an apartment became available, she turned it down.

After the heart attack, Peg remembered that there was a nursing home on the same campus, right next to Providence House, and she arranged to transfer her mother there for short-term rehab. This turned out to be a good move: Mrs. Wunderlich liked the brand-new building and the staff; she regained strength and balance over two weeks, and she heard other patients and visitors praising the affiliated assisted living next door.

"So that's the dance we're in right now," Peg said, preparing to launch another discussion about moving to Providence House. Mrs. Wunderlich was still on the waiting list for a studio.

True, she seemed to be doing reasonably well back in her apartment. It helped that, like Mr. Dutton, she had a geriatric care manager: Peg had learned of Elder Resources in Newton through a friend and hired one of its experienced people to help assess her mother's needs and set up home care after rehab. Thus, a trained aide was waiting when Mrs. Wunderlich came home to Arlington and spent half a day there for the next two weeks. A nurse came to monitor her every week or two at no charge, a service of the local council on aging that the geriatric care manager had discovered. "She knew that world," Peg said, singing her praises.

But even with both her husband and her mother resuming their lives, Peg was unraveling. "I'll admit that my capacity to manage all this stuff is diminishing; I can feel it shrink," she confessed with a weary laugh. She was afraid of the next time her mother, alone in her apartment, had heart trouble or left the stove on or fell.

Assisted living—"personal safety, supervision, meals being prepared, someone checking on her, a network of support"—was sounding more attractive to Peg all the time. Her brother Fred in Virginia (their older brother had died, too young, a couple of years before) also liked the idea.

Peg wouldn't force her mother into Providence House—as if that were possible!—but she was making tactical plans. "It's the next conversation we have to have," she said. "Because I can see what's happening: She's settling in again and feeling like, 'I don't need anyone.'"

But Peg thought she did.

Not a Nursing Home

Assisted living is an idea defined largely by what it isn't: It's not a nursing home. Nobody wants to go to a nursing home, indispensable as they sometimes are; seniors and their families tend to shudder at the very phrase.

Yet elderly people increasingly survive illnesses that used to prove fatal; they live longer but also face chronic diseases, frailty, extended periods of disability. Remaining in their own homes—the choice almost everyone prefers—isn't always practicable.

So the development of an in-between option has proved enormously appealing. When Karen Love was the director of new assisted living facilities in suburban Virginia in the early 1990s, "we had people from all over the world—Japan, Italy, Australia—coming through on tours," she recalls. "It was a new way to provide care for the aging. The growth was going through the roof, and everyone wanted to come see what it looked like." Assisted living "was seen as almost-home; it filled that intermediate spot."

Take Goddard House, the assisted living complex Mr. Dutton was mulling, which opened in 1996. It's tucked into a small parcel of land in one of Boston's close-in suburbs, a short stroll from a popular park. Designed to play well architecturally with neighboring homes, it's a gabled gray clapboard building, very New England, with a long front porch lined with, yes, wooden rocking chairs. Like many of the newer assisted living facilities, it could pass for an upscale apartment complex or perhaps a small hotel, with landscaped lawns, flower beds, and the inevitable gazebo.

Inside, past the desk where the receptionist calls hello to residents and visiting family by name, the lobby features elegant upholstered furniture, a grand staircase that few residents can use (they take the elevator) but that heightens the feeling of a traditional home, Oriental-patterned carpeting and drapes. Concerts take place in the Palm Court, where there's a baby grand in one corner; exercise classes and discussion groups, in the cozier library. On the afternoon I first visited, five women were putting the finishing touches on a crafts project—cones of bright silk flowers for May Day. The dining room staff was beginning to lay out tablecloths and cloth napkins for the first of two dinner seatings. Seventy-five residents live in studio and one-bedroom apartments here, each with a private bath and kitchenette; an attached dementia unit is home to another 40 people.

Certain design elements have become so standard in assisted

living that people in the field joke about them—the gas fireplace and brass chandelier, the aviary housing parakeets or lovebirds, the gazebo. More significant, though, is what one doesn't find: no long, tiled, hospital-like corridors with nurses' stations, no residents trailing IV poles, no PA system paging anyone.

"I look around and I say, 'This is such a great way to live,'" said Goddard House's enthusiastic director, Nancy Shapiro, giving me the tour. "It's like going to a country inn." That was a stretch—but assisted living has indeed proved an attractive alternative. The model proliferated so quickly through the 1990s, as major corporations stampeded into the business, that such facilities now house close to a million seniors.

Upscale complexes like this one are only part of the picture. The idea of "almost-home" goes back decades, and the smaller places that used to serve that function are still around, known by a variety of names—board and care homes, residential care facilities, adult homes. Some are literal mom-and-pop operations—an expanded house on a suburban street, say, run by a family with a couple of other employees—that house five or six people.

Such differences make it hard to talk about assisted living, what it offers, how well it succeeds. The house down the block and the five-story stucco buildings sprouting along suburban highways are very dissimilar environments. The financial underpinnings vary, too: Goddard House, built by a venerable Boston charity, is a nonprofit entity, but more than 60 percent of assisted living facilities are for-profit businesses, many owned by national or regional chains. Moreover, families looking at facilities encounter all kinds of hybrids: assisted living attached to nursing homes, assisted living with separate dementia wings, assisted living on campuses that also include independent living apartments and nursing homes—a graduated arrangement sometimes called a continuing care community.

But assisted living does have an overall philosophy: It aims to provide personal care, 24-hour supervision and assistance, activities, and health services in a homelike setting. It's supposed to adapt to residents' changing needs, minimizing the need to move to another facility (the phrase often used is "aging in place"). And it emphasizes residents' "dignity, autonomy, privacy, independence, and safety."

In practical terms, this means residents can usually expect private living quarters they can furnish and decorate themselves. The staff prepares and serves their meals, cleans their rooms or apartments, changes their linens. "You don't have to ever make your bed again," a Goddard House nurse had promised Mr. Dutton.

Residents get help with activities of daily living like bathing, dressing, using the toilet, and taking medications. Someone's around in case of emergencies. The facilities usually provide transportation to doctors' appointments and sometimes to stores, and offer recreational outings and activities from bingo and art projects to July 4 barbecues. The larger ones usually have nurses on staff and amenities like beauty salons; Goddard House has a Bank of America branch open one morning a week. Dentists, podiatrists, physicians, and physical therapists often make house calls.

The price tag for all this makes families gulp: the monthly fee for a private one-bedroom apartment was about $3,000 in 2008, a national average that concealed great regional variation from about $2,200 a month in South Dakota to more than $4,500 in Chicago. They gulp again when they realize that a number of services—like incontinence care and personal laundry—can involve additional costs.

Unlike nursing homes, where most residents' bills are paid—initially or eventually—by Medicaid, assisted living is largely a private-pay affair. Though some facilities charge a flat payment, most use tiered pricing, so that monthly costs rise as a resident requires additional hours of staff help.

And they may very well need more assistance as the months pass. In marketing brochures, assisted living is a cheery enclave of well-groomed, healthy-looking older people, photographed while painting or strolling but rarely shown using wheelchairs or walkers. For years, that's what investors and builders had in mind, housing for active elders with financial means and without much need for expensive services.

Instead, the industry has learned, seniors stubbornly stay in their own homes for as long as they possibly can. By the time they or their children decide to investigate assisted living, either because the seniors aren't doing well at home or because they're leaving a hospital or rehab center and can't go home again—most are no longer vigorous golfers and square dancers.

⁓

This is a frail and quite elderly population, mostly female, mostly widowed. The average occupant has already celebrated her 85th birthday. Almost 70 percent of assisted living residents need help with bathing and about half with dressing, according to a 2006 industry survey; about a third can't use a toilet without assistance. Only about a quarter walk totally unaided; the rest use a cane, walker, or wheelchair. About a third have some degree of urinary incontinence. Health problems like high blood pressure, arthritis, and osteoporosis are common; estimates of those suffering depression range from 24 to 40 percent or more. Residents therefore take an average of nine drugs, both prescription and over the counter, and nearly all need help remembering when and how to take them.

That's because, in addition to their physical problems, "just about everybody has some level of cognitive impairment," recognized or unrecognized, says Philip Sloane of the University of North Carolina, who for almost 30 years has studied long-term dementia care.

Seniors enter assisted living, he points out, because they can no longer handle such complexities as coordinating their medical care or running a household; otherwise, even with physical restrictions, they could probably put together sufficient care at home. "We refer to that as 'executive function' problems," Sloane explained, "and that is one of the characteristics of what we call mild cognitive impairment." His studies indicate that 90 percent of residents exhibit at least this low level of impairment. As for the more severe disorder known as dementia—hard to measure because facilities often misdiagnose it—he estimates the proportion at between 40 and 50 percent.

"Years ago, everybody thought it was just going to be this nice fancy place where you could go and not worry about cooking," notes Sheryl Zimmerman, codirector of the Program on Aging, Disability and Long-Term Care at the University of North Carolina, Chapel Hill, who codirects the largest, most comprehensive study of assisted living ever undertaken. But residents aren't like hotel guests, it's turned out; they have considerable needs. "They look like what nursing home residents looked like 10 or 15 years ago," Zimmerman says. In fact, you sometimes hear assisted living sardonically called a nursing home with a chandelier.

For all these reasons, assisted living more often serves as a way station than a long-term home. Because seniors wait until they're in their 80s, physically dependent, and cognitively impaired before they move in, they don't stay long—just 27 months, on average. Turnover is so high that of those celebrating at the Fourth of July barbecue, as many as 40 to 50 percent will not be there for the next Independence Day.

About 30 percent die while in residence (one mordant resident I knew, a retired physician, genially referred to his facility as "assisted dying"), and some move to other assisted living facilities or to relatives' homes. But the largest proportion leave for nursing homes—rarely because they can no longer afford assisted living, but because they've come to need more care than it provides.

This may not be what children expect as they carefully shop for the most attractive assisted living they can find, with the most amenities, the most reassuring reputation. They believe they're selecting their parents' final homes and ensuring, as the brochures promise, "peace of mind"; the reality is often different.

Still, it's good news that a variety of options have cropped up between staying at home (which often means being alone) and entering a skilled nursing facility (filled, only a couple of decades ago, with people who really didn't need such medicalized environments but had nowhere else to go). Assisted living residents, though cognizant of both their own problems and their facilities' shortcomings (more on this in a bit), tell researchers that they're reasonably satisfied with their care, that the staff treats them with respect and affection, that they value the privacy and autonomy of this type of senior living. They and their children are voting with their feet for a place that's Not a Nursing Home.

One common challenge, though, is timing. "I love the model of the assisted living facility," says Barbara Moscowitz, senior social worker at the Massachusetts General Hospital Geriatric Medicine Unit. "I have seen people flourish magnificently, freed of the worry of shopping and cooking, freed of the fear of being alone . . .

"The question is, how can you help older adults choose to make the move when they are well enough that they can still engage in active living? People move into ALFs when they are sick, too sick to make connections, and so it *can* feel like they are waiting to die."

It's not hard to see why seniors resist. Relocation, stressful for anyone, is particularly hard on older adults. The sheer tasks involved—deciding what to take, packing what you want, discarding what you don't—are daunting. And cognitively impaired seniors, Moscowitz points out, are often afraid to leave what's familiar, reluctant to expose their infirmity to others.

Residents new to assisted living usually do rebound from an initial period of uncertainty or confusion, studies indicate, but those who move voluntarily, who have a sense of control over the transition, make better adjustments.

❧

Which would include someone like Mr. Dutton. "There isn't a crying need for him to make the decision," his onetime geriatric care manager Suzanne Modigliani recognized. Though they hadn't spoken recently, she sometimes got secondhand reports from helpers she'd referred him to, or from Goddard House.

Modigliani thought he'd do well there; she also thought he could stay at home in Newton, with some additional help. What she wasn't particularly at ease with, not that anyone was asking her, was the status quo. "Sometimes kids' pressure is a force, but his kids are placing zero pressure on him," she added.

Pressuring parents is a tricky thing. They're adults, their children reason, and unless they're suffering from significant cognitive problems, they should be permitted to reach their own decisions. Baby boomers, a generation once known for bumper stickers that read "QUESTION AUTHORITY," don't seem at ease playing the authoritarian.

Yet some children have told me they initially thought they were respecting a parent's autonomy by not pushing for a change, then came to feel they were leaving an elderly person to face an overwhelming decision alone. Their parents actually seemed to find it a relief, they thought, to cede some aspects of decision-making.

"Did you ever feel you *wanted* Paul or Steve to tell you what to do about moving?" I asked Mr. Dutton at one point.

He nodded, yes. "But then I'd probably turn around and resent it, if they said, 'You must do this.' "

Hmmm. "What if they didn't say 'you must'? What if they said, 'I strongly urge you to move into Goddard House?' "

Yes, he thought that would have been a help. But no one had urged. So matters had drifted along—until late April.

Mr. Dutton

"What day of the week is it?" asked Kim, the nurse from Goddard House, sitting in Mr. Dutton's sunroom with a clipboard.

"Wednesday."

"What date and what month?"

"May 2." He also knew the season and his town, county, and state. He could identify items Kim was pointing to ("wristwatch") and holding up ("pen"). He could follow directions when she asked him to take a sheet of paper in his right hand, fold it in half, and throw it on the floor.

"I'm going to name three objects. Keep them in your brain," Kim went on, after which she asked him to spell "world" backward.

"I might have trouble with this," Mr. Dutton said. But the temporary distraction of coming up with d-l-r-o-w didn't prevent his remembering the three objects: "Apple. Table. Penny."

This was the Mini-Mental State Examination, a ten-minute test of cognitive functioning sometimes administered to those entering assisted living.

Kim had already gone over a long list of questions about Mr. Dutton's health and medications, his diet, the activities he enjoyed. She wanted to know which ADLs he might need help with, but except for having someone nearby while he showered, and help with maneuvering drops into his eyes, he would be almost entirely independent. "If that's your biggest problem, we're all set," Kim assured him. His monthly fee included 45 minutes of personal care a day; it sounded like he would use few of them.

And he'd just aced the Mini-Mental. "Guess what you got on your test—100 percent!" Kim announced. "A perfect score of 30 . . . So welcome to Goddard House, Mr. Dutton."

I found the interview startling. "No one says, 'Home Sweet Nursing Home,'" Mr. Dutton had pointed out just a few weeks earlier, talking about his desire to stay in his house. Now, suddenly, he was leaving it.

The immediate cause, he explained, was a call from Goddard House: A one-bedroom had opened on the first floor; did he want to take a look? He and Paul drove over on a Saturday to check it out. Though the apartment was actually a bit smaller, in square footage, than the one he'd earlier rejected, he liked the layout better. But that only partly accounted for his change of heart.

Another factor was an offer from Judy Hersh, "my clutter expert." The proprietor of an organizing business called All Together Now, she'd listened to Mr. Dutton debate such a move for two years and was quietly in favor. She went along as he looked at the apartment a second time.

Having spent hours helping him organize his old photos and letters and LPs, "I see him in his house alone, nobody much to talk to," she told me. "He's very social; he loves to talk to people. At Goddard House there's classical music at least four times a week;

he's going to eat it up. He'll have dinner with people, and I think he'll eat much better."

But Judy also understood that leaving his home was "a huge leap." Once she saw Mr. Dutton getting serious, therefore, "I told him I could take charge of the whole move. That it was an easy move, because we didn't have to pack up his whole house. That I could help with every piece of it, the packing, the movers, the unpacking. He realized he didn't have to be responsible for every detail." The clincher: she'd give him a 20 percent discount on her usual $60 an hour rate. He thought it over and agreed, sounding "very relieved."

Moreover, Mr. Dutton finally sat down with a financial advisor who came to the house, then ran the numbers. The calculations were reassuring: If he continued to contribute to the upkeep of the house, where Paul would still live, Mr. Dutton could easily afford Goddard House until he reached 94. If he stopped contributing, he could stay until age 98, and if he sold the house, he could pay for assisted living "indefinitely." Though Mr. Dutton already half-knew he had enough money, he liked hearing an expert's confirmation, even though "I hate to see it go $4,500 at a time."

Then there was his sense, Mr. Dutton conceded, that he was losing physical stamina. "I'm not very energetic anymore; the simplest thing seems a big effort," he said. Moving was "something I've got to do sometime, and it'll get more and more difficult if I wait."

A need for more help, enough money, someone to handle the move—this time, the decision seemed to add up differently. Mr. Dutton took Apartment 105. He was, he said, both apprehensive and excited. Using The Ride, he could still go to church, see his doctors, take in an occasional concert. He was particularly looking forward to letting somebody else make dinner and do the dishes each night.

I wondered if he sometimes had second thoughts.

"Oh, all the time," he said cheerily.

"So basically, you're still ambivalent. Before, you were ambivalent and staying, and now you're ambivalent and going."

"Yep."

On moving day, a gorgeous late May morning, the house was awhirl. Judy Hersh had already ordered and assembled a bookcase, bought linens for the single bed Mr. Dutton found (half price!) at Mattress Discounters, and put yellow stickers on everything the movers would take. Steve Dutton, up from New York to help, took charge of electronics and was disassembling the stereo and TV. He'd seen Goddard House for the first time two days earlier, and though he liked the idea of his father having people around him, "It hit me a bit—God, where are we putting him? . . . He's going to live in two rooms." Paul Dutton appeared anxious and fidgety.

But Mr. Dutton watched with his usual stoicism as the burly movers arrived and, under Judy's supervision, left empty spaces in the living room and on the walls. It took just a couple of hours to load everything.

"I want a minute," Mr. Dutton said, and he walked slowly up the stairs for a look around. He'd be back now and again—he could even move back for good, should he dislike his new residence—but nobody really expected him to live here again.

"It's sad. I'm losing my roommate," Paul said, waiting down-stairs, grappling with his own ambivalence. "I know it's the right thing to do. But it's so much money! They'd better be good for $4,500 a month."

When Mr. Dutton walked into Goddard House, everybody from the receptionist and Kim the nurse to director Nancy Sha-piro made a point of saying hello and welcome. "Everyone seems to know you already," Paul marveled. He had lunch with his father while Steve and Judy got the boxes emptied.

The dining room supervisor asked about mealtimes, and Mr. Dutton selected the later of the two seatings, one o'clock for lunch and six for dinner (breakfast was more informal). He learned he would share a table with several "lovely ladies" and that for the first three days, a staffer would come to his apartment to be sure he knew where to go.

Afterward, he sat down with the nurse to go over the individual care plan that a quality assisted living will design for each resident and update periodically. The marketing director handed him an activities calendar. "Ah, they play *Jeopardy* here," he noticed, interested.

Then he signed his contract and passed the marketing director two painfully large checks for the deposit and first month's rent, including everything except phone service, cable TV, and haircuts at the third-floor salon.

In the meantime, Steve and Judy had arranged his small living room with his desk and computer by the window, through which he could see shade trees and azaleas, dogwalkers, bikers, and runners. Judy would return in a couple of days to help him hang his paintings and photos. Steve, preparing to drive back to New York for a business meeting the next day, gave his father a hug. "I always picture you on Shornecliffe Road," he said, naming the street he'd grown up on. "And tonight, you won't be there."

Mr. Dutton wasn't the sort to volunteer what he was feeling. The nurse had asked if he was happy to be moving into Goddard House, and of course he'd politely said he was. But lately, he'd been thinking about the old television series *The Golden Girls*, and how the character played by Estelle Getty had earlier lived in, and heartily disliked, an old-folk's home called Shady Pines. Now, Mr. Dutton felt like he'd moved into Shady Pines himself and, as his helper and his children said goodbye and promised they'd see him soon, he wondered if he'd done the right thing.

Mrs. Wunderlich

Meanwhile, another studio apartment opened at Providence House and the marketing director needed a yes or no by June 1. Peg Sprague and her mother talked it over. Mrs. Wunderlich felt—no surprise—that she couldn't make a decision so quickly. Anyway, she was doing fine on her own.

The Providence House marketing director left me a voice mail message. "Ninety-five-year-old Mrs. Wunderlich is not yet ready for assisted living," she announced, sounding more amused than exasperated. "But I remain optimistic that she will move in before *I'm* ready for assisted living."

Maybe, maybe not.

Mrs. Wunderlich explained to me all the reasons a move felt premature. What they mostly came down to, of course, was money. Peg calculated that with her savings and Social Security, Mrs. Wunderlich could handle two years' rent. "I say, 'Let's take a chance, Ma. You're 95.'" No dice.

If Providence House charged, say, $500 a month, Mrs. Wunderlich acknowledged, she'd be there in a flash. But she didn't want to chance having to accept money from her children. She didn't want to take money from "the government." (I refrained from pointing out that almost everything about the way she lived—from her subsidized apartment to her Social Security check and Medicare coverage—already involved money from "the government.") So she wasn't about to pay $2,100 for a studio, even though Providence House was offering her a great bargain. (The market rate for a one-bedroom was $4,950.) "I don't want to be in a position where I feel I have to *ask*," Mrs. Wunderlich declared. "I'd rather be without."

At times, she wavered. I came in one Monday morning—Cheryl, her "A Number-One Homemaker," was there for her weekly three hours, flitting around with a dustcloth—and for the first time found Mrs. Wunderlich looking distressed, wearing a blue housecoat and no wig. She was complaining about a sudden "bellyache" apparently caused by constipation. ("It was like giving birth! It was awful!")

"Today is a bad day," she said. Even after the bellyache passed, "I felt lazy. I didn't want to do anything. I wanted someone to make my bed. I wanted someone to hand me my breakfast." Which of course sounded much like assisted living—and as if reading my thoughts, Mrs. Wunderlich confessed that if someone at Providence House had called this morning, "I would've said, 'Have you got a room right now?'"

Yet when Cheryl suddenly realized that she was due at her

next client's but hadn't yet vacuumed, Mrs. Wunderlich urged her to run along. "Don't knock yourself out! Just leave the vacuum cleaner there and I'll finish. I've got the rest of the day to push it around." Cooking and doing chores let her feel competent, even as she sometimes announced that she was sick of them.

Over time, Peg was growing more philosophical about her mother's opposition. "If I insisted, if I said, 'You must do this, I can't stand it anymore,' I believe she would move. But I don't want to do that," she said. We were at a soothingly quiet, candlelit lounge near her condo at the end of her long workday, having a couple of glasses of chardonnay.

"I know the struggle going on with my mother. It would mean relinquishing a level of autonomy and control she still has and wants desperately to hold on to, and I respect that," Peg mused. "This is a fierce fight she's having within herself."

At the moment, she didn't think Mrs. Wunderlich was in danger, living alone. Her doctor said she was doing well, though she didn't have much appetite and had lost 10 or 15 pounds since her hospitalization. Her diabetes was under control. A nurse still came twice a month to check on her and, at Peg's insistence, Meals on Wheels delivered three days a week. Mrs. Wunderlich was managing fairly well. For now.

She had found the past few months enlightening in a way, Peg went on, "the most intense experience I've ever had with my mother . . . In many ways I feel closer to her than ever." Seeing her through illness and recovery had made Peg feel more sensitive to "what it feels like for her to be vulnerable, to be increasingly dependent, to be trying to accept the fact that she'll be dying soon . . . It's deepened the relationship."

The one time in her adult life she could remember her mother saying she loved her was when Mrs. Wunderlich was leaving rehab, going home. Even now, her mother was tenderer, less brusque, more grateful. "She's not a gushy, effusive person . . . But she says to me, 'You're the reason I'm here. You're the one keeping me alive.' It's her way of saying, 'I appreciate all you do,'" Peg saw, and she was moved by that.

What You See and What You Get

I first spoke with Karen Love when I was researching a story for the *Washington Post Magazine*. I wanted to know how well these assisted living "communities," as they like to call themselves, cared for their elderly charges. Love, founder of the Consumer Consortium on Assisted Living, tartly graded the industry a C, with "occasional glimpses of excellence."

Five years later, she was managing director of the Center for Excellence in Assisted Living, a collaborative formed by 11 national organizations bent on improving the industry. What mark would she give assisted living now? I asked.

She mulled the question. "I'd say a B-minus," she said. "Certain pockets of improvements. A lot of room for growth. And some outliers doing incredible work."

Though one can hear or read horror stories, I've encountered few people in the field who see the majority of assisted living residences as dangerous, or even of poor quality. They seem to be doing an okay job, overall. But it's an industry, one analyst told me, that "overpromises."

Translation: The folks writing those hefty checks every month (a third of the time, the family is the primary payer) expect more than not-bad care for a little over two years. They think they're purchasing something different: the last home seniors will need, experienced and skilled caregivers who will come to know and love them, the elusive state called "peace of mind." Even in quality facilities, they're likely to be disappointed.

"The heavy marketing oversells to worried families the amount of care that will be given," is Barbara Moscowitz's take.

"I see families getting more educated and more thoughtful" about assisted living decisions, agrees Catherine Hawes, a longtime researcher at Texas A&M. "But they're often deluded by the environment, because it looks so nice."

There's far more variation among assisted living facilities, regulated by each state with differing levels of intensity, than among nursing homes, subject to strict federal regulations. Many advocates and owners want assisted living to retain more flexibility than federal regulation might allow. But for families, recognizing where expectations conflict with realities could lead to more informed choices. In Pennsylvania, for example, assisted living communities weren't even required to have awake staff on duty 24 hours a day, until a *Philadelphia Inquirer* exposé led to new regulations in 2007.

One realm where misconceptions crop up is central: health care. Larger assisted living facilities usually have a staff nurse, but these can be varying relationships—full or part-time, licensed practical or vocational nurses, or RNs. Only about 40 percent have an RN on staff 40 hours a week, a landmark national survey led by Catherine Hawes and Charles Phillips discovered several years ago. They also found that a full-time registered nurse greatly reduces the odds of relocating; residents in facilities with full-time RNs were half as likely to move to a nursing home as those in facilities without them. Even small increases in RN hours lowered the risk of hospitalization, according to another large study.

What a staff nurse can actually do depends on state laws and a facility's policies, however. Few assisted living facilities can provide the close monitoring that unstable diabetics require, for instance. A staff nurse's job may consist primarily of monthly weight and blood pressure checks. Having a nurse "on call" evenings and weekends may mean that she will answer questions by phone, but not necessarily come see residents with problems.

In most cases, a fever or a fall will prompt a call for an ambulance, and then a call to the family member who's the designated emergency contact, even if a nurse *is* on the scene. "It's an easy way to handle the liability," Love says. So while a mishap or illness probably won't result in a resident's lying untreated on her floor for hours—the nightmare scenario children so often fear for parents living alone—"the health care for most assisted living is 911," Love says.

As for the aides who provide the hands-on bathing, dressing, and toileting, they work under the same constraints that affect other parts of the long-term care industry: they're undertrained, poorly paid, and often lack benefits, and there generally aren't enough of them to allow unhurried time with each resident. Hawes and Phillips found most aides "almost completely unaware of what constitutes normal aging," thus apt to shrug at conditions—sudden incontinence, say—that should be investigated and can be treated. A spate of state legislation has probably brought some improvement since then. Still, aides too often leave their jobs in frustration, causing high turnover rates and, for elderly residents, too many strangers performing intimate tasks.

Another concern: Those jolly activities calendars posted in the lobby, each weekday crammed with games, classes, and visiting entertainers. When you're shopping around for a facility, you soon realize there's a circuit; the same local yoga teachers and pianists show up at Whatever Court on Mondays and at Whichever Gardens on Wednesdays.

Activities matter; they promote social engagement and interaction and improve many measures of physical and mental functioning. But how many residents participate? Does the staff remind them of what's happening in the community room and help them get there?

And does what's happening in the community room reflect what residents really want to do with their days? In the Hawes study, nearly 60 percent of residents said the staff rarely asked about their preferences. Relying on "the cruise ship model," as Karen Love calls it, can feel forced. "That's not how we live our lives," she notes. "Even on a cruise ship, it gets old."

Probably the most important issue for families, and one of the least discussed in real detail, is the question of who can enter and who can stay. Assisted living balances on a tricky fulcrum: It admits residents who need help, but not too much help. It wants to help people age in place, up to a point.

The ideal new resident, Catherine Hawes says—sort of joking, sort of not—is Miss Daisy. Remember the movie starring Jessica Tandy? Miss Daisy was lucid and mobile, a fierce advocate for herself; what she needed was transportation, light housework and meal preparation, and companionship from the courtly, attentive

Morgan Freeman. Any assisted living facility would be happy to have her move in, so long as she could pay the fees.

For seniors who aren't in as good shape, though, facilities adopt a bewildering variety of policies. "Moderate physical limitations," like using a wheelchair or needing help walking, are usually acceptable, the Hawes survey showed. But few administrators will admit someone who can't "transfer"—move himself from bed to chair or wheelchair; in many states, regulations prohibit facilities from serving such residents. Mild to moderate cognitive problems are common, but fewer than half the administrators in the Hawes study said they'd accept a resident whose cognitive impairment was moderate to severe. And residents whose wanderings cause problems, who become threatening or disruptive, are almost always unwelcome, except in facilities specializing in dementia care (and sometimes not even there).

Much of the time, administrators answered researchers' questions about this with a vague "it depends." They may be less fussy about admission when they have more vacant apartments than usual. They may try to retain a long-term resident with a particular need when a newcomer with the same problem would get turned away. "They want to be as accommodating as they can," says Hawes. But *it depends* "is not a good answer for consumers."

"The biggest problems tend to be, how long can people stay?" agrees Susan Reinhard, director of AARP's Public Policy Institute. "Is aging in place really going to happen there? . . . People get very upset when they're told they can't stay; they definitely didn't expect that."

❧

Assisted living faces an inherent predicament: Over time, seniors decline. A facility that accepts or keeps too many people with serious disabilities can't continue to look or feel like not-a-nursing-home. If it keeps discharging people when they need more care, on the other hand, it can't encourage aging in place. In fact, the National Center for Assisted Living, the industry group, now discourages use of that phrase. Two of the industry's major philosophical tenets are in conflict, and not-a-nursing-home usually wins out.

Residents themselves reflect this contradiction; they complain about neighbors who are in worse physical or mental health than they are. Yet they're indignant at the idea that they themselves, should they develop greater infirmities, would be asked to leave; the great majority expect to stay as long as they want.

In reality, however, residents who need nursing care for more than two weeks, or in other ways require more help than assisted living is designed to provide, are usually discharged. Residents with severe cognitive impairment are more than twice as likely, according to one national survey, to move to a nursing home as those with little or no impairment. The behavioral problems that sometimes accompany advancing dementia are among the most-cited reasons residents are asked to leave.

Can you forestall an unwanted discharge? Some families manage by hiring private aides to supplement the care the facility provides. It's an expensive solution.

Another possibility: a legal document called a negotiated risk agreement. An NRA recognizes that while safety is a prime concern, residents may choose to accept certain risks. Say Mrs. X refuses to use a walker, even if that means she's more apt to fall. She or her family can discuss her preferences and their potential risks with the administrators; if they can reach resolution, the facility may permit her to deviate from its policies and still remain in residence.

It's a controversial option. The AARP is on record as supporting NRAs. "It's very adult and I think we should emphasize being an adult," Susan Reinhard told me. Opponents, including the National Senior Citizens Law Center, fear that facility owners and their lawyers will merely use NRAs to avoid liability for substandard care.

Still another alternative: multi-facility campuses that include independent and assisted living, nursing homes, and dementia care—or some combination thereof. When a resident can't safely remain in assisted living, the nursing home or dementia unit is across the driveway or on the third floor, not miles away. If he can't truly age in place, he can at least age right down the hall.

We don't know how well this model, which sounds so sensible, really works for seniors, though. The presence of an affiliated nursing home, for example, results in residents being nearly twice as likely to be transferred as other assisted living residents, one large study shows. Is that an advantage?

It's also unclear whether adapting to new quarters and new faces on the same campus is any less distressing for residents than adapting across town. There's a stigma to having to leave one level of care for the next, wherever it is, researcher Sheryl Zimmerman points out. "It's still leaving your home," she says. "It still feels like a transition, and people usually don't want to make it."

As for separate dementia units, becoming quite common, there's surprisingly little evidence that they do a better job than assisted living in general. In theory, a supportive and carefully designed environment, with staffers especially trained to work with dementia patients, could be extremely helpful.

But in practice, "when we compare specialized units with non-specialized environments, we don't see much difference in outcomes," says Philip Sloane. "Whether it's quality of life, length of life, hospitalization rates—all those things don't seem to be that different." The specialized units, he theorizes, may reassure families, but they're probably not really so special—except that the doors lock.

ℜ

In fact, here's a pretty stunning finding from Zimmerman and Sloane and their team, who followed nearly 2,100 residents in 193 facilities for a year, part of the largest assisted living study to date:

Many attributes of assisted living make less difference than we'd think in how a parent fares. Given a reasonable level of quality, characteristics like the type of facility, its size or age, how attractive its neighborhood is, whether it's part of a chain—none of these have a significant or consistent relationship to residents' risk of death or illness, to their odds of entering a hospital or nursing home. Seniors in large, upscale buildings with gazebos and chandeliers showed no less decline—in matters like cognitive function, social withdrawal, the number of ADLs they needed help with—than residents of smaller, old-fashioned residences.

What's most significant, the researchers repeatedly found, is residents' physical health and cognitive status. Surroundings and activities may contribute to quality of life, but "in terms of Mom or Dad's overall well-being, the big picture of how well they're going to do—it has a lot more to do with who they are, as opposed to the care they're going to get," Zimmerman told me.

Maybe it's not so startling, when you think it over, that a healthier, more lucid resident is likely to do better after a stint in assisted living, regardless of the place, than someone more frail and disoriented. But the finding does take some of the pressure off. Most people going into long-term care have progressive diseases, and it's the disease rather than the facility that most determines a resident's future.

"In a way, that could be liberating for families," says Philip Sloane. He was careful to point out that a negligent or dismal facility isn't good for anyone. But in comparing assisted living options, "families can look a bit more for where residents are going to be *happy*," rather than trying to parse staff ratios. And such a place, he maintains, isn't as hard to recognize as one might think.

Reconnaissance

How to select assisted living? We know that seniors who feel their move is voluntary and who help make the decision adjust better to their new surroundings, but we also know that 40 percent of those entering assisted living are coming directly from hospitals or rehab facilities and are in no condition to comparison shop. A substantial proportion of newcomers also suffer from cognitive impairment. Children therefore wind up doing a lot of the advance work and, as marketing directors are well aware, heavily influence the decision.

So perhaps it's comforting that, as Sloane puts it, "there's no best facility type, no matter how you cut it." A small, less expensive board and care home on a residential street, with half a dozen bedrooms, might serve quite well. "They are like little houses," Sloane says. "For some people, it's wonderful because they feel like they're at home and they feel comfortable with everybody. They can walk into the kitchen and grab something out of the refrigerator. The staff blends with them well. Some of those places are fabulous."

But they probably don't have a nurse on staff, so may not be suitable for someone with more medical needs, or for someone who wanders and would benefit from room to roam securely. Conversely, someone intellectually adventurous enough to crave lectures by local professors and field trips to museums might do better in one of the newer, larger facilities. "They're vibrant," says Karen Love. "Lots of people with different interests. If you're trying to put together a bridge game, you may need a larger group."

As a starting point, Love suggests collecting recommendations from a geriatric care manager with long connections in the area ("the best $200 or $300 you'll ever spend"). The local area agency on aging may have helpful information, too, though some are more knowledgeable than others. The firsthand experience of friends, neighbors, fellow book club members is often valuable.

Once you've narrowed the field (in rural areas it may be fairly narrow to start with), "go for the regular tour and then come back in the evening after dinner, 6:30 or 7, unannounced," Love advises. "What does it feel like as you walk through? What do the residents look like? Do you hear laughing and life happening? When you see people just biding their time, that's not a good placement. Use your senses. How does it smell? It shouldn't smell like urine; it shouldn't smell like Clorox, either."

Sloane urges visitors to notice the interactions between staff members and the elders in their charge. "As in most other aspects of life, it's really the relationships that matter, " he says. "The best thing you can do is meet and talk to the staff, see how they behave, see if they're treating the people there the way you'd want to be treated." Professionals in the field talk about "person-centered care," a phrase, Sloane explains, that merely means: "Are you treating people like they matter? Like their feelings matter? Like their preferences matter?"

You'll know it when you see it, Zimmerman adds. "My dad recently moved into an assisted living setting, and it's just so clear. I don't need any of my measures to go in and say, 'This is a person who generates warmth,' or 'This is a person who doesn't understand who my dad is and doesn't even really care.' "

When it comes to nursing homes, there's considerable evidence that, overall, nonprofit facilities do a better job than for-profit ones. *Overall* is worth emphasizing, because there are high-quality homes operated for profit and lousy nonprofits; nevertheless, the research is generally consistent. In assisted living, where about a third of facilities are nonprofit, there's less research and the differences are less clear. Still, some findings indicate that residents of nonprofits are less likely to move or be discharged, thus better able to age in place.

When it's time to talk with the director or marketing director about your parent's needs, very specific questions help. Incontinence is common in assisted living, so if a daughter says, " 'My mother's incontinent, will you be able to handle that?' the facility director will say yes," Catherine Hawes explains. "And what the facility means is, 'As long as she can wear Depends and manage on her own, we're happy to have her.' And what the daughter means is, 'My mother needs help managing her adult incontinent supplies and she needs to have her sheets changed every morning.' So they talk right past each other."

Ask specifically, too, about the reasons a resident can be discharged. Marketing directors don't disabuse newcomers of the idea that this will be home for many years. They may proudly point to Mrs. Whoever who's been there for six years. But that's unusual; see what the average stay is.

(One warning: Being state-licensed may not in itself ensure high quality, because states vary so widely in oversight and enforcement. California, for instance, inspects only 20 percent of its licensed facilities each year, so it could be five years between state surveyors' visits.)

As with any lease, which is essentially what you're signing, what's in writing supersedes anything you're told. The Consumer Consortium for Assisted Living recommends that a family not only read the contract but have a lawyer review it as well, preferably an eldercare attorney.

And of course, moving day is only the beginning. Families continue to be highly involved with seniors in assisted living. They visit regularly, most at least weekly, several studies show. They call. They take their relatives on outings. They monitor their health and moods, make medical appointments and get prescriptions filled, handle their finances, confer with the staff. In one survey, a quarter of them did the laundry.

"Some children think, 'Great, Mom or Dad will be taken care of and I don't have to be the caregiver," says Barbara Moscowitz. What they find is that "it's just a new kind of caregiving, it reshapes itself. You're still in charge. For some people that's a disappointment, for some it's a relief. But it's the reality."

It may be more difficult, in fact, than having a parent in a nursing home, where there's so much more hour-to-hour monitoring. When a team of researchers looked at family caregivers of residents with dementia in assisted living versus demented relatives in nursing homes, they found that both sets of family members spent an average four hours a week visiting residents or talking by phone. But the assisted living group reported feeling more involved and also more burdened; they were assuming greater responsibility to assure their relatives' safety and well-being. They stepped in to compensate for the difference between assisted living and nursing home care, the researchers suggested, and that might have allowed their loved ones to remain in assisted living longer.

At Goddard House, Mr. Dutton decided he would do his own laundry ("It's not one of the things that's free"). He intended to handle his own finances, too, especially since there was a branch of his own bank on the premises.

Still, on moving day his son Paul made a point of telling the director, "You'll see a lot of me."

"Good," she said. "Family is good."

Mr. Dutton

When it came to *Jeopardy*, Mr. Dutton was a killer. He'd been watching for years on television, and besides, "I'm kind of a nut for trivia." So he was one of the first into the library this morning—nine contestants eventually showed up—for the weekly game.

He picked "Famous Nicknames" to start and rolled right through the questions. The Peekaboo Girl? "Veronica Lake," he said calmly, old movies being one of his specialties. The Blonde Bombshell? "Jean Harlow." The Last of the Red-Hot Mamas? He guessed Mae West—a mistake that a competitor swooped in to correct. "Sophie Tucker!"

The sports category was trickier for this crowd, but Mr. Dutton knew the date when Jesse Owens ran in the Olympic Games (1936). And when it came to quotes, he knew instantly who'd said, "Take my wife—please."

A young staffer named Kate read the questions aloud, using a handheld microphone so everyone could hear, though she still got a lot of *whats?* Goddard House rules dispensed with the answer-in-the-form-of-a-question requirement; it was enough that people rummaged through their memories and had a good time.

"That round, John was far ahead of anyone else!" Kate announced, tallying the final score. "Blew away the competition! John, I don't suppose you want the beads"—one of the gewgaws offered as prizes.

"I'll take a notepad," Mr. Dutton said.

He had lived at Goddard House for three months at this point, and director Nancy Shapiro thought he'd adjusted beautifully. "He's delightful," she said. "He is what people wanted for assisted living—independent, active, cognitively intact." Assisted living wasn't really like that anymore, but Goddard House still wanted such recruits, and Mr. Dutton was "a pretty good specimen."

His son, too, was pleased. "I think it's working out fine," Paul said. "There's no question it's the kind of place he needs." Perhaps Paul needed it, too. He saw his father slowing, but because he was no longer alone in the house when Paul traveled, "I worry less," he acknowledged. "He fell asleep the other day and missed lunch, and someone came and knocked on the door . . . There are people around."

And what did Mr. Dutton think?

I drove up to see him every few weeks that summer. He was taking advantage of what Goddard House could offer. Since it had a small private dining room, he hosted a thank-you dinner for seven, complete with wine, for the cousin's son-in-law who'd been bringing him Tuesday dinner for so long, plus a few other relatives. Besides playing *Jeopardy*, he frequented a discussion group called "Practicing Your Faith," led by a retired minister. A physical therapist came to the facility several times a week, and Mr. Dutton arranged for appointments to see if he could improve his balance.

Some assisted living residents rarely leave their building, but he occasionally took The Ride back to Newton to have dinner with neighbors. His son Steve drove him to Vermont for the reunion of the Hartford High School Class of 1938, a happy event though his classmates had dwindled to a handful. When Goddard House took a vanload of people to the much-ballyhooed Edward Hopper exhibit at the Boston Museum of Fine Arts, Mr. Dutton loved the show ("It's remarkable what he can do painting an empty room"), though walking the long corridors proved tiring.

One Sunday morning, I tagged along as The Ride picked him up for his almost-weekly excursion to Old South Church. His pastor and many friends greeted him with smiles and handshakes; he seemed happy to be there, hearing the old hymns, sharing cake and lemonade after the service.

Back at Goddard House, we sat out on the shaded patio, where several residents maintained small flower gardens in raised beds. I asked if he was glad to have made this move. He gave his usual considered response, which essentially boiled down to: Sometimes.

"There are days when I say, 'Why am I here? Do I need to be here? I'm capable of doing more,'" he said, still in his gray sport coat, white shirt, and tie.

He seemed to find the matter of dependence versus independence almost a moral issue. "It's laziness to take the easy way out and pay to have things done for me," he said. On days he felt vigorous, he scolded himself for being "coddled."

"Then when I think rationally, that goes away," he added. "And I'm glad I'm here."

Did he need to be here? I remembered a bright spring day we'd been sitting out front, chatting in the sunshine. When we walked back onto the porch, Mr. Dutton suddenly grew so dizzy he had to grab my arm. It took time for his eyes to readjust to the shade, he later explained. Maybe, I thought, being here did make sense.

Since he still didn't require personal care, Mr. Dutton hadn't experienced any of the problems that sometimes arose when assisted living residents have too long a wait for an aide to provide help. He had minor complaints of the sort that surface when dozens of people live together—the person who belched loudly in the dining room, the petty grumbling at the residents' council meetings, some activities that "could use a little boost."

I'd seen him quietly leave an opera lecture that consisted of a woman reading the plot of *La Bohème* aloud and fumbling fruitlessly with the large screen television to play a videotaped performance. Mr. Dutton had seen *Bohème* many times at the Met and the Boston Opera, and he preferred Verdi anyway.

On the whole, however, despite occasional gibes about Shady Pines, he felt satisfied. I never heard enormous enthusiasm for assisted living, but I did hear him acknowledge, "It's a good practical solution for me."

The women he ate with were in accord. Mr. Dutton admired

the unstoppable Evelyn, who at 94 still walked briskly around nearby Jamaica Pond every morning, and the equally indomitable May, who signed on for every Goddard House field trip despite her wheelchair. (I've changed his dining companions' names.) They genially allowed me to join them at lunch one day.

"To me, assisted living is a solution," Evelyn declared in her authoritative manner. "When we can no longer maintain our houses, what do we do? Move in with our children? That would be *most* uncomfortable." She paused long enough to order corn chowder and a fruit salad, then crisply enumerated several things she liked about Goddard House: the lobby was "fairly elegant in appearance," she grew phlox and dahlias in her flower garden, the cuisine was quite good, and the staff "wonderful."

"I didn't have any adjustment at all," May put in. In her former apartment, "I was cooking on one foot, and I said, 'This is ridiculous.'"

And yet, Evelyn admitted a bit wistfully, after three years here, "I still wish I lived at home. I miss being in my own house. I miss being able to come and go as I please. I miss my Siamese cats, beautiful creatures." Cats were permitted at Goddard House, but Evelyn thought her small apartment too confining for them. "You can't have everything."

With that, they moved on to discuss their current book club selection, *The Kite Runner*, and invited Mr. Dutton to join their afternoon Scrabble game; he declined.

But what they'd said resonated with him. However much it resembles a Holiday Inn, an assisted living facility is still an institution, one most older people probably hope they won't need. It's not home, and it's an imperfect substitute in both significant and minor ways. But when well-run, it can serve as a decent compromise.

Mr. Dutton, about to turn 87, didn't miss his Newton house as much as he'd expected to, he told me. The couple of times he'd pondered, still a bit ambivalent, whether he should move back, he decided that would be "really impractical . . . I'd be back in the same mess I was trying to get away from." So he didn't regret his decision.

"But are you *happy* here?" I wanted to pin him down, I guess. A flicker of a smile. "I still don't know the answer myself."

Mrs. Wunderlich

"Peggy and her husband are coming over," Mrs. Wunderlich reported when I called to wish her a happy 95th birthday. "And they're bringing lobster rolls and an Italian rum cake from the North End. She said, 'You can only have a little piece.' I said, 'It's my birthday and I'm going to eat as much as I want!'" Her next doctor's appointment was a full two weeks off, Mrs. Wunderlich had calculated; she could feast today and still have decent blood glucose readings by then.

The celebration had begun early. Mrs. Wunderlich put on a silky purple dress printed with pansies and an elegant wig. Enormous bouquets arrived from the grandchildren. All afternoon, people were calling with congratulations: her nephew's wife from New Jersey, a 97-year-old friend in New Hampshire, her son Fred, Fred's two children and Peg's two. "I didn't think I was that popular," she said, sounding pleased.

Surreptitiously, Peg had arranged to have Mrs. Wunderlich's best chums in the building join the festivities. "All of a sudden, a knock comes at the door and all my neighbors are there singing 'Happy Birthday,' five of them," Mrs. Wunderlich later reported. Peg planted one candle per decade atop the cake, and Mrs. Wunderlich blew them all out with a single puff and read every birthday card aloud. "She was in her glory," Peg said.

Nobody was in a hurry to leave. The guests reminisced about moving to this building years ago, gossiped about neighbors past and present. They were clearly enjoying the conversation, which somehow eddied around to assisted living.

"I'm going to wait till the next opportunity at Providence House," Peg was startled to hear her mother announce, only a couple of weeks after she'd turned down an apartment there for the second time. "The next time around, I'm really going to go."

"Ma, you have six witnesses here," Peg pointed out.

Was Mrs. Wunderlich really ready to move? She'd said the very same thing the last time she'd rejected Providence House, Peg's husband pointed out as they drove home. Besides, Providence House's policy was that its next available low-income studio would go to a current resident; six months or more might pass before Mrs. Wunderlich got another shot.

We had several conversations about assisted living as the summer passed. She was, in some ways, clear-eyed about her situation. She noticed a few hints of forgetfulness. One evening, she lost track of time and overbaked a pork chop until "it was like charcoal." She invited a friend for supper and dried out the chicken, lamenting, "In my life, I never had a meal I made turn out so badly." She'd had a few minor mix-ups while paying her bills, too, so Peg took over the task.

But Peg already had so much to do and to worry about. She might relax a bit, her mother knew, if she took the next apartment at Providence House. "These vacancies don't crop up like daisies," Mrs. Wunderlich said. "The next one, I have to take it whether I like it or not, because I'm not getting any younger."

But then I'd come by and find her happily yakking with her best pal Mary, a stripling of 80 who visited her daily and went shopping with her, and who regularly listed all the reasons Mrs. Wunderlich didn't need assisted living. And that would make sense to her, too.

"I'm with it and then I'm against it," Mrs. Wunderlich said one afternoon. "That's where I drive Peggy crazy."

In truth, though, Peg no longer seemed so intent on persuading her mother to move. The past few months had made her think more about mortality, which could come at any age, and about her mother's fierce self-determination.

"She has integrity and strength," Peg said. This was a woman who, if she'd been born 50 years later and gotten more education, could probably have run Bethlehem Steel. But she was not going to live much longer, Peg suspected, and Peg was coming to terms with that.

"It's not unhinging me," she said. "I'm not in panic mode." In fact, she was grateful to be able to look at her mother's life and her own, "to be able to think about dying and not have the heebie-jeebies. The more you're around old people, the more you're in these conversations." It was healthy, she thought.

So she spent time with her mother, ferrying her to medical appointments but also taking her to the farm market she loved, having dinner at her apartment, just being around. And if Mrs. Wunderlich was still contemplating assisted living, Peg rarely raised the subject any longer. It didn't seem so important. What would happen, would happen.

"I don't even talk to her about it anymore," Peg said. "I just wait for the phone to ring."

SOME QUESTIONS TO CONSIDER ABOUT ASSISTED LIVING:

Does your parent need help with housekeeping, meal preparation, and such activities of daily living as bathing, dressing, and re-membering medications? Assisted living is primarily designed for seniors requiring this level of assistance.

Is she otherwise able to live comfortably in her own room or small apartment? Can she feed herself? Use a toilet or manage her own incontinence garments? If not, your parent may need more help and supervision than most assisted living residences provide.

Is she mobile enough, with a cane, walker, or wheelchair, to go to and from the dining room and to participate in activities and outings?

Does she require vigilant daily health monitoring (of blood glucose levels, for instance) or regular skilled nursing care? Most assisted living facilities don't provide such services, even if there is a nurse on the staff.

Can your parent or family afford steep monthly fees? In most cases, assisted living residents pay privately. But Medicaid will pay part of the tab in some states, and some facilities offer subsidized apartments; have you looked into such arrangements?

Can family members, trusted friends, or a geriatric care manager visit your parent weekly or more often, not only to spend time with her but to monitor her care? Can they come on varying days and at odd times?

Is your parent social enough to form relationships with staffers and friendships with fellow residents? Is she adaptable enough for a group residence?

FOUR

WHAT ELSE IS THERE TO FEAR?

Nursing Homes

First-time visitors to Greenwood House, a rambling beige-brick building on the outskirts of Trenton, New Jersey, tend to walk through the automatic doors with their noses on high alert. But there's no smell of urine, nor of the antiseptics some nursing homes use to cover it up. There's no smell, period. "It's the only one I've been in that has no odor," one resident's daughter said, surprised.

Past the lobby, they come to a crossroads near the nurses' station, where the dining and activity areas and the residents' hallways intersect; it's called the North Lounge.

Much of the day, something is going on here. An affable staffer named Lamar might be dealing hands for Texas Hold 'Em in the atrium; at the next table, gamblers no longer able to grasp the intricacies of poker might be tossing oversize foam dice to win play money. If it's time for Cocktails with Carol, aides pass around cups of ginger ale spiked with cranberry or grapefruit juice, while Carol plinks "Fly Me to the Moon" on the upright piano. On Thursdays, a social worker leads a "hot topics" discussion in the adjacent auditorium; Fridays, residents shape the twisted loaves of challah traditionally served with Sabbath dinner.

The skylit atrium, with its huge potted ficus tree, generally makes some seasonal statement, a reminder of the year's milestones. The staff fastens orange construction-paper leaves on the tree in autumn and scatters red hearts around in February. A large aquarium stands eye-level for those in wheelchairs; in the hallway outside, the inevitable bird—a cockatiel named Faigele, in this case—hops about its cage.

Sometimes, visitors catch a bit of banter.

"You sure you should be working today?" a guy in a baseball cap, riding past in his power chair, asks the pregnant nurse dispensing meds. He's a physician who worked here at Greenwood House years ago; now he's among its residents.

"I would miss you if I didn't," she returns. She's been getting lots of commentary.

"Remember, I'm here in case of an emergency," he says, scooting off.

Meanwhile, the nurse wheels her cart to her next patient and announces, "Hello, gorgeous. Would you step into my office, sweet thing? I have something for you. Guess—is it a million dollars? Is it a new car? Or is it—a pill?"

Not everything visitors see is so cheery, of course. It takes staffers a long time to move dozens of elders in wheelchairs into the dining room for meals or the auditorium for a concert, then back out again. Besides, they don't want residents spending hours in their rooms. So the North Lounge often contains a cluster of people in wheelchairs, doing nothing much, nodding off or calling out things that don't seem logical, parked in neutral. It's supposed to encourage engagement and socializing, but some patients seem beyond repartee.

Past this hub is where the residents live, paired up in—one of health care's great euphemisms—semiprivate rooms. The corridors look scrupulously clean but, as in most nursing homes, institutional, hospital-like, with their tiled floors and fluorescent lights.

The living quarters, divided by striped curtains, are confining, barely able to hold a hospital bed, a small bureau, a television if the family brings one, perhaps a chair. "I've made half a room into my home," one resident told me, not complaining, just stating reality.

On this Sunday afternoon in July, I found Sari G. wheeling her father, Henry B., down the hallway toward the auditorium, where unspecified "musical entertainment" was scheduled to begin at 2. "Here's the gift shop, Dad," she said, pointing out landmarks as they passed. "Want to go in? Maybe they have a candy bar."

He'd moved here three days earlier, after spending several years with Sari, her husband and two daughters, and an expanding roster of hired aides. He was 84 and growing increasingly disabled from Parkinson's disease. All kinds of people—Sari's husband, her mother-in-law, her siblings—kept telling her that bringing her father to Greenwood House, where he would have around-the-clock care, was the right thing to do. She remained unconvinced. The night before he moved in, she sat up labeling her father's clothes with a Sharpie and crying.

Greenwood House is probably one of the better nursing homes in the region. It boasts not only a sterling reputation within the local Jewish community, which has supported it for decades as a nonprofit institution, but high ratings on the government Websites intended to help families locate quality facilities.

Federal law requires that every 9 to 15 months, state inspectors pay an unannounced visit to each nursing home that receives Medicare and Medicaid funding; their findings—including any "deficiencies" the surveyors see, from failing to prevent bedsores to not keeping accurate medical records—appear on the medicare.gov Website. The national average in 2006 was eight deficiencies per nursing home; here in New Jersey, it was six. Greenwood House had no deficiencies, zero; it received just one in the previous four years. (A few minor deficiencies turned up the following year, but were quickly corrected.) By comparison, the for-profit nursing home just down the street received ten deficiencies in 2006 and 20 the year before.

New Jersey also compiles a Nursing Home Report Card, found on its state Department of Health and Senior Services Website, derived from the same data. Out of a possible 100 points, Greenwood House scored 99.

Yet most families look for a way, any way, to avoid such places. "It's the stigma," said the home's longtime executive director, Rick

Goldstein. Often, adult children considering placing their parents "call me three or four times over a period of a year and a half; they're trying to convince themselves." He understands their reluctance: "They've heard how bad nursing homes are—and there *are* a lot of bad nursing homes."

Families view such facilities as the threshold to the grave, where once-robust elders grow ever more incapacitated, until they die. And they're not completely wrong: Long-term inhabitants of nursing homes, including this one, are an increasingly frail and elderly group. Greenwood House's 132 residents are 88 years old, on average, with multiple health problems. Over the course of a year, some may experience improved health, but 35 to 45 residents will die, either here or in a hospital.

(While we often think of a nursing home as a long-term residence, most of today's nursing facilities also provide short-term stays for patients leaving hospitals after a health crisis or after surgery. These patients aren't moving in for good; they need rehabilitation for a few weeks or months, then return home. Nursing homes are increasingly geared toward such "post-acute" stays because they're more lucrative. Greenwood House, something of an anomaly, still defines itself as a permanent residence for the Jewish aged.)

Goldstein is proud of his nursing home, but he knows how it's viewed. "I hate to use the term 'the place of last resort,' but no one wants to come to a nursing home," he says. When someone does, it's usually because a family decides it has no real choice.

Sari wasn't sure about that.

Mr. B.

The afternoon in late spring when I first drove up to Sari's expansive new house, in a development in Bucks County, Pennsylvania, Mr. B. had just risen from a nap. "Pleased to meet you," he said hoarsely, as she steered him into the bathroom to brush his teeth.

Then it was time for a snack and Sari was darting around her elegant kitchen preparing food, administering drugs, talking to her father, talking to me. She tied a piece of terry cloth around Mr. B.'s neck—"Let's keep that shirt looking spiffy"—and brought him a cup of potato soup. "Careful, Dad, it's hot." He could, haltingly, lift a spoon to his mouth.

She stirred a powder called Thick-It into a glass of water; all his liquids had to be thickened to keep him from choking and inhaling fluid into his lungs, which could cause pneumonia. "Want a piece of lemon in here, Dad?" Next, she cut up some fruit and added yogurt. "Is that good? Refreshing?" And then, a few moments later, "Dad, the prednisone. Shall I put it in chocolate pudding? Or maybe applesauce?"

Slender in her trim jeans, tank top, and heeled sandals, Sari was a youthful 52. She kept her russet hair trimmed to chic shapeliness, her nails polished, her makeup fresh. She had great energy, and she needed it: She'd taken both her ailing parents into her home, following a stint in assisted living. After her mother's death from heart disease and colon cancer, she'd continued caring for her father.

"It turned into more of a job than I'd expected," she acknowledged. A year or two ago, Mr. B. could make his way around the house, sometimes using a cane, and function fairly independently; now he needed assistance to get out of bed, to dress, to take a shower and use a toilet. In the past few months, he'd been hospitalized for pneumonia, taken some falls, made several emergency room visits.

Sari brought in a succession of helpers; home aides now spent five hours a day with her father. He'd had the foresight, years ago, to buy a long-term care insurance policy—a rarity among his generation—that helped pay the tab.

Still, "you pretty much have to be around, on the phone, supervising," Sari said. "You're the staff person, the scheduler. You do payroll . . . I feel like I've gotten honorary degrees in physical therapy, speech therapy, preventing falls, medical supplies."

Mr. B. was gaunt and snowy-haired. He had occasional periods of confusion, but mostly was quite aware, a daily newspaper reader and TV news viewer. His dark eyes retained their curiosity and intensity, even if his arms trembled as he ate. "His body has deteriorated much faster than his mind," was the way Sari's husband put it.

While Sari thickened a glass of juice—I rarely saw her stop bustling when her father was awake and nearby—Mr. B. told me a bit about his life in 1950s New York. He'd come from Poland in 1949, a survivor of the Nazi camps, and arrived here without money, family, or English.

At first, he said, apologizing for his feeble voice (Parkinson's made it hard to clear his throat), "I had a grocery store in Brooklyn." He and his wife, Bluma, another Holocaust survivor, ran the place together and lived upstairs. After a few years, they bought an appetizing store ("lox, whitefish") in Queens and bought a house. Sari, the middle of the three children, finally got her own room. When Mr. B. sold his deli, "I was too young to retire," he said. "Believe it or not, I drove a cab. I didn't get one ticket in five years!"

"Little sips, Dad," Sari coached, delivering the thickened juice. "Keep your chin down."

Not until the afternoon aide—I'll call her Odette—arrived to help shift Mr. B. from the dining room chair to his walker, escort him to the bathroom, then guide him into his room to watch the news, did Sari take a seat, on the shady patio behind the house, and talk about Greenwood House.

She'd gone to see it several times, once with her father; they'd put his name on the waiting list for a room. But she couldn't shake her uncertainty. "I'm having such a hard time," she confessed. "I have too many emotions to juggle. I keep throwing up my hands and saying, 'What am I supposed to do?'"

For nearly five years now, she'd been deeply involved in caring for her parents; for much of that time, they'd lived in Sari's home. It was causing mounting tensions. The very features that had attracted Sari and her husband to this house—its airy, open floor plan, with one space flowing into another—made it hard to have much privacy with her father ensconced just off the living room. Mr. B.'s equipment and supplies and clustered pill bottles had spread across much of the first floor. Throwing an 18th birthday party for their younger daughter and her friends had required moving Mr. B. and one of his aides to a hotel for a night, which so disoriented him that Sari wasn't about to try it again. Feeling tethered to the house, she had trouble finding time to exercise or go out with her husband; travel was becoming impossible.

"My husband feels justified in saying he can't live like this anymore," she said. "He doesn't feel at home in his house. There's always people around, aides, nurses, physical therapists. And I'm always distracted, because I'm concerned about my dad."

"I haven't been a very happy camper," her husband, Roy, later confirmed. He didn't, for example, appreciate having a baby monitor in their bedroom, so that Sari could hear if her father called at night. "I'm trying to be supportive, but I'm angry at the same time."

Then there was the imminent departure of Erica, their younger daughter, heading for college out of state. "Honestly, I'd love to have a summer with her," Sari said a little wistfully. "She's going away in August and I don't want to miss driving her up and going to orientation; I don't want to feel cheated of that."

Tending to her father had been very satisfying for the first year or so after he was widowed. "He'd been sitting at the hospital all day," with his wife, Sari recalled. "He wasn't eating properly . . . He didn't look well, he wasn't thriving. So it felt good to take care of him, to build him up, to provide a place that was comfortable." She had always been her family's caregiver, the one who even as a child cooked and cleaned and half-raised her younger sister, who in her 20s went home to Queens when her mother had a heart attack. She'd earned two college degrees, but having opted to stay at home with her daughters, she'd been out of the workforce for years. "It has, at times, felt easier to care for other people than to figure out what the hell to do with my own life," she recognized.

But being the caregiver had lately become "so much more of a chore." Her father needed increasing assistance. Yet despite her

tireless efforts, and the antidepressants he took, Mr. B. declared
from time to time that this was no way to live, that he wished it
was "over." Her sister, who had a demanding career and two young
children and couldn't really share the workload, assured Sari that
Greenwood House would be good for their father and also help
restore normalcy at home.

So Mr. B.'s name was on the list. At some point, Sari mused
as the backyard trees rustled—it was the first time she'd sat out
on this lovely patio all season—Greenwood's social worker, Joan
Rubin-Kritz, would call to say there was a room available. And
then what?

Mr. B. had left the decision to his children. "You'll know the
right thing to do," he said the one time that Sari and her sister and
brother swallowed hard and asked what he thought.

But Sari wasn't sure she could actually institutionalize him. All
those rules, all those strangers. The home employed a nurse's aide
for every seven patients, she'd been told. That was fine if you were
first or second in line for something, Sari thought, but "horrible"
if you were seventh. Last night, Mr. B. had awakened at 2 a.m.
and asked for something to eat; if he wanted a predawn snack at
Greenwood House, would someone oblige him? Wasn't he entitled
to such small comforts toward the end of a long, sometimes sorrowful life?

"I'd almost feel like I was abandoning him," Sari fretted. "All
the gifts I have—that we're comfortable, that I have room, that I
have an education and the ability to do certain things, that I have
the luxury of not working . . . what *good* is what I have, if I can't
use it to make my parents' lives more comfortable?"

She went around and around about it. Some days, she said, "I
feel like I'm in a vise."

And then, barely two weeks after this conversation, the social
worker did call. It was a Monday; Greenwood wanted Mr. B. to
move in Thursday morning. Other families were eager to take the
room if he didn't.

So he did, and now Sari was sitting with him and her brother
in the auditorium on Sunday afternoon, awaiting a concert that,

as the moments ticked by, seemed unlikely to materialize. Aides passed out ice pops while the roomful of people waited. Eventually, Sari wheeled her father back to his room for a nap. As he dozed, she sat by his bed, describing to me all the problems she was already unhappy about—she'd been here every day for hours—and her doubts that he belonged here at all.

Mr. B. woke up uncertain about where he was. "This is Greenwood House. Greenwood is a nursing facility," Sari explained, displaying far more enthusiasm than she felt. "People live here if they have medical needs or they need therapy. They try to take care of you, whatever you need."

"Who talked me into this?" her father said in his faint voice. He sounded more puzzled than angry.

"We looked at it together a couple of times, remember? And you said it might be easier. Because it's hard to get help. People don't always show up. And you weren't getting out so often."

He had more questions; she tried to respond. "Remember, we said we'd wait a while," she said finally, "and see if there were benefits to being here."

Mrs. Gordon

Joel Gordon got the same sort of phone call from the same social worker a couple of weeks later. He happened to be on a boat, taking a sightseeing cruise around the harbor in Annapolis, Maryland, with his wife, Marlene—they'd driven down for a summer wedding—when his cell phone vibrated. Greenwood House was ready to admit Pauline Gordon, age 96.

"Oh, shit," was his response.

"It sounds like you're not happy to hear this," said Joan Rubin-Kritz.

Perhaps "happy" is never the best description for a family's reaction when this transition looms. But the Gordons faced particular challenges: Joel's mother had been diagnosed with obsessive-compulsive disorder, and as it intensified and her physical health declined, she had grown increasingly difficult to handle. The assisted living facility where she'd lived for five years had issued an ultimatum: She could remain only if she hired private aides around the clock.

Mrs. Gordon was, no question, a handful. She shrieked in alarm and outrage over such transgressions as not replacing a knickknack in its proper spot on her shelf. She imperiously ordered housekeepers out ("Who's the boss in this apartment?") and sometimes threatened suicide when she felt thwarted. So what would ensue when Joel told her she would be moving from her facility outside Princeton to a nursing home? "Nagasaki," was his prediction.

That's why he hadn't told his mother that he'd applied for a room at Greenwood House, not yet. Mrs. Gordon's dementia was growing more severe, but it hadn't reached the point where she didn't know where she was.

"Making her get out of her apartment is the worst punishment in the world. I'm not looking forward to doing that," Joel told me. He found it hard to empathize with her overwhelming concern with her small dwelling, its tchotchkes and furnishings, the sheaf of schedules and menus she laboriously maintained—symptoms, in part, of her illness. But he tried.

"If someone told me that I could never read again, that I could never listen to music again, that I'd forget everything I knew about science—that would be the worst thing *I* could imagine," said Joel. A molecular biologist, he spent much of his leisure immersed in books and newspapers, and kept the sound system in his West Windsor home tuned to a classical music station. "This is the equivalent thing for her. You have to respect that."

Now, the move was upon them. Joel asked Rubin-Kritz to drop them down her waiting list a slot or two to give him time to prepare his mother and to map out strategies to minimize the disruption of a move. Rubin-Kritz assented. For his part, Joel agreed to break the news and to bring his mother to Greenwood for a visit. It seemed that nobody wanted to tick off this very elderly, but apparently still very potent woman.

"She's not warm and fuzzy," Marlene cautioned before she took me over to meet Mrs. Gordon one weekend. They never knew, on a given day, what frame of mind she'd be in. Joel stayed home this afternoon; his presence, he'd found, often set off rounds of recriminations. Marlene, patient and smiling—she *was* warm and fuzzy—didn't trigger the same anger.

"How are you?" she said brightly, walking into her mother-in-law's apartment.

"Not good," Mrs. Gordon said. "What day is today? I'm very confused. I'm not feeling well today. What did I eat for lunch?"

A turkey sandwich, her aide said.

"What shall I eat for dinner? I don't know what to eat." She consulted the papers on which she recorded, in tiny penciled notations, everything she had done, or supposedly had done, or had yet to do that day, and everything she had eaten or planned to eat. Keeping these records was her "work," so central that she sometimes said she had no time for activities elsewhere in the building or her appointment at the downstairs beauty salon.

"I don't have any jewelry on. I'm not even dressed," Mrs. Gordon continued—though she was dressed in the blue pants and blue print shirt she wore every Saturday. Another of her habits: She put on a particular beige outfit Sunday through Tuesday, black pants and a striped shirt on Wednesday and Thursday, and on weekends this blue ensemble, refusing to vary the uniforms or to replace garments as they frayed. Marlene, who'd seen photos of her wearing the same shirts 20 years earlier, kept mending them.

"Want me to get the necklace you usually wear?" Marlene offered, found the strand of beads, and draped them gently around her neck.

Though she couldn't have weighed 100 pounds, Mrs. Gordon retained a strong, querulous voice that seemed to belong to someone larger. She had hooded gray eyes, behind a pair of glasses that took up half her face, and crimped hair in a pinkish blond shade. It was difficult to steer her onto other subjects beyond meals and calendars, but if you could manage to, she smiled a bit.

The artwork on her walls, for instance. Joel had told me of her artistic side. She'd loved theater and music, directed plays as a camp counselor, played the piano, and had painted these landscapes and still lifes. "I never took lessons; it's a natural gift," Mrs. Gordon declared when I asked about them. She was also proud of the silk flowers she'd assembled in vases around her small living room. "See how beautifully they're arranged?"

Marlene brought over a framed photo of Pauline and her late husband, Sam, who'd sold laundry supplies. In their youth, the Gordons had played bridge together and went ice-skating in Central Park. They took ballroom dancing lessons, and their tangos and fox-trots could clear the floor at a family bar mitzvah as everyone stopped to watch and applaud.

"We led beautiful lives; now I barely recognize him," Mrs. Gordon said sadly. Then she commanded, several times, "Put it back in the same place!" She had actually penciled lines on her white shelves, to ensure that after dusting every object did return to the very same place—as if she was trying, with her strict routines, to keep life's uncertainties at bay.

"You know, I don't want to get that old," Marlene murmured as we said goodbye. "Maybe I should take up drinking and smoking."

⁓

But these symptoms went back decades. As a child, growing up in Queens with his younger brother, Larry, Joel had seen his mother's rigidity as an odd personality trait. Ask him what she'd be serving for dinner on the third Wednesday of the month and he could tell you instantly: liver chow mein. Her insistence on neatness was such that once, outraged at her son's messy bedroom, she'd thrown all his clothes out the second-story window. She was always a bit tyrannical, prone to flying off the handle. Not until he left home for Johns Hopkins and took a course in abnormal psychology did Joel conclude that her behavior went beyond idiosyncrasy.

Nevertheless, she functioned reasonably well for some time, even after losing her husband a decade earlier. When Joel realized that she needed more attention than he could provide long-distance, he moved her from her Florida apartment into this large assisted living facility near his home. At first, she had a few friends, occasionally joined in activities, turned down a suitor named Herbie. She had emotional outbursts, but Joel advised the employees to "please just walk away" when that happened, so they did. It was what he had learned to do himself when she grew agitated and accusatory ("You're no longer my son!") and he didn't want to respond with anger.

"But this last year," he said, "she's showing more deterioration." Mrs. Gordon had stopped getting up for breakfast, started skipping the medications she'd always kept meticulous track of. She'd been hospitalized a few months before with a urinary tract infection, and afterward grew anxious and disoriented, more apt to lash out at helpers. She had a series of falls as well, which led to the director's decree that she needed full-time supervision.

"Get Mother Teresa if you can, because that's what we're going to need," Joel told the agency he called, looking for live-in help; his mother fiercely resisted intruders in her space. But the agency sent a woman he considered "a gem," and she'd been on the job for a couple of months.

Still, was this "quality of life"? Mrs. Gordon hated having an aide and regularly lambasted her. Except at mealtimes, it was growing difficult to cajole her into leaving her apartment. And the combined cost of assisted living plus a private aide—more than $100,000 a year, because the aide insisted on a higher-than-normal wage, a kind of combat pay—would quickly deplete the money she'd need to enter a good nursing home. (Greenwood House, like most nursing homes, gave preference to new patients who could pay their way for at least a few months before they "spent down" and qualified for Medicaid.)

Joel had anguished over the question of where his mother should live. Sometimes she seemed quite rational, while at others she might ask five times in a row what day it was. "I'd really like to have four or five siblings," he told me one night, reflecting on the responsibility he faced. Siblings might squabble, true, "but then I could say, 'Fine, *you* handle it.' But there's no one to hand it off to." His brother lived in Chicago and wasn't in great health himself.

In August, Joan Rubin-Kritz called again: Greenwood House had come up with a private room, one of its few, for Mrs. Gordon. It would cost $600 more each month than a semiprivate one, but much less than she was paying now, and it might ease the shift to a new environment.

Maybe no facility could make his mother happy anymore, but the people at Greenwood House could keep her safe and comfortable, Joel thought. His fear that assisted-living-plus-aides would ultimately prove untenable had just been confirmed by, of all things, a late-summer thunderstorm.

The deluge caused a ceiling leak over Mrs. Gordon's bed, and when the maintenance people came in to move the furniture and clean up, she panicked. Yelling and flailing, she hit her aide, who emerged with a scratched arm and informed Joel that if he hadn't already been planning to move his mother, she would have quit her job.

So what else was there to do? "You're faced with a spectrum of lousy options," Joel said. He told Joan to reserve the room. And he repeated to himself his new mantra. It came from a golfing buddy who told him, "You've got to leave this to the professionals or it's going to drive you crazy."

Good advice, Joel thought. He was toting too much psychological baggage, growing tense and overwrought. Leave it to the professionals.

Adjusting

Of course people grow fearful and emotional. They have dreaded this moment.

For years they've heard and read stories about what miserable places too many nursing homes are, even after decades of attempts to reform them. (More on this shortly.) They look at the horrifying costs and wonder who in the world can pay $68,408 a year, the average charge for a semiprivate room in 2008. They balk because the move seems so final. Perhaps in the past a parent extracted that familiar vow, "Promise you'll never put me in a nursing home." For any or all of these reasons, families make strenuous efforts to keep their parents out.

And their efforts, along with demographic and economic and governmental changes, are paying off: The percentage of those over 65 in nursing homes dropped from 4.2 percent in 1985 to 3.6 percent in 2004 (including short-term rehab patients) and the downward trend appears to have continued since. Even among people over 85, nursing home use fell sharply, to less than 14 percent.

Partly that's because the elderly are less disabled than they used to be, or at least better able to cope with their disabilities. They're more affluent, and as poverty rates have fallen, more seniors can afford alternatives like assisted living, which has siphoned off about a million people once probably destined for nursing homes. Some have benefited from a growing number of state and local programs focusing on assisted living or home care, which may save taxpayers some of the billions currently spent on nursing facilities.

At the same time, family care continues at high levels, delaying nursing home admissions. Drawing on data from a national survey of Americans over 70, researchers Anthony LoSasso and Richard Johnson confirmed that over a two-year period, seniors who usually received help from a child with at least one activity of daily living, such as bathing or dressing, were nearly 60 percent less likely to enter nursing homes than those without such help.

It's good news, the rise of a less disabled, more advantaged elderly population less prone to nursing home use. But it also means that those who *do* enter nursing homes, about 1.4 million people at last count, are older, sicker, and more incapacitated than in the past. They're the ones too ill or too poor to take advantage of alternatives, or unable to rely on others for the considerable amount of help they need.

To some extent it's their high level of disability, as much as or more than the condition of the facilities, that can make nursing homes depressing places to visit. In today's homes (average size: 108 residents), even those that smell fresh and look cheerful, more than half of patients are wheelchair bound, according to federal data analyzed by a University of California, San Francisco, team. More than half have urinary incontinence more than once a week. Forty-five percent suffer from dementia, though many studies put that proportion much higher. Clinical depression is widespread.

Sometimes, there's a limit to how long families' determination and alternate kinds of long-term care can keep people out of nursing homes. When an elderly person can no longer turn over in bed, and thus needs someone to reposition her every two hours to prevent pressure sores from developing, the options narrow abruptly.

"There's no one here anymore that doesn't need to be here," said Rick Goldstein of Greenwood House. In 1987, when he became its director, about a third of patients were incontinent, he estimates; now it's closer to two-thirds. Most current residents have some degree of dementia; for those in the advanced stages, he opened a 20-bed dementia unit. The activities staff years back consisted of three people; he's doubled it because residents "want and need things to do, but they're not as self-directed. They can't sit and read a book. They're more impaired."

Yet even for very disabled seniors and their families, who may see no other choice, the decision to move in remains extraordinarily difficult—"wrenching," in Joel Gordon's description.

For the resident, "Chances are, if you're in this situation, you have severe dementia, or you're incontinent, or you have behavioral problems—or you have no family," says Susan Reinhard, director of AARP's Public Policy Institute. "That's when you are at the highest risk of being in nursing home care."

For the caregiver, studies show, the decision usually reflects a combination of the elderly person's high needs, which may increasingly tax her capacity to meet them, and the pressures she feels herself, including the toll on her own health.

In a study of chronically disabled seniors, Urban Institute investigators Brenda Spillman and Sharon Long identified a category of caregivers, almost 20 percent, who were highly stressed—experiencing physical strain, disturbed sleep, and financial hardships. They were already in fair or poor health, these caregivers said, and their health was declining. These were the people significantly more likely to turn to nursing homes. In the first year, 7 percent of the seniors in the study entered a nursing home, rising to 13 percent after two years. Among the highly stressed caregivers, though, 11 percent institutionalized their elderly relatives the first year, and 17 percent within two years.

Looking at those statistics, what struck me was that even among the group shouldering the greatest burdens, so many *still* didn't opt for nursing homes. "It is overwhelming to think what people are undertaking," Brenda Spillman agreed when we spoke. After all, 83 percent of even the highly stressed caregivers remained on the job, still caring for their relatives two years later.

We also know that when caregivers do decide to place relatives in nursing homes, they grapple with varying degrees of anger, depression, and guilt. The decision can spark conflicts with other family members. Caregivers may experience relief from the physical tasks they've faced, but the new environment brings a different set of anxieties and challenges. They sometimes conclude that they've failed, broken an implicit or explicit pledge, deserted those relying on them.

It's a response that dismays Elinor Ginzler of AARP, who has worked on eldercare issues for 25 years. "We do ourselves a huge injustice," she protests. Naturally she thinks family members should devote considerable effort to finding a high-quality facility. Nevertheless, "I think there are circumstances where someone needs to be in a nursing home . . .

"Think about it . . . You're caring for a parent at home, and that parent needs 24-hour supervision. In a facility, it's provided by a staff—a nutritionist, a physical therapist, certified nursing assistants on shifts, a registered nurse, a physician—somewhere between five and ten people . . . And you are *one*. You've probably been doing a gargantuan task"—and to keep doing it indefinitely may be "unrealistic."

Frail seniors may actually fare better at Greenwood House than at home, the staff there is convinced, especially if they've been living alone. A lot of elderly people spend hours in front of their TV sets, Rick Goldstein points out; they don't always eat well, take their prescribed meds on schedule, or get out to see people. He thinks they get better medical supervision, better personal care, more stimulation in his facility.

Still, the industry rule of thumb, Joan Rubin-Kritz advises newcomers and their families, is that someone moving into a nursing home needs three to six months to adjust. New residents are "dealing with loss, with a capital L-O-S-S," she says. "Not just of their physical abilities, their senses, their independence, but their homes, their houses or apartments, their possessions." Possibly they're mourning the person who cared for them until now. Perhaps, too, they're aware of oncoming dementia, the fading of "their memory, their ability to make decisions for themselves."

Their children have to adapt, too, Rubin-Kritz adds, and that means maintaining reasonable expectations. An unexpected fact of life at Greenwood House is that administrators spend lots of time assuring new families of the fine job the staff will do, but also explaining the numerous things it can't do.

"We start at the preadmission meeting"—a 90-minute session during which the incoming patient and family meet staff people, see the resident's room, do preliminary paperwork so that moving day will be less hectic. That's when Rubin-Kritz and her colleagues also begin clarifying their limitations.

"We talk about things like bathing," she says. "People say their mother is used to a shower every day. Right then and there we say, 'That's not possible. No nursing home gives full baths or showers more than twice a week.'" Bathing remains one of those low-tech, labor-intensive jobs that an aide can perform for only one resident at a time—and there aren't enough aides to bathe everyone more often.

"We make sure people are clean—they have bed baths or

are washed in the bathroom every day," Rubin-Kritz hastens to add, but that doesn't always assuage families. "People get very upset."

The children also want to know how quickly a call bell will summon help. "It shouldn't take longer than ten minutes," Rubin-Kritz tells them. "We hope it's ten minutes." That can sound, and feel, like a long wait if a senior needs to be taken to the bathroom, but the home considers it a reasonable response time. (Emergencies like possible falls, signaled by bed and chair alarms, get immediate action, of course. And every resident is supposed to be changed or taken to the toilet every two hours, even if he or she doesn't ask.)

As for such matters as when to get up and when to eat—habits that critics think a facility should accommodate—there's not much flexibility. Breakfast trays arrive between 7:30 and 8. A helpful aide may bring someone's tray first, or last, but those accustomed to sleeping late and brunching at 10:30—or having 7 o'clock dinners—are out of luck. Someone will bring them a sandwich from the fridge, but the schedule stands.

"There's definitely some compromise," Rubin-Kritz advises. "It's not home. It *is* an institution."

Mrs. Gordon

Joel Gordon was 66, old enough (barely) to collect Social Security, but he looked younger, wiry from golf games and gym workouts, with a trim beard and silvery close-cropped hair. He'd retired from Johnson & Johnson a few years earlier but grew restive and joined the advisory board of a biotech start-up, a position that could become quite demanding when deadlines loomed. Marlene, a few years his junior, supervised accounting for a law office. They sometimes shook their heads at the fact that they'd each already survived a frightening health crisis—her breast cancer at 48, his prostate cancer at 63—while his mother had remained in good physical condition well into her 90s.

Their illnesses had served to draw the Gordons, always a tight, well-functioning duo, still closer. Before long, they thought, they'd be able to ratchet back their work commitments, spend more time traveling with friends, cherish their leisure. He had a particular yen to see Australia.

Two pieces of unfinished family business remained. Planning a spring wedding for their daughter was the happy task. (Their son had already married.) The less-happy one was moving Pauline Gordon, swiftly and with the least possible turmoil, into Greenwood House. "It's not a trip to the grocery store," Joel sighed. He'd come to regret the strategy he'd used earlier to persuade her to accept an aide. If she didn't, he had pointed out, she'd be headed for a nursing home. Now she was heading for a nursing home anyway.

When he and Marlene sat down for The Talk, however, he avoided that term. Instead, explaining to his mother that she needed more help than assisted living could provide, he carefully referred to the new place as "a long-term care facility." It would be safer, he explained, and more affordable.

Mrs. Gordon listened for a while, asked why her current arrangement couldn't continue, then announced she'd kill herself.

"That's not an option," Joel said, trying to stay calm.

The discussion deteriorated from there. "I hate you, you're no longer my son! Who ever heard of a child not taking care of their parents?" When the aide tried to comfort her with a touch, Mrs. Gordon shouted, "Take your hands off me!"

The subsequent visit to Greenwood House didn't begin promisingly, either. Offered a wheelchair for a tour, Mrs. Gordon rode around the building with her hands clapped over her eyes. "I don't want to see anything," she declared. "I don't want to move. I want to stay in my place."

Unfazed, Joan Rubin-Kritz, the social worker, brought her into her office, where they talked for nearly 45 minutes about Mrs. Gordon's anxieties and about all the things she might like at Greenwood: the religious services, the kosher food, the weekly discussion group on Judaism. "Joan was absolutely wonderful with her," Marlene said afterward. Mrs. Gordon, mollified, asked a few questions about what time lunch and dinner were served, met a couple of residents including one gallant man who kissed her hand. Maybe this could work, Marlene thought; maybe she would actually enjoy aspects of the place.

Afterward, Joel sat in his family room for a while and let music wash over and restore him.

It was a sad thing to take no pleasure in the time spent with his aged mother, and to feel that his dutiful visits brought her no pleasure, either. She'd always been somewhat intimidating but also, if he thought back far enough, warm and funny and "gorgeous." In his boyhood, she took him to concerts and plays in Manhattan, to the Metropolitan Museum and the Museum of Natural History—catnip for a future biologist.

"My whole love of music comes from experiences with her," he remembered. She taught him the rudiments of cooking, too, and he still liked to cook. "We joked around; at times, I could make her laugh. It was basically a normal life, except for these behaviors. And as she got older, they got worse."

He'd hoped, when she first moved up from Florida, that he could now return the favor, take *her* to concerts and the theater. But she'd lost interest; she even rejected his offer of a radio. Her world had narrowed to her apartment and a few key sheets of paper.

"Don't try to make things right, because you can't make them right," Marlene had urged. "Just shut up and listen." So Joel had learned not to argue with his mother's complaints, to simply sit and hear her out.

At times, driving to see her, he thought, "Maybe we'll have a nice conversation today. That would be enough." He couldn't remember the last time it had happened.

None of that, however, lessened the immense pressure he felt to do the best he could for her, partly for the simple reason that she was his mother, but also because it was what his father, whom he revered and missed, would have expected. "There was an ethical and moral framework he taught me, by word and by example," Joel said. "So he didn't have to tell me, 'Take care of your mother.' It's the right thing to do."

Now he was summoning all his scientist's precision to arrange the smoothest possible move in September. He wanted her new room almost completely set up when she arrived. "I don't want it to look like a hospital room, I want it to look like home," he decided. "She's making this big transition. I want her to be comfortable and have her stuff around her." So he'd measured carefully, devising a schematic to show where the bookshelves would fit, which paintings would hang on which wall. He'd recruited a colleague with an SUV to help him ferry everything to the new location.

The plan, developed with Mrs. Gordon's gerontologist, called for a temporarily increased dose of Risperdal, the antipsychotic drug she took to reduce agitation and anxiety. Otherwise, "you can predict that at some point my mother will totally lose control," Joel said.

On moving day, Joel and his friend would hustle her belongings into the van while Marlene drove Mrs. Gordon to Greenwood House. There they'd have a leisurely lunch and meet the staff while Joel readied her new quarters. "I'll move the furniture and Marlene will move my mother."

It worked more or less as planned. Mrs. Gordon grandly told Rubin-Kritz that she was happy to be at Greenwood House. "I won't have someone sitting in my room, watching me all the time, watching television," she said, free of her aide at last. She grew loudly uneasy at the delay while Joel finished preparing her room, then immersed herself in contemplating the dinner menu and didn't appear to notice when he and Marlene said goodbye.

The problems began that very evening, with a call from the night nurse reporting that Mrs. Gordon refused to let the staff ready her for bed. Irascible, uncooperative, she slept in her clothes, and the next day resisted attempts at bathing, shouting at the aides. "We're going to have to teach her some limits," Rubin-Kritz, staying in close communication, told Joel.

That was okay with him: Let the professionals handle it. "These people *are* professionals, even more than in assisted living," he concluded after a nerve-wracking first week. "There, the attitude was, 'She's becoming uncontrollable, we can't handle her, find something else to do.' Now, it's 'She's difficult to handle, just hang in there and *we'll* find something to do.'"

The nurse who most often cared for Mrs. Gordon, a sunny and extremely patient LPN named Takesha Smith, had a knack for knowing when to be firm and when to yield. She tried to give Mrs. Gordon choices—Wear the white sweater or the black one? Take the pill now or in ten minutes?—but she insisted on courtesy. When Mrs. Gordon raised her voice, "I say, 'I can't listen to you when you yell at me. I'm going to leave and come back when you're not yelling,'" Smith explained to me. "And as I'm walking out she says, 'I'm sorry, I won't yell anymore.'"

Except for bathing—that intimate act, one Mrs. Gordon never accepted without protest—she seemed to be coping with the new place and its routines. As Joel had predicted, she wasn't happy—she only occasionally joined the goings-on in the atrium—but he thought she was being well cared for. "You get a real sense that they care deeply about the people in their charge," he said.

Over the ensuing months, as I went to see Mrs. Gordon—knowing she wouldn't remember who I was—I saw what Joel and Marlene meant by "the lottery": You could chance upon a good day or, just as randomly, hit a real nightmare.

One fall afternoon, I had a brief sample of the "nice conversation" Joel so often wished for. The usual question about what day it was—Thursday, I said—somehow triggered recollections about Friday, the Sabbath. "Friday night in the Jewish religion, we light the candles," Mrs. Gordon declared. "Friday, I wear blue and white. I have a table all set. I have the candles out and I say the prayer. They bring a challah up from downstairs. I make a real Sabbath dinner. I have chicken."

I asked if she went to services on Friday; she assured me that she did. She even chuckled a bit when I observed that women seemed to work awfully hard to prepare for the day of rest. Much of what she'd told me was no longer true, but in her memories, it was.

But then came the day I arrived to find Mrs. Gordon, her hair askew and her eyes wide with alarm, restlessly declaring, "I need help. I need to prepare. I need to get ready. I'm ready to give orders and there's no one to give them to." It wasn't clear, at least to me, what she meant. "Nothing was taken care of. Everything got mixed up and nobody came."

Conversation was impossible. I asked if she'd like a drink of cold water—the only thing I could think to offer—and when I returned from the ice machine, she was lying on her bed, even more distressed. "I don't know what's going on, what went on all day. I'm lost." She had stopped keeping her careful daily notations; perhaps that made her feel unmoored.

"I wish I were dead! I wish I were dead! I'm 90 years old. I try to keep in contact with things but I just can't . . . I don't know what to eat, what to drink. My nose is running. And I'm cold, I'm very cold. I'm a mess."

Meals seemed to calm her. The staff had decided she should have them in the atrium with residents who needed help eating, not because she couldn't feed herself but because the servers in the main dining room upset her when they approached the table. Simply giving her a tray of food, rather than allowing her to dither endlessly about menu choices, also simplified the process. With Joel and Marlene's help, the dining staff had compiled a list of her likes and dislikes.

I sat with her one evening as she spread chopped liver on bread and chewed meditatively; she was as peaceful as I'd ever seen her. She'd actually gained two pounds in her first month at Greenwood House.

Persuading her to leave her room for meals was a challenge, though, and sometimes a bit of an Abbott & Costello routine. "Hellooo, Miss Pauline, how's my pretty girl?" Takesha Smith crooned to her late one afternoon. "Are you coming to eat in the dining room with me tonight?"

"Okay," Mrs. Gordon said, after some back and forth. Some advocacy groups are uneasy about workers using endearments like "sweetheart" or "darling," instead of a resident's name. Smith used them liberally—and effectively.

"*Thank* you. We can go now, or you can wait. Want me to come back in ten minutes?"

She did.

"Ready?" Smith asked, returning to a host of questions about what was being served for supper. Grilled cheese and tomato sandwiches, she said, and soup and fresh string beans.

"Grilled cheese?"

"Come on, let's go see, before it gets cold," Smith urged, trying to avoid a long food discussion. "C'mon, gorgeous."

They moved toward the hallway, Mrs. Gordon wielding her walker, when she suddenly stopped. "I don't have my keys. Where are my keys?"

"I'll close the door, no one will come in," Smith said. Mrs. Gordon wasn't buying it.

The keys weren't in her purse or on her dresser. Smith eventually found them on the corner cabinet. "Here, Mommy."

"What am I having?"

"Let's go see."

"I'm having cheese?"

"Grilled cheese."

"What's today, Thursday?"

"Wonderful Thursday!" Smith sang out, and they walked slowly down the hall to supper.

As for Joel, he was more relaxed than he'd been in months, less likely to grow edgy and uncommunicative on visiting days or to snap at Marlene. He still didn't enjoy visiting his mother—but he did anyway, at least weekly, keeping an attentive eye on her. He worried about what would happen when her money ran out and she became dependent on Medicaid, which wouldn't pay for a private room. Mrs. Gordon's being forced to share living space was not a happy prospect. But in the meanwhile, he'd had "an epiphany."

For five years, whenever he got a call from his mother's assisted living facility reporting one problem or another, "I'd get terribly upset. It would ruin the day, and the day after. Why? Because I was worried that we'd have to put her in a nursing home. And now, she's *in* a nursing home, and they're taking care of her. So what else is there to fear?"

Mr. B.

Sari, on the other hand, couldn't relax at all. She was at Greenwood House for hours each day, and she continued to pay her father's private aides to come in from 5 until 11 p.m.; if she could have afforded it, she would have hired someone to stay overnight as well.

Private help was very unusual at this nursing home, but without it, "I don't think they're going to give him that personal attention," she worried. "I wanted to believe what everyone told me, that people adjust. But I think what they really mean is, you'll get used to it"—and not complain.

She came dashing in one afternoon at her usual speedy pace, found her father having a drink in the atrium and kissed him—"Hi, Daddy!"—on the forehead. Then she excused herself to stash the food she was bringing—a container of cherries, a piece of Muenster cheese wrapped in foil—in the picnic cooler she kept in his room, so he'd have a supply of favorite snacks. He'd been in residence about two weeks at this point; she had a clearer idea of what might make things more pleasant.

"Want a top and a straw for that?" asked the nurse, the pregnant one, who'd prepared his drink.

"If it's the same price, I'll take it," Mr. B. said, a whispery quip.

"It's the same price. Here you are, darling."

He could joke, and he could read the copy of the *Bucks County Courier Times* that Sari brought daily, if someone handed him his eyeglasses and propped the newspaper on the tray of his chair. One afternoon, sitting outside with his aide enjoying the summer warmth, Mr. B. asked me whether the truce in the Middle East was holding.

On the other hand, he'd just told the nurse—giving her belly a pat—that he had two sons. He had one, and two daughters. In its later stages, Parkinson's could cause mental confusion as well as physical symptoms.

Sari's cooler caused some grumbling, because Greenwood House adhered to the Jewish dietary laws and wouldn't permit any nonkosher foods, but she swore that everything she brought was kosher.

Nor was she at ease with the ban on all outside drugs, even over-the-counter remedies. Federal regulations don't permit most residents to self-medicate: A resident might take the wrong dose, or a neighbor might wander in and take someone else's pills; there might be interactions with patients' prescription drugs. So when one of the nurses spotted a bottle of Mylanta in Mr. B.'s dresser drawer, she told Sari to take it home. "They don't want you to do *anything*," Sari said. "But if he has a headache, I don't care, I'm going to give him a Tylenol."

A low-level guerrilla conflict was under way, it seemed, about who could or should do what for Mr. B. Sari was miffed when the staff issued prohibitions about things like thickening her father's beverage, which she'd probably only done about five thousand times. "If I'm around, I can make it not too thick," she said. "Otherwise, he won't drink it and it just sits. Then I'm concerned about his dehydrating"—a common problem in nursing homes.

A much bigger issue was that the staff had assessed Mr. B. as a "two-person transfer," which meant that a single individual— whether a Greenwood House nursing assistant, his private aide Odette, or his daughter—could not safely get him out of bed or take him to the bathroom. The wait for not one, but two assistants to disentangle themselves from other tasks and come help him could seem awfully long.

Yet even if Sari or Odette (who of course had single-handedly helped him to the toilet numberless times at home) were with him, they were not to move him themselves. If he couldn't wait, he was supposed to urinate in the Depends-style undergarment he wore as a precaution. "Here's someone *trying* to be continent, and they're not encouraging it," Sari complained. "It takes away his dignity."

Tensions between staff and family aren't uncommon in nursing homes. Sari naturally felt she knew her father's needs and preferences better than any staffer who'd met him two weeks ago. Greenwood House, for its part, put an extremely high premium on safety, and was also constrained by volumes of federal and state regulations.

She didn't want people repeatedly coming into his room through the night, interrupting her father's sleep, for instance. Yet employees were required to turn him every two hours to prevent pressure sores, since he couldn't turn himself; they risked getting a deficiency from state inspectors if they didn't.

"You are the guest now," a nursing supervisor told Sari. "You have to get out of that caretaker mode." Possibly she meant the remark kindly—you can finally relinquish some of the hard work and worry—but it sounded to Sari like criticism. She tried to keep her response measured: "I have no problem being a guest, if I see my dad's being cared for."

How to handle this stuff? Sari was trying to be tactful and cooperative. If she questioned or complained too often—as on the day she arrived at 11:30 and found her father still in bed, unwashed and undressed, because the aides had given priority to residents with morning appointments in physical therapy or at the beauty parlor—"I'll be a pariah here," she worried. Maybe she already was; maybe the staff saw Mr. B.'s private aides as an implicit reproach.

"Everybody has to have that opportunity to develop relationships with the staff on their own," said Joan Rubin-Kritz, who worked to smooth over family/staff conflicts. "The staff are not themselves, they're not relaxed and at ease around the resident, if the family is always there and they feel the family is always judging them, criticizing every little thing they do."

Still, Sari chafed at the rules. The day before, for instance, she and her sister spontaneously took their father and his aide out to dinner at Antonio's, just down the road, and had a grand time. Along with his chicken piccata, her father savored a glass of white Zinfandel and a cup of clam chowder, both forbidden him at the nursing home—the former because he hadn't yet obtained written permission from his doctor allowing him to drink alcohol, the latter because shellfish aren't kosher. "He was so happy," Sari reported. "He said, 'I have to come here more often.'"

Afterward, though, the nursing supervisor told Sari that she should give 24 hours' notice before taking her father away from Greenwood House for more than an hour or two, so that the pharmacy could order packaged medications to take along. "They're driving me crazy," Sari muttered.

※

Not that the picture was entirely bleak. Sari appreciated the occupational therapist who'd worked overtime to adapt a comfortable reclining wheelchair with head and foot supports; she also thought the physical therapist had "a heart of gold." If someone came to fetch him for activities—sometimes they did, sometimes not—Mr. B. enjoyed Lamar's poker games and some of the musicales. He was happy when staffers took the time to kibbitz with him.

At home, things were certainly easier. Sari could sleep without a monitor in the bedroom. Her husband felt he could reclaim his house and his wife. Their older daughter Nicole came home from her campus for a weekend, cooked an enchilada casserole for dinner, and the family all sat around the kitchen table playing a biographical guessing game called Botticelli.

"It was so much fun," Nicole told me afterward. "When Poppy was here, Mom tended to have a split focus, understandably. She'd be listening or running back and forth; she was always very, very vigilant. And she was very good at it, but it was exhausting. This was nice, in a selfish sort of way. She was just there, physically, emotionally, just present. We got all of her for a while."

Sari had cherished the evening, too. And she was looking forward to a couple of family events, spending a few days in Florida, taking Erica to college.

Nevertheless, she'd begun contemplating bringing her father home. He had too little control in the nursing home and not enough to do, in her opinion. The employees seemed pleasant and wanted to be helpful, but were often too busy to respond to calls as promptly as she thought they should.

One night, "I went home and lost it," Sari confessed. "Couldn't stop crying, just thinking about his situation . . . It's torture to me, to have him there." She told him, more than once, that if he wanted to, he could return to her house.

♋

There was another layer to this story, Joan Rubin-Kritz was convinced. Most residents and families, she said, were quite satisfied with Greenwood House. (I spoke with several who agreed.) To her mind, Sari's responses reflected not only the expected adjustment but her personal history as the child of two Holocaust survivors. "I think that's a huge factor," Rubin-Kritz told me.

She'd done some Internet research, printing out a study from the *American Journal of Psychiatry* and one by social workers at a Toronto geriatric center. "Children of survivors seem to have consciously and unconsciously absorbed their parents' Holocaust experiences into their lives," Rubin-Kritz read aloud from the Toronto study. "Children are often troubled by guilt . . . for not being able to undo their parents' early life traumas." In the other article, she'd highlighted a reference to survivors' children's "inappropriate hypervigilance and distrust."

Sari would "come right out and say it," Rubin-Kritz went on. "Because her father had lost so much, suffered so much, had so little control during the Holocaust, she felt she had to provide him with as much control as she could . . . She felt guilty if she did anything less."

Sari was, indeed, aware of the effect of her parents' sorrows. "I heard horrible things," she said. "I feel like I've spent my whole life trying to make it up to them, trying to make their lives better."

Yet she also thought a nursing home simply couldn't give her father enough attention and comfort. Greenwood House seemed to regard her as an overanxious daughter with unrealistic expectations, micromanaging tasks that were no longer her responsibility. Sari saw a fragile man reliant on an overtaxed staff. "You have people whose hearts are in it and they really care—but they *can't* really care," she concluded. "They have to move on to the next person, or they won't get done."

A few weeks into Mr. B.'s stay, Rubin-Kritz asked Sari to come to a meeting. She sat in the library for an hour with Rubin-Kritz, the nursing supervisor of her father's wing, and the director of nursing, talking over the things that bothered Sari, the things that bothered Greenwood House, and how they might resolve their disagreements. Everyone was very courteous.

"I just want what's best for Henry," the supervisor concluded.

"That's nice to hear; so do I," said Sari.

But she was still pondering possible alternatives. Maybe she could rent an apartment somewhere for him and a live-in aide, giving him more care while protecting her own household's privacy. But then he'd be too isolated, and who knew what might go on when she wasn't there?

"There's no good answer, is there?" she concluded.

"How Did My Mom Do Today?"

The fact is, you don't have to be overprotective or psychologically damaged to feel the need for continuing vigilance when your parent is in a nursing home. A few facilities—the executive director of NCCNHR, formerly known as the National Citizens' Coalition for Nursing Home Reform, informally estimated the proportion at 10 to 15 percent—do a very good job. A larger group provides the sort of substandard care that amply justifies families' fears: The U.S. Government Accountability Office reported that in 2006, "almost one in five nursing homes was cited for serious deficiencies, those that caused actual harm or placed residents in immediate jeopardy." Some of these places, despite stepped-up federal enforcement, were chronic offenders; sanctioned for harming patients, they temporarily corrected the problems, then were later cited for the same failures—over and over again.

That leaves most nursing homes in the middle, not dangerous but hardly beacons of quality. Most residents and family members—in a survey completed by more than 146,000 people—rank their facilities as "good" (51 percent) or "excellent" (31 percent). Professionals and researchers in the field are less complimentary; they consider most homes adequate but distinctly second-rate.

"My concern is not the bad performers, the really bad apples, where you'd be afraid to have your family member live there," says Robyn Stone, a veteran long-term care researcher with the American Association of Homes and Services for the Aging, which represents nonprofits. "It's this really nagging level of mediocrity."

Reformers inside and outside government have been trying to raise standards for decades. Nursing home horror stories cropped up so persistently in the 1970s and 1980s that Congress passed the sweeping Nursing Home Reform Act in 1987. It established residents' legal rights, set stringent standards, and established inspections and enforcement mechanisms—all meant to ensure that facilities receiving Medicare or Medicaid payments (as nearly all nursing homes do) provide quality care. It was supposed to enable residents to reach their "highest practicable" levels of physical, mental, and psychosocial well-being. Critics, whistle-blowers, prosecutors, residents, and families have been protesting ever since that it doesn't.

There has been measurable progress.

The number of nursing homes where inspectors found "serious deficiencies," the GAO reported, fell from 28 percent in 2000 to a low of 16 percent in 2004, then crept up again to 19 percent.

The use of restraints that restrict physical movement—vests, wrist or ankle bands, chairs with locking trays—became a particular target for reform. Alice Hedt of NCCNHR was a long-term care ombudsman in North Carolina in the 1980s. "I'd walk into a nursing home," she recalls, "and it wouldn't be unusual to see 30 percent of the residents tied to wheelchairs with bed sheets. It was the greatest indignity I could imagine."

The rationale was that restraints would stop patients from falling or wandering, but research has demonstrated that such practices (along with the inappropriate use of psychotropic drugs, sometimes referred to as "chemical restraints") actually cause more injuries than they prevent. Their use nationwide has plummeted from nearly 40 percent of residents before the 1987 legislation to less than 7 percent.

Hedt also applauds "the whole concept of residents' rights" that the Act created: "If you have a problem, you can pursue it and the law is on your side." Those rights include participation in resident and family groups, which Hedt and her colleagues find valuable. "Family members often feel like lonely voices," she noted. "They don't feel equipped to talk to the facilities. They fear retaliation."

Nearly all nursing homes now have resident councils and almost 40 percent have family councils in which to explore common dilemmas. That doesn't always translate to action, Hedt knows too well, but "a good administrator will be responsive"—and there are enforcement strategies to pursue if he or she isn't.

Many problems remain, however. Nursing homes still receive frequent deficiencies from government surveyors for not preventing accidents or controlling infections, for not exercising patients' limbs to prevent painful muscle contractures, for not providing enough help with meals so that patients can maintain their weight. The proportion of residents with pressure ulcers (aka bedsores), which are both dangerous and largely preventable, has remained fairly constant at more than 7 percent for nearly a decade. The actual picture may be more disturbing, since there's continuing evidence that inspectors understate the serious deficiencies they find.

In a Massachusetts study of 18 nursing homes, researchers reviewing patients' charts tallied well over 500 "adverse drug events" in a year, meaning errors in prescribing, ordering, dispensing, or monitoring medications. An anthropological study of 40 residents in two California nursing homes found that almost none were drinking enough liquids; over the two years that researchers observed their care, 25 of the 40 developed conditions that might have been related to dehydration. The extent of actual elder abuse in nursing homes, from verbal insults and rough handling to hitting or shoving, has gone largely unmeasured but is believed to be a serious problem.

What underlies nearly all these defects is a severe, ongoing shortage of well-trained staff, the single greatest factor in poor-quality care. "That's what a nursing home is all about, the staffing," says Charlene Harrington of the University of California, San Francisco, who has published dozens of studies on the issue. "Nursing homes don't have enough staff to get the work done, so they don't get people to the toilet, they don't get people out of bed, they don't help them eat."

The evidence has been piling up for years: Higher ratios of staff to residents are associated with "a lower mortality rate, less weight loss, fewer injuries," Harrington says. "Fewer rehospitalizations. Fewer ER visits. Almost any clinical measure you can think of has been found to be related to better staffing." The level of registered nurses is particularly significant, because "RNs are trained to catch problems. They can tell if somebody's getting in trouble, if their blood pressure's going up; they're better at preventing infections."

After all, the hands-on workers who provide the bulk of care to residents, variously known as certified nursing assistants, personal care assistants, or nurses' aides, are required by federal law to complete just 75 hours—two weeks—of training, though some states impose higher standards. Critics are fond of pointing out that state standards are often far stricter for manicurists and dog groomers.

Nursing home aides have very tough jobs, with some of the highest workplace injury rates of any occupation. Because the demands are high, their training generally inadequate, their average wages low, and benefits frequently nonexistent, they tend to leave their jobs in droves. A 2006 survey of more than 100,000 nursing home employees found that only about half of nurses and nursing assistants were satisfied with their jobs. "Turnover in some places is well over 100 percent" a year, says AARP's Susan Reinhard. "So you don't know who is, literally, laying hands on you."

Without a stable workforce, Reinhard says, families' conversations with caregivers are likely to be exercises in frustration: " 'How did my mom do today?' 'I don't know, who's your mom?' Or 'How did she do yesterday?' 'I wasn't here yesterday; I might not be here tomorrow.' It's very difficult."

How many nurses does it take to staff a good nursing home? In 1998, a New York University conference—drawing researchers, economists, administrators, and consumer advocates—reviewed the many previous studies and federal survey data and came up with a series of guidelines, including this one: Quality care requires at least 4.55 hours of total nursing time—from registered nurses, licensed practical or vocational nurses, and aides combined—per resident per day. A few years later, a report from the federal Centers for Medicare and Medicaid Services put the minimum at 4.1 hours per resident day. Fewer than 10 percent of the nation's nursing homes could meet those standards then, and the hours of registered nurses' care has declined since.

Even Greenwood House, with its excellent survey reports, falls short of those benchmarks. In 2006, the year Mr. B. and Mrs. Gordon came to live there, it reported a total of 3 hours and 51 minutes of nursing per resident per day. That exceeded the state and national averages, with considerably higher RN hours, but it was "definitely not good enough," Charlene Harrington said when I told her the numbers.

Greenwood's administrators themselves wish for more nurses, though with a nationwide nursing shortage it's already difficult to hire as many as they need, despite relatively high pay scales and solid benefit packages. "It would be wonderful to have one aide for five patients," the nursing director told me. "Six, max." But the ratio is one to seven. There's no money for more, administrators say; Greenwood House already operates at a deficit.

Critics and reformers have urged a focus on improving the workplace—with better training and supervision, plus emphasis on "soft skills" like communication. Staff members, after all, can be the victims of physical and verbal attacks, especially from residents with dementia, not only the perpetrators. Staffing "is not just about numbers," Stone points out. "It's about whether there's a workplace that supports these frontline caregivers."

The staff issue arises at every monthly meeting of Greenwood's resident council (along with complaints about being served far too much chicken), its president told me. Evelyn Nade, who was 82 with multiple health problems, used a wheelchair and needed a lot of physical help—but was mentally sharp enough to run for Congress.

A poker player and ceramicist, "I'm as happy here as I could be anywhere," she assured her anxious daughters, both fans of the place. It was too lonely being at home with hired aides, she found, and she needed too much care to move in with her children. Here she had friends, founded a chapter of the Red Hat Society, bonded with an aide named Elizabeth. A relentlessly sunny woman, she felt respected and well treated, yet she understood why a family member might grumble.

"Some people complain they don't get enough attention," she said. "When they ring the bell . . . sometimes they wait five minutes, sometimes it's 20 minutes." Like Mr. B., Mrs. Nade was a two-person transfer, which often meant a longer wait. "Many times I've lost it; I've wet myself," she said. "They're very nice, they change me and wash me. But it's something that's happened to all of us here."

"There's Life There."

Because of such persistent shortcomings, and because families remain families no matter where their eldest members live, children's sense of responsibility rarely ends at the nursing home door. They relinquish many of the hands-on chores—but they face a new set of trials as they try to figure out their roles in this new environment.

Finding a facility is the initial challenge. The Gordons and Sari had the luxury of time to ask around and look around, but if a senior has had a health crisis, is being discharged from a hospital but can't go home, families may have just days to locate a facility.

It's easier to find information about nursing home quality than it used to be, using tools like the medicare.gov Website, state-issued report cards, and conversations with long-term care ombudsmen (there are almost 600 ombudsman programs, at least one in each state).

But it's still not simple. "A lot of information still isn't available," says Alice Hedt of NCCNHR. "It's not public who owns a facility, who manages it. If a facility has been sanctioned, fined $250,000 for poor care, Nursing Home Compare"—the findings posted on medicare.gov—"doesn't show that."

So the pros urge families to talk to others with relatives in a facility, to get a sense of what people at local senior centers or hospital discharge offices think, to do whatever background homework they can. Then, there's no substitute for walking through the place yourself.

"Are there cars in the parking lot? Are people visiting? That's a really important sign," says Susan Reinhard of AARP. "You want to hear lively things, not just the sound of a TV. You'll see the recreation person doing senior exercises, you'll see activity . . . You want to see staff who—I'm not saying they're smiling all the time—but who generally have a good demeanor. There could be pets, or flowers growing. There's life there."

Talking to residents and visitors, watching how the staff interacts with patients, seeing what happens when call bells go off— "unobtrusive observation is a really good thing for families to do," agrees Robyn Stone. And she suggests observing not only during the day, when activity and staff levels are higher, but also during the evening, when there's far less of both.

❧

Some factors are known to correlate with better care—ownership, for example. About two-thirds of nursing homes are for-profit institutions, most owned by chains. But nonprofit homes, research has repeatedly shown, generally do a superior job. For instance, a review of the federal survey data in 1998, encompassing nearly 14,000 facilities, found that nonprofit and government nursing homes provided more nurses and averaged fewer and less serious deficiencies.

Ownership isn't an infallible guide; there are poor-quality non-profit facilities, as well as excellent for-profit ones. But "a for-profit nursing home is a business," Rick Goldstein of Greenwood House points out. "Owners are trying to maximize their returns. Some of the chains have stockholders and *they* want to maximize their returns."

Staff is always the largest part of a nursing home's operating cost, so keeping staff levels lower helps push profits higher. Greenwood House, by contrast, faces a nearly $600,000 deficit each year, even with a volunteer board of directors and lower-than-usual staff turnover. It relies on grants from local charities, fund-raising events, and memorial bequests from grateful families to bridge the gap, as many nonprofits do. For-profits can't bolster their budgets with philanthropy; nobody's going to hold charity auctions for a chain like Manor Care.

The proportion of Medicaid residents is another signal worth paying attention to. A majority of long-term patients in most facilities will be Medicaid recipients; it's the nation's largest purchaser of nursing home services. At Greenwood, for instance, 30 to 35 percent are private-pay residents—higher than at most for-profits—and a few temporarily receive Medicare, but the majority rely on Medicaid.

Medicaid reimbursement amounts vary from one state to another, but as state governments try to hold down costs, those rates are substantially below what patients pay privately, and sometimes below what it actually costs to provide care. Nursing homes with very high Medicaid populations, therefore, often can't maintain the same quality care as those with more balanced populations.

When researchers looked at nursing homes where 85 percent or more of residents were Medicaid-supported—such "lower-tier" facilities represented between 13 and 15 percent of nursing homes in the 1990s—they saw significantly fewer registered nurses and other professional staff, significantly more deficiencies, more pressure ulcers, and greater use of restraints.

Because heavily Medicaid-dependent nursing homes tend to be located in the poorest urban and rural counties, and serve a disproportionately African-American population, the researchers pointedly entitled their article "Driven to Tiers." The United States, they argued, has permitted a stratified nursing home system, with one level of care for minorities and the poor and another for the comparatively wealthier.

Families steering clear of nursing homes where nearly everyone is a Medicaid recipient are doing nothing to address this inequality—but they are probably finding better care for their parents.

Even in higher-quality facilities, the professionals I've interviewed universally agree, continued involvement by family members can be crucial. Not only does the resident need ongoing contact with loved ones for emotional sustenance; she also needs them to tell her new caretakers things they ought to know, especially if she's unable to supply much reliable information herself.

"Very often they're the fonts of knowledge," Reinhard says of family caregivers. "If you don't respect them and work with them carefully, the patient can be harmed. There won't be enough information exchanged."

In fact, Reinhard goes on, family visitors provide a service to other residents as well, just by being watchful and on the scene. "It adds a level of oversight," she explains. "It's harder to have serious problems if there's a lot of people walking around."

Staff members appear to notice who has regular visitors. When pressed for time, as nursing home workers commonly are, "it's the residents whose family members come who get the most attention," says Janet Wells of NCCNHR, voicing a widely held conviction. "If family visit, the resident will be up and clean and dressed. If no one visits, they're more neglected." (Friends, volunteers, pastors, case managers, or geriatric care managers who drop in and spend time can also serve that purpose.)

Yet family involvement can also prove tricky. Families hope to form their own relationships with staffers who will recognize

them, share information about their relatives' conditions, listen to
and respond to their concerns. Perhaps even more than they value
their technical competence, relatives want staff members to treat
their loved ones as people, not tasks. Ideally, what should result
are harmonious interactions that further the mutual goal: caring
sensitively and skillfully for patients.

Sometimes, that happens. But a number of researchers have
documented the strains that can also arise. They've found problems like "role ambiguity," confusion about who's responsible for
which duties, or "an overly rigid division of labor" that prevents
family from participating in elders' care. They report families'
frustrations when the information they seek to provide—about
not only their relatives' medical histories but who they are, what
their lives have been like, their preferences—seem ignored.

Yet families fear that complaining will brand them as trouble-
makers, that relatives will pay a toll in substandard care, even puni-
tive behavior—illegal actions, but they can occur.

Suspicion and anger flow in both directions. Staff members
often see family expectations as unrealistic; they dislike feeling
mistrusted and monitored. Sometimes racial and ethnic differences play a role; elders who grew up with language and attitudes
now deemed unacceptable can say hurtful things, especially when
they're disinhibited by dementia.

In one survey of Florida nursing homes, administrators at 46
facilities reported that over a six-month period in the 1990s,
they'd recorded nearly 1,200 cases of verbal aggression by family
members insulting or berating staff members, cursing or yelling,
name-calling or threatening. Eight administrators said that family members had occasionally been physically aggressive, shoving,
punching, or slapping staff.

Yikes.

Gerontologists at Cornell have developed communications
workshops for staff and family members to help ease these strains.
Family members who participated saw staff members as more empathetic; staff regarded families more positively and were also less
likely to quit their jobs; conflicts abated. Whether such interven-

tions can improve the lot of patients themselves, however, remains an unanswered question.

At Greenwood House, Joel Gordon—very conscious of the difficult job he was entrusting to the staff—had few complaints. He was frustrated at his inability, despite repeated requests, to arrange a discussion with the facility's psychiatrist about whether the increased Risperdal dose prescribed to help Mrs. Gordon through the move should now be reduced. On the whole, though, he thought Mrs. Gordon was being well cared for, and he felt appreciative.

Sari was another story.

Mr. B.

Over Labor Day, I knew, Sari and her husband were taking their daughter Erica to college. So I waited until a few days later before calling to see how things were going.

Roy answered the phone. "Does it feel quiet there?" I asked, thinking about a couple with no children in residence for the first time in more than 20 years.

A pause. "Not exactly," he said. "Things have changed a little. Henry is back home."

Returning from Erica's campus, Sari had brought Mr. B. to the house, as she did periodically, for lunch. "And lunch," Roy said, "got really long."

In Rick Goldstein's 20-year tenure at Greenwood House, he could recall only three or four residents who had voluntarily left; now there was one more.

The next time I drove to Bucks County, on a sunny September day, Mr. B. and his aide Odette were sitting outside, playing the simple card game Uno.

"Your turn, Henry," she prompted. His cheeks looked more sunken than before, to my untrained eye.

"My turn? I just went," he said. And then, in another moment, "It's a little chilly." Odette offered to bring out a blanket, but he'd had enough.

"Okay, at least we got some fresh air, right?" She steered his wheelchair up the walk to take him into the house.

Sari had told me that lately, Mr. B. sometimes thought he was working in New York, or staying in a Catskills hotel. There were days when he recalled having lived at Greenwood House, days when he didn't.

He agreed to talk with me about it, but he didn't have a lot to say. "I liked the cleanliness," he said, his voice soft as always. "Nice bunch of people." On the other hand, "the food was not always right."

Did he feel lonely there?

There were long silences between his responses. "Not really."

And the people who worked there, did they help when he needed them?

"I don't remember any more."

Did he like living here better?

"Much better."

In a little while, Sari came sprinting in from an expedition to the mall. It had been fun, picking up odds and ends for care packages to send to her girls. She was trying to force herself to get out more.

At times while her father was away, she acknowledged, it had felt great to drive into Manhattan with her husband for a play, to help Erica settle into her dorm, to feel liberated from the constant responsibility. "I was getting used to having my life back." But that pleasure was outweighed by her worry about her father in a nursing home—most likely, she acknowledged, any nursing home.

He was like a new man the minute she brought him home for lunch, Sari insisted. He didn't remember having lived here before, yet he walked up the steps into the house with his walker, ate his meal with no help, seemed chattier. "He slept like a baby that first night," she said. "It was so gratifying to me; he looked so peaceful and comfortable." The next morning, when she asked if he'd prefer to stay here, he said he would. Sari called the nursing supervisor on duty and informed her, "He doesn't want to come back and I'm not forcing him."

Now that she was once again hiring aides—even more of them this time, to provide around-the-clock care—she was hoping to manage things differently. "I don't want to do hands-on anymore, the bathing, the changing, the toileting, the breathing treatment," she said. She would train and supervise instead.

Plus, she wanted to curtain off a front room for Mr. B. and his growing retinue, complete with furniture and TV, "so that can be his sitting room and we can reclaim part of the house."

She still felt tired. There were inevitably days when an aide couldn't make it—a car with a dead battery, a sick child, whatever—and Sari had to either scramble for a replacement or take over herself. She'd been very late meeting her husband at a restaurant last night, because Mr. B. was having trouble eating, and she had to show the aide what to do. "I need to get out, I do," she said. "But you get sucked into what's going on."

But if having Mr. B. at home again was hard for her, she had no doubt it was better for him. "I know he's okay. I know he's comfortable. He can have something special, like the aide soaks his foot in a little spa. If he's hungry, he comes in and eats. At night, I know that if he wakes up, someone's there with him. He has personal attention.

"I'm here to see to it, minute by minute, day to day."

Mrs. Gordon

Something was changing, Joel thought as winter came. Maybe it was because his mother was adjusting, or maybe it was because of continued cognitive decline. She seemed less anxious, "much more mellow." She could still fly into a rage, but if he timed his visits around meals—when she was up and alert and enjoying her food—they felt less tense.

One Saturday in January, they had a fairly long conversation about being old. Mrs. Gordon knew she was in her 90s, and when Joel supplied the actual number—96—she appeared proud. "That's pretty good, to live that long," she said, and reminisced a bit about other family members with great longevity. Joel was startled, and pleased.

He and Marlene had come to rely a great deal on Takesha Smith, the nurse who most often cared for Mrs. Gordon. "She's our conduit to what's going on, the one who can handle my mother best, the one that reports problems to us," Joel said. "She doesn't get upset when my mother's agitated. She gets my mother to laugh. And my mother responds and does things for her." It was a skill he'd never have, he'd accepted that long ago, but he was glad that someone did.

Sadly, Smith was not around on a Sunday afternoon in February—red and silver foil hearts decorated the lobby—when Joel arrived, toting a new pack of incontinence briefs. "Hi, Mom, how are you?" he said, finding her sitting in the atrium after the lunch trays had been cleared.

"I don't know whether I'm coming or going," was her fretful response. "What's today?"

"Today's Sunday."

"Sunday?"

"Yes."

"Sunday?"

"Yes. Did you just finish lunch?"

"I thought it was Friday."

So it was going to be one of those kinds of visits. Mrs. Gordon wasn't angry, so much as lost. "I'm all mixed up, I don't know whether I'm coming or going," she lamented.

"I know," Joel said, taking a seat at the table.

"I'm just sitting here doing nothing. I should be doing something. I have a lot of work to do, to keep the records up to date. I'm way behind."

"I understand, it's hard." What else was there to say? After a while, Joel went off in search of an aide to help his mother back to her room, then kissed the top of her head and said he'd see her Wednesday.

"An average day," he said to me, leaving the building.

Better, perhaps, to remember New Year's Eve. Like all holiday celebrations at Greenwood House, this one took place very early—about 5 p.m. Family members were invited for dinner and entertainment, and Joel and Marlene, their expectations modest, decided they'd go.

The staff had clearly put considerable effort into this event. They'd set the tables with white cloths, hung swags of twinkle lights across the dining room, and set out festive hats and noise-makers. The servers brought hors d'oeuvres—egg rolls, hot dogs in blankets, and little knishes—then bowls of matzoh ball soup. "The food was actually good, plain but good," Joel said. Moreover, "my mother was in a really mellow mood." She was beginning to have trouble manipulating utensils, so he and Marlene helped her eat.

Somewhere between the soup, the pot roast, and the petit fours, an instrumental combo swung into standards from the 1940s, big-band numbers played by a small band. A bunch of staffers—plus family members, and even a few residents—got up to jitterbug.

"My mother went into a sort of reverie," Joel said. "Dancing with my father was really important to them. They were great dancers; they loved being the center of attention."

He thought she might be remembering that, doing the samba or the cha-cha with Sam while the family watched and clapped. "We tried to get her to talk about it; she didn't much. But she had a beatific look on her face. She said she liked the music, it was nice. It was good to see her seemingly happy, even if it was a simple sort of happiness."

It was an image, a memory, to hold on to.

SOME QUESTIONS TO CONSIDER ABOUT NURSING HOMES:

Does your parent need help with almost all activities, including moving around his room and eating meals? Does he need two helpers in order to safely take a shower or use a toilet? A nursing home is the most likely facility to provide this much assistance.

Does he require hour-by-hour monitoring and nursing care, during the day and at night—more assistance than most families can afford to hire at home and more than most assisted living facilities offer?

Does he need physical or occupational therapy, or help from a social worker? Nursing homes generally have such specialized care available onsite; other facilities may not.

Has he exhausted his assets, or will he soon, so that he will be eligible for Medicaid? Skilled nursing facilities are the only long-term care option that Medicaid will pay for regardless of the state your parent lives in; coverage for other alternatives, like home care or assisted living, varies from state to state.

Can family members, trusted friends, or a geriatric care manager check on your parent regularly, sometimes at odd hours, to be sure he is receiving the care he needs? Can you locate a nursing home with a family council, so that family members can support one another and communicate with administrators as a group?

FIVE

A WEDDING AND TWO FUNERALS

Hospice Care

IT WAS ALWAYS FUN TO SEE WHAT MRS. NOTO, FOR WHOM CLOTHing and accessories were not casual decisions, might be wearing. The first time we met, she was padding around her little apartment, in a subsidized senior building outside Baltimore, in a silky red-patterned shirt, bright red pants and red socks, plus three ornate rings, a sparkly bracelet, and a long necklace of faux rubies.

"Red is my favorite color," she explained.

But pink was her second favorite, which made the ensemble she'd just bought—at the nearby Goodwill store, source of much of her wardrobe—for her daughter Debbie's wedding, all the more perfect.

"It's fuchsia," she announced, proudly lifting the vibrant dress and its matching jacket from the hall closet. There were pink pearls scattered across the satin fabric. "It needs dry cleaning, but I've got time."

Dolores Noto was delighted by Deb's engagement. Debbie was her only child—"a blessing, thank God for her"—and had been divorced for quite a while when a tall guy with a moustache joined her Friday night bowling team and was quickly smitten.

Two months ago, "they were in the bowling alley, and he got down on one knee and proposed in front of their whole league! And everyone cheered," her mother recounted, relishing the story.

She liked Doug Mueller, his teasing sense of humor, his eagerness to relieve her of chores like getting her car serviced. And she was enormously glad that Deb, who was 43, would have someone to love and care for her.

The family had been awhirl ever since, Deb juggling two jobs and her intensifying concern for her mother with the thousand details of a wedding she and Doug were largely arranging themselves to hold down costs. She and Doug (who also held two jobs) were always off buying materials for centerpieces at craft shops or auditioning deejays, or else she and her girlfriends were cruising bridal shops for dresses. Mrs. Noto, too, had a great deal to attend to: she needed shoes and faced the vexing question of just when to have her hair permed.

"I tell her about everything that's going on, every time I make a phone call to anyone about anything, the cake or a caterer," Deb Noto said to me. "She wanted to go to the florist with me, and I think she was sorry because we were there for *three hours*. She's included as much as she wants to be," which was a lot.

Yet Mrs. Noto, about to turn 79, was gravely ill. A few days earlier, at the weekly meeting where the Hospice of Baltimore staff reviewed the physical and emotional status of every patient, her nurse and social worker reported that Mrs. Noto seemed to be losing weight. The cancer invading her tongue made eating increasingly difficult. She was in fine spirits, but could she survive until an October wedding, still more than three months away? Possibly. She'd already been a hospice patient—which requires a physician to certify that a patient is likely to die within six months—since the previous September, an unusually long tenure. But possibly not. "We're all just hoping that she'll make it," said the social worker Laura Vermillion.

Laura and Pat Dykes, the RN, were due at Mrs. Noto's apartment this morning to check on her. Pat came weekly, Laura every other week, and the hospice chaplain called regularly and visited perhaps once a month. Hospice provided Mrs. Noto's drugs, including something called Magic Mouthwash that numbed her mouth and reduced pain. A hospice volunteer sometimes drove her to doctors' appointments; Mrs. Noto still piloted her massive old Buick around her neighborhood in Belair, but didn't want to brave the highways. As she needed more assistance, they could all come more frequently. Hospice could arrange to deliver equipment like a walker or a commode, and would add a home health aide to the team.

Like a lot of people, Mrs. Noto had vaguely heard of hospice and initially thought of it as a place, a facility. This made some sense: Hospice of Baltimore (now known as Gilchrist Hospice Care) does maintain a residence, a beautifully designed building for the minority of patients whose symptoms can't be managed at home. But hospice is really a program, an approach to the end of life that most often involves bringing professionals and services to patients in their own homes, which is where Americans overwhelmingly say they would prefer to die, but where fewer than a quarter do.

When Mrs. Noto first learned that she didn't have to leave her little flat with the rococo lamps and lace curtains and family photos, that instead hospice workers would come to her, she wept with relief. She'd lived here for eight years, since she was widowed. She liked the people, the beauty parlor down the hall, the pastor who came regularly and played the accordion for residents.

Laura, the hospice social worker, was the first to arrive this summer day; she breezed in looking tanned and curvy, a sharp contrast to her patient.

In her youth, Mrs. Noto's father had dubbed her Chub. Now the nickname no longer fit. She'd grown very thin, her chin jutting sharply and her cheeks gaunt, and quite pale. Because her mouth was a narrow slit—the tumors made it difficult for her to open it fully—her speech sometimes sounded a bit distorted. She rarely grumbled about anything, but she'd confided to Laura, at her last visit, that since she could no longer wear "my plates" (her dentures), she felt unattractive. "You're a beautiful lady, inside and out," Laura had told her.

Now they chatted companionably on the couch, Mrs. Noto sipping from the glass of Boost she always kept nearby, Laura asking about her latest excursion to find bridesmaids' gowns. "Oh my Lord." Mrs. Noto sighed, not really complaining. "What one liked, the other didn't. What they both liked, Deb didn't like. It was trying."

"You're a trouper," Laura said, laughing.

"Now the main thing is the cake."

Hospice of Baltimore visits appear quite casual; nobody's wearing a uniform or wielding a clipboard. Laura asked if Mrs. Noto had enough Boost, mentioning that some people added ice cream to the supplement to make a milkshake, and it sounded like a recipe tip more than a way to increase a cancer patient's caloric intake. When Pat Dykes knocked at the door—"It's open, hon," Mrs. Noto sang out. "Join the crowd!"—she carried her stethoscope and blood pressure cuff in a very nonmedical flowered tote. Questions about meds and bowels got slipped in between discussions of wrist corsages.

"Angels in disguise," Mrs. Noto said of her visitors, after they'd gone. "Angels in disguise. If I have a problem, I know who to call."

Still, it was clear to everyone that the day was approaching when she would weaken, and couldn't rely on these visits alone. The plan was to move in with Deb and Doug at that point, so Deb—in addition to everything else she was doing—was frantically trying to sell her small condo nearby and buy a house with room for her mother. When Mrs. Noto admitted to worries, which was not often, her fears were less about her own illness than the intense stress her daughter was coping with. "She's so good-hearted," she fretted.

But the fact was, nobody dwelled on such things, not when there were far more exciting prospects at hand. Mrs. Noto was planning to bake her special biscotti, Italian cookies shaped into twists and bow ties and iced in white, for the wedding. It sounded like a major undertaking, involving six pounds of flour and 20 eggs and plenty of sugar and lard ("No margarine, no butter. Lard!"), but she was undaunted. "Every one of them is rolled out by hand, but Deb and her girlfriends will pitch in," she said.

It was inconceivable that she wouldn't be there to supervise.

Mr. Hardaway

Mr. Hardaway felt the same way about home. His was a brick row house with a porch, purchased so long ago, in the years after the Second World War, that neither he nor his family could come up with the exact year. He had worked at Bethlehem Steel, saving diligently to become a homeowner, back when East Baltimore was a thriving blue-collar neighborhood.

Now some of the surrounding streets contained too many boarded-up houses; the kinds of industrial jobs easy to find when veteran Paul Hardaway came home from Europe had long since dried up. But this block was still lively and Paul and Alice Hardaway, both 91, were still here.

"I feel good, just my legs is weak," he said whenever someone asked how he was. Or, "Fine. I'm fine. Just my legs . . ." Then he'd launch into a story about growing up in rural Farmville, Virginia, or about his adventures in the Army, where he served in Germany with "my best friend, my rifle. Kept it with me all the time."

He never showed much interest in discussing his health. But the fact was, his kidneys were failing.

Most patients diagnosed with acute renal failure who don't undergo dialysis measure their remaining life expectancy in weeks, said Kim Stone, his hospice nurse. Since Mr. Hardaway had enrolled with hospice, however, he had already enjoyed—and that was the appropriate word—ten months in his row house with his wife and family.

Though it's not the purpose of hospice care to either shorten or prolong life, it does happen with some frequency that terminally ill patients confound their doctors' expectations. A 2007 comparison found that hospice patients had longer survival (by almost a month, on average) than nonhospice patients with the same conditions; the difference was significant among those with congestive heart failure (who lived 81 days longer) and several types of cancer, though not all. Perhaps that was because hospice patients received better monitoring and treatment, the researchers speculated, or because they avoided aggressive interventions, like surgery or chemotherapy, that in themselves entailed risks.

In the case of Mr. Hardaway, though, Kim thought she knew what was keeping him alive. In her view, it wasn't her twice-weekly visits, at which she checked his blood pressure and heart rate and urine, listened to his lungs, adjusted his medications. It wasn't the hospice aide who came five mornings a week to help him bathe, to tidy the room and keep an eye on things; with Alice Hardaway losing ground to Alzheimer's disease, nobody wanted this elderly couple to spend more than a couple of hours alone.

No, the reason he was still around to banter with her, Kim was convinced, was the unflagging effort by his children and grandchildren, who took seriously Mr. Hardaway's desire to stay at home and Mrs. Hardaway's likely inability to function as well anywhere else. Coordinating this mission was his daughter Patricia Marshall, known to the family as Gail. Committed as they are, hospice workers can't be omnipresent; Gail ensured that a family member was almost always on the scene.

"There've been times that he really hasn't looked good and his blood pressure plummets and you think, 'This is it,'" Kim recalled. "But they'll have someone there 24/7, and he gets better." He'd recovered from a recent urinary tract infection and, astonishingly, from a fall down the cellar stairs (in a moment of confusion, he'd gone looking for his keys) that caused only a few scrapes.

Gail was grateful for the backup from hospice, particularly from Kim, whom her father adored. "Kim's not just my nurse, she's my best friend," he liked to say. It amazed him that if he needed medicine or bandages, Kim would make a call and the items would be delivered—right to his door! But Kim maintained that "without this very caring family, their willingness to give up huge quantities of time, this man wouldn't have lived this long. And his wife would be in an institution."

At the moment, the schedule worked this way: Gail spent her weekends cooking dinners for her own family and her parents, enough to cover Sunday through Wednesday. She took covered dishes along to work—she taught second grade in suburban Baltimore County—and ferried dinner to her parents after school, sitting down with them to make sure her mother took at least a few bites of meat loaf or fried chicken. "My mom eats like a little bird," she said. When she left, she took their laundry with her. And whenever she could override her mother's protests, she cleaned their house.

On Thursdays, to give Gail a break, her older brother, Paul, a mail carrier, took the dinner shift. Fridays and Saturdays, Gail's grown sons brought take-out food.

About 7:30 or 8, after their own dinner, Gail or her husband or brother drove the 20 minutes back to East Baltimore to help Mr. Hardaway get ready for bed. He could no longer climb the stairs to the bedroom, so his helpers unfolded a sofa bed in the den, helped him undress and wash. The next morning, another grandson, Gail's nephew, arrived to help him get up and dressed and eat breakfast, and stayed until about 11. By late afternoon, Gail would be there again.

"My family takes good care of me," Mr. Hardaway said, which was the simple truth. "There's nothing I want."

He was faltering despite that. I found him settled on the recliner where he spent his days, a smiling, sociable man with taut brown skin and wisps of silvery hair. He'd been losing weight despite Gail's constant cooking, so his knit shirt hung on his frame. A catheter tube and bag were tucked discreetly beside the chair; there was no first-floor bathroom, and even if there had been, it wasn't clear he could walk to it.

"He's at about a ten-step maximum," Gail had explained. "He can get from his chair to the dining room table, and then he's about done." Thinking about her parents alone in the house at night troubled her own sleep.

But Mr. Hardaway was where he wanted to be, and he liked watching the news and *The Price Is Right* on television and chatting with the people, relatives and hospice workers alike, who came to care for him.

He told me about the rigors of farm life in rural Virginia where he grew up—his voice was faint, sometimes hard to hear, but his memories were vivid—and also about sleeping on the frozen ground during the war.

"I never was afraid," he declared.

"Why not?" asked Gail, listening attentively to a story she'd heard 500 times. "It seems so dangerous."

"It come natural to me. I lay down at night with my rifle beside me and I'd sleep just as sound . . ."

I mentioned that my father had also served with the Army in Germany in the 1940s. Mr. Hardaway wanted to know how old he was. Nearly 84, I said.

He smiled. "A young man."

Watching the Birds

However carefully families arrange matters, however vigilant they are, no amount of time or money or care can confer immortality. Eventually, seniors' health problems will multiply or intensify; their frailty will increase; the effective medical options will shrink. Though the timing and trajectory may be uncertain, they will face death, and because of the chronic diseases that increasingly claim them, many seniors will know they face death, if they care to know. People have more time than they once did to think about the ends of their lives.

When they do, they express definite preferences about what constitutes "a good death." They want physical comfort, with their pain relieved and their other symptoms controlled as well as possible. They want to feel prepared to die, to have a sense of completion about their lives and of connection with those they love. They want to be clear about the decisions they're making, to have good relationships with the health care professionals who help them reach those decisions and then carry them out. They don't want to prolong the dying process or burden their families.

Ours is not a culture that faces death forthrightly, so such ideas aren't always borne out by what the terminally ill and their families actually do. Patients say they want control over decisions about their care, for instance. But only a minority have prepared advance directives, legal documents that specify the kind of medical treatments and interventions patients want, or don't want, though they're readily available from lawyers, in hospitals and doctors' offices, on Websites.

Even among the severely or terminally ill, fewer than half have advance directives in their medical files. It's not unusual, either, for patients to say they want all available treatments, regardless of the odds of recovery—and also to say that they don't want to be attached to machines that keep them alive.

We know, too, that while the vast majority of people tell researchers that they'd like to die in familiar surroundings at home, about half still die in hospitals (and another quarter in nursing homes).

But if our ideas about a good death sometimes reveal considerable ambivalence—there's a gauzy ideal of a painless yet lucid farewell from one's own bed, with family members clustered around, that somehow occurs without anyone's having had to discuss it much—it's easier to say what constitutes a bad one.

A bad death is marked by pain and fear. If an elderly person feels anxious and alone, attended by bustling strangers with little time to explain or reassure—that's a bad death. If he's subjected to hospital stays and medical procedures that are probably futile and cause trauma and discomfort, because nobody has clarified their purpose or determined whether he really wants them—a bad death.

If there's no one to guide him and his family through this singular experience, to help them find meaning and consolation in his life and its completion, to encourage the conversations that might allow a more peaceful passage, that's an unnecessarily bad death.

"It's still a challenge to get the correct information about the true nature of the illness and to get the patient on the path to good end-of-life care," says Don Schumacher, a hospice administrator for 25 years who now leads the National Hospice and Palliative Care Organization.

"The conversation is still a difficult one to have; many health care providers struggle with how to give that news. And it probably always will be—we're a youth-oriented society, and death is still something people resist."

As a result, a high proportion of the terminally ill do suffer bad deaths. Many experience moderate to severe pain in the final weeks of life, studies persistently show. In hospitals, they and their families complain that they don't get sufficient information, that nurses are too busy to talk to them, that patients have difficulty coping, physically and emotionally. In nursing homes, understaffing frequently means that nurses and aides can barely attend to such basic needs as bathing and feeding, let alone engage in discussions about the meaning of life and death.

Staffers untrained in recognizing the trajectories of terminal illnesses may subject patients to unnecessary tests and procedures and fail to provide adequate pain medication. Families report that they weren't well informed and didn't know what to expect as death approached. Anxiety, depression, and exhaustion seem as integral to the process as sorrow.

Dying doesn't have to happen that way. I know because a decade ago, when my mother's uterine cancer was diagnosed and the specialists told us about the available treatments—unlikely to significantly prolong the life of an 80-year-old, they acknowledged after considerable questioning, and likely to make her final months even more difficult and debilitating—I remembered having read about something called hospice. Hospices were listed in the yellow pages, it turned out.

My parents and I were sitting tensely at the dining room table in their apartment in Vineland, New Jersey, when a nurse from what's now called South Jersey Healthcare Hospice Care first came to talk with us, and to listen to us.

Jane wanted to know not only my mother's medical condition but her interests (bird watching and doing crossword puzzles, my mother said, and watching the ocean as she walked along the boardwalk) and her personality and her fears. My mother never liked to talk about death, before that visit or afterward. But she told Jane that while she wasn't afraid of dying, she was anxious about pain, and she much preferred to avoid hospitals.

Jane assured her that hospice had an excellent record of relieving pain. She also explained the services the team—hospice care does involve a team—could provide: A nurse would begin weekly visits, even though my mother didn't think she really needed one; the idea was that she should get to know the people who would be taking care of her before emergencies struck or symptoms worsened.

A home health aide would come as well, every weekday if

needed, to change the bed linens, help my mother bathe or dress, do some light housekeeping or a load of laundry, and be with her if my dad—who now became known as "the primary caregiver"— needed to dash to the supermarket or the bank. Volunteers were available if he needed a longer break, or she needed a ride to a doctor's office or the beauty parlor.

The team included a chaplain ready to talk with them about spiritual concerns, and a social worker who could help sort out financial issues or family conflicts, and coordinate with other senior services. My mother could still use her own doctors, if she chose, but hospice would deliver all her drugs, along with equipment like a raised toilet seat or a wheelchair. After her death, counselors and support groups would be available to help the bereaved.

And Medicare would pay for all of it.

As she was leaving, signed authorizations in hand, Jane also urged my parents to enjoy these summer days. Let the dirty dishes sit in the sink sometimes, she suggested, having apparently read this couple quite well in just an hour. Spend time watching the birds. Maybe you can take a walk on the boardwalk.

I remember feeling immense relief. Mom could stay at home. She would not have to suffer weeks or months of terrible cancer pain. Dad and my sister and I had someone to call day or night, whenever we had questions or problems or a crisis. We had a different kind of specialist now, specialists in the end of life. We were about to take on the saddest of responsibilities, but we didn't have to handle it alone.

Courageous Conversations

"Hospice excels at courageous conversations," Reggie Bodnar told me. "No one ever likes to talk about death or deliver 'unwanted news' about a patient's condition. But we need to do that, to educate and inform patients and families. And we need to do it with our hearts in the right place."

Hospice care, introduced to this country from Britain in 1974, has grown and changed dramatically in the time since my family used it. In the mid '90s, the National Hospice and Palliative Care Organization counted about 2,500 hospices; now there are more than 4,700. Once a grassroots movement, largely volunteer, with a somewhat antiestablishment attitude, it's taken a capitalist turn: Almost half of hospices are now for-profit businesses, with chains like Vitas (a subsidiary of the corporation formerly called Roto-Rooter), Vistacare, and Odyssey operating dozens of hospices in many states. The population that hospice serves has shifted, too. Early on, the majority of patients had cancer; now, most don't.

Some hospices offer some sort of residence—like this airy stone-and-glass building called the Gilchrist Center, where Bodnar has her office. Named for the philanthropist who founded Hospice of Baltimore, the largest hospice in Maryland, it's filled with plants and art and an aviary, and surrounded by gardens. Up to 24 patients who don't want to die in their homes, or who can no longer be properly cared for there, can end their lives here, instead.

A longtime Baltimorean (hence the small gold earrings shaped like crabs) and a veteran oncology nurse, Regina Bodnar now served as executive director of Hospice of Baltimore, subsequently Gilchrist Hospice Care. But she'd begun as its very first nurse back in 1993, so she knew what it was like when a hospice team made its initial visit—usually within a day of a family's call.

"We get into the home, the patient's in physical distress, the household is chaotic, the family is exhausted. It's *so* hard. . . . They've been adapting, they've been managing, but no one's been orchestrating this care for them. They need that professional touch . . .

"Sometimes, just having the presence of a hospice team member in the home is soothing," she went on. "There are some very modest measures that can help the patient be more comfortable. Sometimes it's just tweaking a medication. When that patient is no longer in pain, no longer struggling to breathe, when the family can get a good night's sleep, let me tell you, the anxiety in that house comes way down."

This philosophy reflects what's come to be called palliative care—aimed not at curing, but at comforting. Hospice patients aren't expected to recover their health; their doctors (or a hospice doctor if they don't have their own physicians) have certified that their illnesses, if untreated, will probably cause their deaths within six months. In reality, most have waited so long to enroll in a hospice program that they don't live nearly that long.

But they can feel better, have their pain controlled and their other symptoms relieved, in many cases find peace, even pleasure, in their remaining days and weeks. This takes some time; Bodnar thinks enrolling in hospice three to six months before patients enter the phase called "actively dying" is the ideal.

Maybe the chaplain will help someone plan her own memorial service. Maybe the social worker will encourage the mending of strained family relationships or help someone say the things she wants to say. Maybe arranging a few days of free "respite care" in a nearby nursing home will allow the patient's caretakers to attend a child's college graduation or take a short, restorative vacation. Maybe the patient can help pick out bridesmaids' dresses, or even live long enough to dance at her daughter's wedding.

The research shows that most of the time, hospice can deliver on its claims. Hospice patients *are* likely to die at home, for example: three-quarters are either in their private residences or in the places they've come to call home (including assisted living apartments or nursing homes). Remaining at home makes it easier to avoid invasive treatments and maintain their daily routines, their familiar caregivers, some sense of control.

The hospice record on pain control is also reassuring. In 2005, the National Hospice and Palliative Care Organization's national survey of patients showed that on average, more than 84 percent of patients reported their pain reaching "a comfortable level" within 48 hours of admission. (Hospice of Baltimore uses a 72-hour benchmark: 89 percent of patients say their pain was resolved by then, Bodnar told me, a statistic with which she was "pleased but not satisfied.")

Compared to those receiving conventional medical care, hospice patients have better pain management and are more involved with decisions about their conditions. They rate the attention given their emotional needs more highly; they're more satisfied with their care.

Families respond with relief and gratitude. In questionnaires administered after patients' deaths in 2006, more than 140,000 family members gave hospice high marks: On a 1 to 10 scale measuring how well the patient's symptoms were "controlled to an acceptable degree," 87 percent gave hospice 9s and 10s. More than 90 percent said that the patient had received "the right amount" of pain medication, and that the family had received "the right amount" of support from their hospice teams before and after their loved ones' deaths.

The organization's researchers noted room for improvement. There was less unanimity among families, for instance, about whether they'd had sufficient communication about the patient's condition (84.5 percent said they had). Only 55 percent said they were "very confident" they knew what to do at the time of death.

About 10 percent were critical of hospice's response to evening and weekend problems. Eleven percent said the family should have been referred to hospice care earlier—a continuing complaint, and backhanded compliment, over the years.

Moreover, if your parent is one of the patients still suffering pain after 48 or 72 hours—a minority, certainly, but not a negligible one—none of the other statistics may provide much comfort.

Still, how many enterprises can cite consumer satisfaction findings like this one? Asked if they'd recommend hospice care to others, 98.5 percent said yes.

Nursing homes, where hospice services have expanded rapidly in recent years, don't fit our idealized notion of a good death. That's not where anybody really wants his or her life to end. Bringing in hospice staffers, with their different mission, has in some cases caused conflicts with nursing home staffs. Skeptics wonder if understaffed nursing homes are using hospice care primarily to provide more nurses and aides, without much attention to its philosophy.

Yet even in institutions, most studies show consistent benefits. Hospice patients in nursing homes undergo fewer hospitalizations, which are often unnecessary and can cause disorientation, mood changes, and other problems sometimes called "transfer trauma." (In fact, in nursing homes with hospice programs, even dying residents who *aren't* hospice patients have fewer hospitalizations.) They undergo fewer invasive treatments, have fewer physical restraints and better pain management; their families report higher quality of care.

"It's not like being in your own living room or your daughter's, where someone's there constantly and their sole goal is to provide what the patient wants and needs," Bodnar acknowledges. But as her squadron of hospice staffers visit nursing homes daily and share what they know, she has found, "it can be done very successfully."

Courageous conversations can take place in any setting, though it's striking how rarely they do. The mere fact that a family has called a local hospice, in itself an act of recognition, seems to allow for questions, and answers, that other health care providers approach only with reluctance. "True or not, the families and patients say, 'The doctor hasn't told us anything,'" Bodnar says. "'He just said you'd be coming and you'd explain.'"

So they do explain—everything from how to use an oxygen tank to why you should keep talking to a semiconscious patient (because hearing is the last sense to fade). Who else will tell you about what is delicately called "mode of exit," by which hospice nurses mean the way someone is actually likely to die? To explain that with liver failure, your father will probably enter a hepatic coma, becoming less and less alert and sleeping more until one day, you won't be able to rouse him and you'll know that he will shortly slip away? Wouldn't that be a helpful thing to know?

In my mother's case, before she could suffer any serious cancer symptoms aside from fatigue, she had a massive stroke and largely lost consciousness. Well-meaning friends urged us to take her to the hospital, where intravenous feeding or a ventilator possibly could have kept her alive a while longer.

But prolonging her life so that she could die of cancer a few months later seemed pointless, inhumane. The nurses and aides who'd been helping for almost three months showed us how to turn her gently with a draw sheet to prevent bedsores, how to crush pills with a spoon so that we could control her seizures, how to moisten her dry mouth with a sponge.

We cared for her at home for two or three more weeks, during which she couldn't eat or drink. We exulted in the brief moment of lucidity when she spoke with us and saw that we were all there. Then came the afternoon the hospice nurse sat us down, a stethoscope still around her neck. My mother's heart had begun racing. "This is incompatible with life," she said. "Do you understand what I'm telling you?" We did.

One image from my mother's months of hospice care that's lodged in my mind: a small, plump doughnut of yellow satin. She lay on this little pillow, she explained, to keep a painful pressure sore from developing on her ear; her aide, Terry, had sewn it for my mother as her energy declined and she spent more time in bed. I would never have anticipated the problem or thought of the solution, but then, I wasn't the expert. I was glad we had someone who was.

"We always say, we want the daughter to be the daughter," was Reggie Bodnar's refrain. "We want the wife to be the wife. Let *us* be the nurses."

Mrs. Noto

Mrs. Noto dressed with particular care on July 31: sunny yellow pants, a pizzazzy red floral shirt with ruffles, an even greater than usual array of rings and bracelets. It was a big night: Debbie and Doug were on their way over to take her out to a birthday dinner at a riverfront restaurant up in Port Deposit.

"Hi, Mom!" Deb called from the doorway, toting two pink gift boxes with big bows. She was an ample woman, young looking, with a fluff of brown hair and a bright smile. "Happy birthday, a few hours early."

"Oh, Debbie, that's *so* pretty, hon."

Mrs. Noto thought she'd save the presents until tomorrow, the actual day she'd turn 79, but Deb wasn't having it. So she agreed to open the top box, Doug snapping photos as she peeled off the wrapping.

"Debbie! Oh, hon, it's beautiful." Reverently, she lifted out a rose-colored evening purse, every square inch covered with sequins and crystals.

"Got it yesterday," Deb said with pride. "I saw it and said, 'That's Mom.' It'll work with that dress; I held it up." Nobody had to specify which dress.

Her hospice social worker Laura theorized that Mrs. Noto's fairly stable condition, the fact that she'd not only survived this long but remained quite active, had everything to do with that upcoming event. "I think that's what's keeping her going," she said. "She wants so much to be at that wedding. I'm keeping my fingers crossed."

"Isn't that beautiful?" Mrs. Noto tucked the glittery bag back into its box. "I'll pass it down to you one of these days."

And off they went. She was looking forward to a scenic drive, to seeing sailboats on the Susquehanna, to ordering dinner. A seafood lover from way back, she could no longer chew anything crunchy. But crab cakes, that staple of Baltimore cuisine, were mushy enough to enjoy.

Mrs. Noto might not have been as willing to accept hospice care, had this not been her second bout with cancer. Or the third, if you counted her husband's lung cancer. "He was a great guy," she often said.

They spent most of their lives in the red brick neighborhoods of Baltimore. Mrs. Noto had abandoned school in ninth grade to help support her family. Some of the jobs she held no longer existed: she was a drugstore soda jerk, then a waitress and hat check girl at the Lord Baltimore Hotel, then an office switchboard operator. She was out with friends at a neighborhood tavern in southwest Baltimore, enjoying a few drinks and cigarettes (and she still smoked, a fact she tried to hide from her daughter, who knew but figured there was little point in nagging about it), when a Navy veteran asked her to dance. He was a smoothie on the dance floor, knew how to jitterbug and tango, and he asked her out. Though she'd never dated an Italian before, she said yes. They married in 1951.

Frank Noto spent a dozen years as a Baltimore cop, then took over his uncle's busy barbershop. Debbie was born in 1963. "God, he was so happy." Mrs. Noto beamed, remembering. "He wanted a girl. He said if it was a boy, he was going to send him back."

The Notos had 46 good years together. Then Frank's health began to fail, and it was while she was sitting in hospital rooms with him that Mrs. Noto felt some pain in her jaw. But her own aches seemed unimportant compared to his long, ultimately fatal illness. By the time Mrs. Noto's doctor performed exploratory surgery and found she'd developed extensive oropharyngeal cancer, "the picture looked pretty bleak," Deb told me. "I thought I'd be taking care of her funeral within a year of my father's."

Mrs. Noto still shuddered when she spoke about that miserable period. Chemotherapy made her so sick that she couldn't continue, and radiation was less nauseating but very debilitating. "It was just awful," said Deb, who for months was feeding her mother pureed foods through a feeding tube in her stomach. "She doesn't remember much of that summer, and that's God's blessing." But the radiation did shrink her tumors. "The doctors hoped they could buy her a few months—and nine years later, she's still here."

Mrs. Noto remembered enough, however, to have developed definite opinions about cancer treatment. A year ago, she thought she'd cut her tongue while eating her way through—what else?—a pile of steamed crabs. After some weeks of soreness, she submitted to a series of tests and biopsies that showed tumors on the back of her tongue. She didn't want chemotherapy again; she wasn't a candidate for further radiation; and she surely didn't want a major portion of her tongue removed, the only surgical option. The doctors determined that the best alternative, therefore, was to call hospice.

"I'm not saying I expect you to die within six months," her oncologist told her, though perhaps he did. "I'm not saying that.

But it's good to have those things in place and have people get to know you."

"It was all Greek to me," Mrs. Noto remembered. She didn't know what to expect; at first, she thought she'd have to pack up and move into the Gilchrist Center. But Deb, an office manager for a medical practice, was familiar with hospice and helped explain how things would work.

"I felt like I would be needing more help as time went by," Mrs. Noto figured. "My daughter's got to work for a living; she can't take care of me. And Deb was saying, 'Mom, it wouldn't hurt you to have some help.'" So, after a meeting with Laura Vermillion, she signed on. "And they've been wonderful to me, everybody. I look forward to seeing them."

The truth was, she still wasn't availing herself of that much help. She hadn't permitted any home aides, for instance. Even though she'd been a patient for ten months at this point, far longer than most patients spent in hospice care, she could still prepare simple meals, do a little housecleaning, handle her personal care, and make an occasional trip to Goodwill (she still needed wedding shoes).

When a lightbulb blew out in the bathroom, she climbed onto a step stool—her daughter trembled to think of it—rather than ask someone else to change it. Uncomplaining, proud of being able to manage her life, she didn't like to "take advantage."

It was clear, nonetheless, that this level of independence would end before long. "It's going to have to be done, sooner or later," she said of the plan to move in with Deb. "I won't be able to do for myself."

Which was why, despite their long workweeks and a raft of wedding chores still to face, Deb Noto and Doug Mueller were clearing out of their condo on a muggy Sunday afternoon. Maybe buyers would flock to the open house their real estate agent had set up. Meanwhile, they'd cruise around Harford County looking for a house, one with a ground floor bedroom and bath for her mother.

"This is how we spend our time," Deb groaned as they climbed into Doug's van. She had her eye on a well-maintained brick ranch nearby; we drove over to see it. "It's got a beautiful backyard with a stone patio," she said wistfully, as we idled in front of it. She hoped her condo would sell before someone else grabbed this place.

In case someone did, though, they'd printed out several other listings. "Nice piece of property," Doug said as they drew up to a colonial set on a half-acre. "It's got dogwoods all around."

"I love dogwoods," his intended said.

When she first learned that her mother faced cancer once more, Deb had talked to her about moving in together, an offer that met with little enthusiasm. "She wasn't ready," Deb decided. More recently, though, she'd shown Mrs. Noto that brick ranch and raised the issue again. "She said, 'Well, I wouldn't want to inconvenience anyone or put you out.' She won't ask. But I definitely got the feeling she was ready now . . . Maybe she feels worse some days than she lets us know."

It would be lovely to share a house, Deb thought. She and her mother had been close, always, and had cherished these recent years of weekend trips to New York, Niagara Falls, and, often, to Ocean City on the Maryland shore. But with work and wedding tasks, Deb didn't get to spend as much time with her mother as she would've liked, couldn't be as helpful with simple things like laundry as she wanted to be.

So she was particularly grateful that Pat and Laura were visiting Mrs. Noto, keeping tabs on her, letting Deb know if anything needed her attention, helping them feel as ready as they could for whatever came next. "It's such a comfort to me," Deb said. "If something is going on and Mom doesn't tell me herself, they will. It's a nice way to keep me in the loop without my constantly breathing down her neck."

She and Doug took note of a few real estate possibilities, then drove past a county-owned manor house to show me where—on what they hoped would be a sparkling October day—they would be married outdoors under an ivy-draped archway. Then they went home to make centerpieces and to learn that absolutely nobody had come by for their open house.

Over the next several weeks, matters grew more tense. Another buyer took the ranch house Deb yearned for. She and Doug made an offer for a different house, but it was contingent on selling the condo—in a housing market that was rapidly deflating. What would happen when it was time for Mrs. Noto to move in?

On top of which, the state of Maryland suddenly informed Mrs. Noto that she was no longer eligible for Medicaid: her reward for living so frugally, saving some of her paltry Social Security check each month, was that she'd accumulated slightly too much money, including a tiny insurance policy meant to pay for her funeral. "It's been *insane*," Deb wailed as the sheer number of things she was trying to handle kept growing. Laura, the social worker, was scrambling to try to find her another insurance program; meanwhile, she gave Deb the names of several eldercare attorneys who might be helpful.

So perhaps it shouldn't have come as a total shock—but it did—that one morning in late August Deb woke up with "all these strange symptoms. I told Doug, 'You'll think this is crazy, but my face hurts. And my *hair* hurts.' And I was really really sensitive to light . . ."

She had shingles, a potentially serious viral infection related to chicken pox; its outbreaks are associated with stress. Blisters, "ugly crusty things," broke out on her face and crept frighteningly close to her eye, causing such pain that heavy-duty drugs barely touched it. "The last thing in the world we needed right now," was the bride's understatement. Antiviral drugs and an emergency visit to an ophthalmologist helped quell the infection quickly.

But the episode served as a caution that caregivers are at increased risk of becoming ill themselves. Counselors and support groups sometimes invoke that airline warning—put your own oxygen mask in place before you attempt to help others.

Life would be easier, and more enjoyable, once they had a house. "It'd be so much fun to have Mom living with us now," Deb said, and Doug agreed. "She'd get such a kick out of everything."

Mrs. Noto was meanwhile showing some signs of decline. For

the first time, visiting on a midmorning, I found her wearing a housecoat and socks; she hadn't yet dressed, combed her hair, or put on her jewelry. And was I imagining that her speech sounded a bit less distinct? Pat Dykes said she'd noticed "subtle changes" as well. "She looks thinner to me. She can't eat much. She's a lot slower when she moves."

And yet, Pat added, she was betting that Mrs. Noto would be front and center, in her fuchsia dress, at the wedding on October 14. She might deteriorate more swiftly thereafter, but "she's going to hang in there for her daughter as long as she can. We all had our doubts for a while. Now, we think she's going to make it."

❦

I drove down in September, three weeks before the big day, to find Deb and Doug, her bridesmaid Sheila, and Mrs. Noto all clustered around Deb's kitchen, making chocolates for wedding favors. They formed a small assembly line: Sheila melted chocolate discs in the microwave, then poured the liquid chocolate into molds. Deb unmolded the candy, squares that now bore messages like To Love, To Honor.

Mrs. Noto, back in high fashion gear in a forest green ensemble with maroon velvet slippers, was fitting sheets of color-coordinated tissue paper into white boxes, on which Doug had painstakingly stenciled a golden M for Mueller. Once the boxes were filled with chocolates, Doug tied the boxes with ribbons and charms—while simultaneously watching the NASCAR races, his other great love.

Mrs. Noto was indeed getting a kick out of things. She'd had a lovely time at Deb's shower brunch the previous weekend, though it tired her, and was chatting happily about how yummy the French toast casserole was. Next week, the assembly line would tackle the biscotti.

"You're doing great, Mom," Deb said fondly, watching. "You're a big help."

"You're welcome, darling."

It had puzzled me, as the months passed, to see Deb Noto submerge herself in these sorts of wedding preparations. She had two jobs; she was getting married; she was hip-deep in real estate matters and her mother, sometimes imperceptibly, was dying of cancer. Did she really need to spend time filling gold organza bags with heart-shaped rice for her guests to throw?

Naturally she wanted her mother at her wedding, but I wondered why she and Doug hadn't opted for a quiet ceremony with their pastor or a justice of the peace. She was a down-to-earth woman, not some narcissistic bridezilla. Why was she making things so hard for herself?

After a while, though, I'd come to understand that these elaborate preparations were, in part, a gift she was giving her mother. She wanted Mrs. Noto to have happy activities to feel part of, to have many excursions and celebrations jotted on her weekly calendar. She wanted her to have something to look forward to.

It would have been simpler, Deb acknowledged, to have planned a spring wedding. Sell condo, buy house, move Mom in, contemplate centerpieces and favors later—that would have been the sensible course. But "later" was too risky.

"Things are going to take a turn one day," Deb said. In the meantime, "I want her to have some laughter in her life."

Mr. Hardaway

"Always glad to see you," Mr. Hardaway half-whispered to Kim Stone, making one of her twice-weekly nursing visits.

"Always glad to see *you*," Kim said, putting a strong hand on his weak one. "I told you, you're my favorite."

"Well, you're *my* favorite." This was so universally recognized that the family had taken to invoking Kim as a means of getting Mr. Hardaway to comply with one directive or another. He wasn't taking in enough fluids on these hot summer days? "Kim says she wants you to drink more water!" his daughter Gail would say. And then he would.

This morning, Kim checked her patient's vital signs, asked

whether the new egg-crate mattress pad she'd ordered had made his mornings less achy, then decided to change a leaky catheter. Joey, the grandson who got up at 6:30 every morning in order to be here by 8 to help with dressing and breakfast, gave her a hand. Meanwhile, Mrs. Hardaway fluttered through the house, a tiny, energetic woman saying things that were sometimes perfectly fitting and other times betrayed profound confusion.

"Take some nice deep breaths," Kim instructed her patient. "Almost done."

"It's all right," said Mr. Hardaway, who tended toward the stoic.

When he and Gail first sat down with a hospice social worker, he'd dutifully responded to all her questions about what treatments he'd want as his condition deteriorated. He'd said no to a ventilator. No to a feeding tube. No to cardiopulmonary resuscitation. He was clear about what was happening and what he was signing.

Since then, though, the word "hospice" had hardly come up. His family merely referred to Kim as his "special nurse"; she, in turn, rarely talked about dying unless a patient broached it. "Every visit, I ask, is there anything we need to talk about? Anything on your mind?" Mr. Hardaway's answer, always, was no.

At times, though, his awareness of his situation seemed to surface. There was, for instance, a day when he looked at his daughter—always so upbeat, with wide eyes and unlined skin that usually made her look much younger than her 53 years—and registered the weariness in her face. "I'm not in a hurry to leave you, but I think I'm working you all hard," he said.

Gail tried humor. "You're not working us, you're keeping us from being bored."

"No. Working you hard."

Seeing that he was serious, she told him what she actually thought: He was holding his family together, and they were grateful.

"Honey, when I close my eyes, you all been good to me."

Once in a while, Mr. Hardaway announced that when God called him, he was ready to go. He didn't want to rush things, he added, but he was ready.

The problem was that for a long time, Gail wasn't sure *she* was ready. That her father had survived all these months, requiring his doctor to recertify him for hospice care several times, was to her mind a great kindness. "God recognized that a sudden departure, I probably couldn't have dealt with," she explained. "He said, 'These folks don't have it together; I'd better give them a little more time, so they can get organized'"—which meant not only preparing to accept her father's death but girding for the task, possibly even more difficult, of caring for her mother afterward.

Gail was no Pollyanna. At times she'd felt angry and afraid, left her parents' house in tears. She'd come through these months buttressed by a strong Baptist faith, but also by a sardonic sense of humor.

She could joke about the appeal of a senior retirement village— for herself and her husband. An attractive new apartment? Someone to clean it and cook all your meals and do the laundry while you played miniature golf? Swell, where could she sign up?

When tensions rose or exhaustion threatened, her preferred therapy was to head to a nail salon at the Eastpoint Mall. "It's either that or go to an analyst," she said. She didn't want to face a single decision there; even selecting a color was too much responsibility. Gail just thrust out her fingertips and told her manicurist, "Make my nails pretty. You can't fix whatever else is going on in my life, but you can fix that." Then she leaned back and closed her eyes.

She admitted to feeling depressed when her father first entered hospice care, and to suffering what's sometimes called "anticipatory grief" as her mother's dementia deepened and the woman she knew, though physically still healthy, began to recede.

Yet demanding as these past months had been, "it's not all negative," Gail said. "Initially, because you're so overwhelmed, you don't see that, but now I do. Now I'm sort of grateful for it. Not grateful that my parents aren't in tip-top health, but grateful to have the time to do for them."

It had been, she told me, a period of "incredible growing." She felt her family strengthening as so many people, including her stepsister Bertha, shared the task of caring for their patriarch. She felt proud of her three sons, the youngest 21 and the eldest 26, for cheerfully taking on such adult responsibilities.

The year before, when her husband, Willie, had undergone surgery for prostate cancer, Gail's fellow teachers at the McCormick Elementary School had responded by collectively preparing two weeks' worth of meals for the Marshalls *and* Gail's parents. Stunned by their generosity, "I started crying and I couldn't stop," she recalled. Now, she thought she appreciated better what friendship meant.

As for her and Willie, who'd recovered well, caregiving "has matured us. Not that we're babies, but it's given us depth. We had a good marriage, but it's become stronger." Any simple getaway, dinner *à deux* at Burger King, had become "a special event."

She credited Kim and the other hospice staffers with making this phase less crushing than she'd feared. "I don't feel like I'm dangling out there alone," she said. "I can call and say, 'He's slower today, Kim. And his voice sounds different.' And she'll either explain it to me or she'll make an additional visit to find out what the problem is. Just knowing that someone is as close as that call . . ." With that help, Mr. Hardaway was "totally peaceful," she added, "and I'm eternally grateful for it."

≫⌐

Perhaps Paula Dukehart, Hospice of Baltimore's nondenominational chaplain, had something to do with that peace. The Hardaways hadn't been to church for a long while, hadn't even left their home in months, but the chaplain made house calls. Not every family wanted or accepted Dukehart's services, but the Hardaways welcomed them. Mrs. Hardaway called her the Prayin' Woman.

I happened to be there during one of her visits. Mr. Hardaway was telling stories about a past in which he must have been a strapping, powerful man. One of five children, he plowed his family's acres back in Farmville, planted and harvested tobacco, tended the pigs and chickens and avoided the snakes ("I was deathly afraid"), took a liking to a neighbor girl with "long plats" (braids) who became his wife. Until recently, when travel became too difficult, he returned annually to Virginia to see the homestead and visit surviving family members.

But he didn't romanticize the past. Life in Baltimore, even with 30 grueling years of cutting steel, was easier, provided more opportunities for the family. Neither of the senior Hardaways had much schooling beyond the seventh grade, but their children and grandchildren had gone to college; Gail had a master's degree in education. Mr. Hardaway was proud of that, and of this house he'd saved so long to buy. He'd painted every room himself.

"You must have been a hard worker, to provide for your family," the chaplain said, sitting on the couch next to his recliner. By now, even I had heard many of these tales of rural life, Army rigors, steel plants.

"I worked night and day, sick and well, for 30 years," he agreed, repeating a bit of favorite family lore: in all those years, he'd missed just two days' work. Then, prompted by further questions from the Prayin' Woman, he talked about his grandchildren and how he'd helped care for them after he retired, taking them to school, staying with them when they were sick. He was in the audience whenever Gail's oldest son, David, a talented gospel singer, gave a recital, and David always closed with "Because He Lives," his grandfather's favorite hymn.

"Now things have been turned around. Now they're the ones helping you," Dukehart observed. "That's what families do."

Mr. Hardaway nodded. "They all take care of me. Every one."

Psychologists and social workers would recognize this exchange; it's called "life review" and it's meant to explore "the things this person, by his own description, has found meaningful," Dukehart explained later. "The things people take pride in, their accomplishments, the legacy they have created. What gives them a sense that life is valuable and that they have a purpose, even at this point in their lives?" Sometimes, as they talked, Mr. Hardaway wept a little, and she couldn't ascertain exactly why. But her understanding wasn't as important, she concluded, as his feeling listened to.

After a while, seeing him tire a bit, the chaplain asked if the family would like to pray. She kneeled, mostly so that Mr. Hardaway could hear her. Gail kneeled, too, and her mother stood. They clasped one another's hands and bowed their heads.

"We come before you today, dear God, creator of us all. Jesus our lord and savior. And Holy Spirit and comforter," Dukehart began. She always tried to tailor her prayers, weaving in whatever had arisen in her conversation with the patient. "We come before you with hearts full, overflowing with thanks and praise. We thank you for the gift of this day. We thank you for this precious gift of life, of love, of family and friends.

"We thank you for the gift of faith that helps us to bear confidently the burdens, and to rejoice in the blessings, because we know that you are the guide that abides with us. . . .

"And we come to you today thanking you for the wonderful gift of memory. Memory that helps us to look back, to be amazed, to be filled with wonder and with blessed relief when we see how you have come with us and are still with us.

"For all these blessings, we do thank you and we come seeking your continued care. We pray today for Mr. and Mrs. Hardaway, for all their children and grandchildren—you know them each by name. Bless them, surround them with your love. And help us, each of us who enter this home, to do so only in ways that bring comfort and joy and peace. Let us be your instruments. We pray in Jesus' name. Amen."

"Amen," echoed Mrs. Hardaway, her restlessness stilled for a bit. "Beautiful. Beautiful."

Mr. Hardaway wiped away a few tears. "Thank you," he said.

"So Much More to Do."

Scenes like that make you wonder: If hospices, though they will have inevitable lapses and imperfections, can provide the kind of help that leads virtually every family in a large national survey to recommend them, why don't more people use them? And why don't they call hospice sooner?

The movement has seen real growth in the 25 years since Congress enacted the legislation that allowed Medicare to cover hospice services. By 2007, more than a third of the nation's deaths involved hospice care. But the National Hospice and Palliative Care Organization estimates that 70 percent of dying Americans could use hospice. In other words, says its research director, Stephen Connor, "For every person getting hospice care, there's one that should be."

Certain parts of the country, particularly remote rural areas and inner cities, still aren't adequately served by hospices; that's one explanation. But even where there are plenty of hospices, studies show that people often don't know what hospice does, or misperceive its role.

I was surprised recently, talking with an exceedingly well-educated friend who'd been shuttling between Boston and Boca Raton to care for her dying mother, by her response to my suggestion that she call a hospice. "We'd like to keep her at home," my friend said. Why should she know that keeping a patient at home is exactly what hospice strives to do? Most of us don't have much direct experience with end-of-life issues before we face a family crisis; there's no dress rehearsal.

Researchers have also found that ethnic, religious, and cultural differences play a part in families' attitudes. African-Americans, for instance, are more reluctant than whites to discuss treatment choices at the end of life or to decline treatments when they're terminally ill. Beliefs about suffering, understandings about individuality versus kinship, the very definitions of self and family—all are subject to cultural variation, so that the traditional hospice emphasis on openness, choice, and patient autonomy can prove unwelcome.

For instance, while the great majority of blacks and whites said they would want an honest prognosis if they had a fatal illness, according to a survey of 800 elderly Los Angeles residents, 45 percent of Korean-Americans and 65 percent of Mexican-Americans would not want to be told. Such differences appear to lessen as immigrant families grow more acculturated.

It's true, too, that physicians—still the main source of referrals to hospices—aren't as skilled at calculating when people are approaching death, and therefore might benefit from hospice care, as they and their patients might expect. Cancer, the illness that early on brought most patients into hospice, has a more predictable course than the chronic diseases that most elderly hospice patients have now. Doctors may find it more difficult, therefore, to say that a patient with congestive heart failure or advancing dementia is likely to die within six months.

In fact, physicians are overoptimistic in general about their patients' likelihood of survival, studies have consistently shown, and patients overestimate the ability of various treatments to keep them alive.

At work here, however, is not only the difficulty of knowing when death will come, but a still deep-seated resistance to contemplating, acknowledging, or discussing it. Doctors, after all, see their mission as curing disease, preserving life. To suggest, however gently, that a family summon hospice help may seem an unacceptable admission of failure, a move depriving a patient of hope. Hospice administrators notice that a high proportion of their referrals come from certain medical practices, while other practices evidently avoid such conversations.

Sociologist and physician Nicholas Christakis passes along a bit of dark humor from hospice nurses: "Why are coffins nailed shut? To keep doctors from administering more chemotherapy."

The other side of this equation, though, is that patients and their families are sometimes unwilling to truly hear or accept what's being said, even when a social worker, nurse, or physician does recommend hospice. These professionals may need to sharpen their communications skills, but patients and families aren't always eager for courageous conversations, either.

They may see hospice as giving up, abandoning the fight to live. Framing end-of-life decisions as a series of choices sometimes doesn't make clear, as bioethicists Theresa Drought and Barbara Koenig have written, that ultimately nobody has "the choice not to die of a terminal illness."

Such attitudes have unfortunate consequences. Whether it's because they don't know much about it, because no one's explained, because they don't understand when it's time, because they see it as a kind of capitulation—most families who do call hospice wait until very late in the process.

Medicare will initially pay for six months of care, and patients can be recertified for additional periods beyond that. Nationally, however, the median "length of service" for a hospice patient in 2007 was just 20 days, which means that half of patients had longer enrollments, but half had shorter ones. Every hospice takes in significant numbers of patients who are within a week, or even within hours, of death. Hospice of Baltimore, Reggie Bodnar told me—and she wasn't happy about it—had an extremely short median stay that year, just 16 days.

If they scramble and they're lucky, hospice staffers may be able to relieve a dying person's pain within a few hours, and offer other kinds of limited help. But the kind of trust that developed between Paul Hardaway and Kim Stone, the kinds of support that Dolores Noto received from her social worker, nurse, and volunteers, can't be forged in a week.

When a patient is that close to death, perhaps no longer even conscious, hospice can provide mostly "crisis management," Bodnar said. "We have months of work to do in days . . . The number one negative comment we get back on surveys is, 'We wish we had known about you sooner.'"

There's evidence that families also suffer from short stays. Hospice care has been shown to reduce caregivers' anxiety, increase their satisfaction, and help them adjust better to their losses. But when a research team led by Yale public health specialist Elizabeth Bradley interviewed families of patients at a Connecticut hospice, they found that caregivers of patients who'd been enrolled for three days or less were significantly more likely to suffer a major depressive disorder within 6 months of the death. And the National Hospice and Palliative Care Organization's national survey shows that families who feel referred to hospice "too late" were less satisfied with the care, support, and information.

One way that Hospice of Baltimore, and a number of others, are responding to the conviction that more people could use their services, and use them earlier, is by rethinking what's required to enroll. Maybe the notion that to become a hospice patient, one must relinquish certain medical treatments creates too high a barrier. Maybe patients and families would be more willing to come aboard, and receive the demonstrated benefits, if they didn't think they immediately had to discontinue or forswear their other options.

So Hospice of Baltimore, now Gilchrist Hospice Care, is a "concurrent care" program, sometimes also called "open access." "We tend to be very liberal," Bodnar explained. "When you have a black-and-white list of things you can do and can't do, that just creates a hurdle. Patients and families walk away."

Virtually any procedure that's palliative, aimed at soothing a patient, is permitted in this program: IVs for nutrition, radiation to shrink tumors that cause pain or obstructions, blood transfusions. (Such treatments may not be covered by Medicare or other insurers during hospice care, however.) "We always ask, what's the goal of the treatment? If the goal is to make this tumor go away so Dad can go back to work, no," Bodnar said. This hypothetical Dad's physicians, after all, have already decided they can't make that happen. "But if it's to promote patient comfort, absolutely."

It's a real change for a movement that grew out of consumers' desire to avoid many of these very same procedures—yet not always as big a change as it appears. Often, Bodnar explained, her staff recognizes that a family is overwhelmed, distraught, angry ("at the disease, at whatever, it has nothing to do with us"), and in no mood to waive their rights to do anything—even things the professionals deem futile and likely to cause a patient distress. But over time, even a few days, as a patient grows calmer and more comfortable and gets to know his hospice caretakers, discussions resume.

"That's where the education comes in, providing guidance, helping people make informed decisions," Bodnar said. This hospice, for instance, asks patients if they want cardiopulmonary resuscitation. To restart the heart of a terminally ill patient would seem contrary to the whole spirit of the enterprise. At one time, in fact, many hospices required patients to have Do Not Resuscitate orders. Now, patients can opt for CPR—but their nurses map out the pros and cons.

"It will start your heart," Bodnar explains. "Depending on how long it stopped, you may need to be on a breathing machine. Depending on how long it stopped, you may or may not wake up again. If there was pain present before, there will be pain after your heart is restarted; the other symptoms that were there will remain." Moreover, Bodnar went on, the chest compressions involved can cause bruising, broken ribs, even lacerations to internal organs. So, while CPR is an option her patients can choose, the reality is that eventually, nearly all decide against it.

Open access represents a more flexible approach. It also means that since hospices now differ in what they offer and allow, people who live in areas with multiple programs, like Baltimore, can do some hospice-shopping.

Does someone want a hospice with a religious affiliation? Though all hospices that take Medicare are nondenominational in the services they offer, having a chaplain of one's own religious background may be important to some patients.

What about a for-profit versus a nonprofit hospice? Longtime hospice workers tend to be suspicious of the for-profit chains, especially given the generally superior performance of nonprofit nursing homes. A study of almost 2,100 people cared for at more than 400 hospices in 1998 showed that at for-profit hospices, patients received a significantly narrower range of services. But that doesn't mean that any particular nonprofit hospice does a better job than a for-profit one; consumers have to compare. The need to consider these options is another argument for looking into hospice sooner, rather than later.

"Physicians say, 'There's nothing more I can do; call hospice,'" Bodnar said. "I always say, 'There's *so* much more to do.'" The idea that a patient who seeks hospice care is abandoning hope has always struck her as misguided.

Instead, she said, you're changing what you hope for. Perhaps you no longer hope for a cure, for an aging parent to regain health and vigor. But you can hope for her comfort and peace of mind, for good days that will be enjoyable and meaningful, for conversations that express the things you rarely say. For a good death.

Mrs. Noto

She danced at her daughter's wedding.

Not for very long, because her feet were troubling her. And in the excitement, nobody could remember the name of the song. But she and Doug managed a few steps together on a crystalline autumn day. "The sun was so bright," Mrs. Noto said dreamily. "Everything was so pretty."

We were looking, while Mrs. Noto narrated, at a few preliminary photos of the happy event: The four-layer, flower-bedecked cake ("out of this world") with Dolores and Frank Noto's own wedding portrait displayed next to it. Mrs. Noto in her fuchsia ensemble, accessorized with a wrist corsage ("it turned out lovely") and a cane. Deb in her long train ("she looked so beautiful"), with her father's rosary tucked into her bouquet. Doug in his tux and boutonniere.

It had been a windy day, so blowy that the tablecloths ballooned and the vows became a little hard for the older guests to hear, but nobody seemed to care. Everyone had danced like mad.

"And people were crazy over those cookies!" Mrs. Noto added, meaning her biscotti. She and Doug, drafted as assistant pastry chef, had rolled out and baked several hundred, and they'd all vanished. "No shortening, no Crisco, no butter," she reminded me, in case I should ever try the recipe. "Just lard."

We were in Deb's living room, where a hospital bed had replaced the couch. Things had not been easy since that golden afternoon. Mrs. Noto had kept her strength up through Thanksgiving, through Christmas Day. Then I got a call from her social worker, Laura: "We're seeing a pretty significant change. Her disease is progressing."

At her most recent visit, "I wasn't able to engage her in conversation as often," Laura found. "Usually, she likes to chat. But she was very tired; sometimes her eyes would close. You could tell she was just worn out."

A series of emergencies ensued. A bout of severe diarrhea weakened her to the extent that it had become unsafe for her to stay alone in her apartment. All thoughts about finding the perfect house were set aside; Deb and Doug moved Mrs. Noto into their condo, putting enough living room furniture in storage to make space for a hospital bed, a commode, and an oxygen tank, all supplied by hospice.

Pat Dykes, her nurse, and Laura stepped up their visits; a home health aide started coming several mornings a week. Deb worked from home when she could; when she had to go to her office, a cousin came over. Mrs. Noto's hospice volunteer filled in for a few hours, too.

Just after New Year's, Mrs. Noto spent four days in the hospital while a urologist tried to determine what was causing profuse bleeding when she urinated. "It could be an easy fix, something that could be taken care of," Deb reasoned. If it wasn't, she worried that she wouldn't be able to care for her mother at home. The urologist found a large bladder tumor and cauterized it; the bleeding stopped, and Mrs. Noto went home to her daughter's.

"I really thought she'd be bedridden," Deb told me. "But she started eating and drinking and partying." Mrs. Noto's color improved; she was up moving around the apartment with a walker.

Then that weekend, Deb saw "some changes, weird things. She's staring, fussing with the blankets; she repeats the same question over and over." A transient ischemic attack, Pat said, also known as a mini-stroke; the cancer was probably entering her brain.

She rebounded once more. I was startled, calling Deb's number one day for an update, when Mrs. Noto herself picked up the phone. "I had a scare, but I feel good, thank God," she reported. She and Deb were plotting an outing to a nearby mall that featured a big aquarium; Mrs. Noto liked to look at the bright tropical fish.

Now it was a January afternoon, blustery and growing dark, and we were chatting about the wedding photos as Deb sat nearby, working on her laptop.

Mrs. Noto, wearing a robe and slippers, sometimes felt too enervated to walk to and from the bathroom, so she had a catheter. But she'd tucked her hair behind a spiffy leopard-spotted headband nonetheless, and put on a few rings, though they were sliding around on her thin fingers.

"Everyone's so surprised at how well I'm doing," she said, nursing a mug of tea. "Thank God for this girl."

She disliked being so housebound. The newlyweds, she pointed out, never went out alone anymore, not even to bowl; someone always stayed at home with her.

"Mom, we knew this would be part of the process eventually," said Deb. It occurred to me that if she and Doug could weather these crises in their first weeks of married life, they'd likely be together for the next 40 years.

"I try not to be a burden to you."

"How long did *you* take care of *me*?"

There was some sort of injection the urologist wanted to try, Deb said, to prevent the bleeding from recurring. But her mother wasn't interested. "No more," she said. "God has given me what he's going to give me."

When it was time to leave, I hugged Mrs. Noto very gently: She was so thin, I thought a real squeeze might crack one of her ribs. I wasn't sure I'd see her again.

Mr. Hardaway

As it happened, Mr. Hardaway died first.

Gail had seen him flagging as the holidays approached. Because fluid was collecting in his lungs despite diuretics, "he's been coughing for weeks," she told me in December. "His appetite is not what it was. He has good days and very, very lethargic days." His nurse Kim also saw him losing stamina. The onetime steelworker now weighed 117 pounds.

Yet when Gail arrived with dinner, after a day's teaching, "I anxiously stick my head around the corner and say, 'How you doin', Dad?' His typical response is, 'I'm still here, so I'm blessed!' So what can I say? He *is* blessed."

She cooked for 15 people at Thanksgiving, and the plan was for her brother and nephew to literally carry Mr. Hardaway out of the house and into a car, then drive him around the Beltway to dinner. He wanted to come. But the day dawned rainy and raw and he didn't seem up to it. The family brought turkey and stuffing, crab cakes, vegetables, and sweet potato pie to their parents' house instead. Christmas was the same, family visiting in shifts, bringing dinner and practical gifts of pajamas and socks.

After the holidays, Kim made a difficult phone call. Mr. Hardaway was declining rapidly now, she told Gail. She thought this was "the beginning of the end," and that the end might come within a couple of weeks.

"Of course, I knew it," Gail said. "But she was true to what I had asked—'Be straight with me. Tell me what you see.' I needed to know."

In the days that followed, her father lost his ability to stand and to slide himself from chair to commode. He sputtered and coughed when he tried to eat or drink. She grew uneasy, wondering whether her family could somehow provide still more care than it already did.

One Thursday evening, after he'd eaten nothing but a couple of spoonfuls of applesauce at dinnertime, it took three people to bathe him, get him into his pajamas and into bed; two grandchildren slept in the house until morning.

"I cried and prayed half the night," Gail remembered. "We wanted to keep him at home—but even if I stayed there all day, I couldn't physically attend to his needs. What were we going to do?"

Friday morning, as she was telling her principal she needed a leave of absence, "God decided." Her husband and nephew were helping Paul Hardaway up for the day when he took a deep breath and died. Gail arrived a few minutes later, and her son David, sobbing. Kim Stone came to be with the family, so heartbroken, yet so relieved.

Hospice nurses soon learn that however they might like to, they can't attend every patient's funeral. There are too many. But Kim went to Mr. Hardaway's viewing ("so, so dear of her," Gail thought), at a funeral chapel in West Baltimore. When family members gratefully introduced her, people knew just who she was. "You're Kim! His favorite nurse and his best friend!"

He was buried in Farmville, Virginia, in a family plot next to the High Rock Baptist Church. Though he was the last surviving member of his family, local people remembered him; a crowd turned out to say goodbye.

His six grandsons served as his pallbearers. Three uniformed soldiers played taps and ceremonially folded the American flag that covered his coffin. And Gail's son David somehow managed to sing, beautifully, "Because He Lives."

Gail, however stricken, however conscious that she now had to intensify her efforts to care for her mother, allowed herself this consolation: "Dad knew, until he left, that we'd honored his wishes . . . It was a tall order, but we did it.

"Now, I'm not sure if the easier part is behind us, or ahead of us."

Mrs. Noto

"I'm just sitting here with her," Deb told me on the phone in late February. "She's lying quietly. She doesn't seem to be in pain at all . . .

"I still talk to her. I don't know if she can hear. But I tell her that I'm here."

It was very hard, Deb confessed. She knew that her mother was where she wanted to be. Yet she felt helpless, as if there were more she should be able to do. "No matter what, my mother appreciated what I did," she told herself.

Mrs. Noto died early the next morning.

They had managed that final outing to the aquarium at the mall, where Mrs. Noto bought herself "a really cute pair of snow boots," Deb reported. The odds of her ever needing to wade through snow again seemed slight, but Deb understood the appeal: the boots were on the clearance table, and they were pink.

Mrs. Noto had long ago assembled, in a garment bag, the clothing she wanted to wear at her funeral. Deb helped dress her in a mauve dress she'd never seen before, plus a pin and earrings.

"I had a chuckle," Deb said. "How could we think of putting her in her coffin without her jewelry?" After the funeral at the Holy Communion Lutheran Church, where her social worker Laura was among the mourners, Mrs. Noto was cremated, as she had specified and as her husband had been.

On a stormy March day, Deb and Doug drove to Ocean City, Maryland, a place she and her mother had spent many good times, to scatter her ashes. The waves were churning and the winds harsh. Bundled up against the cold, she and Doug walked along the beach, wondering where to perform this ritual.

"The wind stopped suddenly; it got completely still," Deb said. "I had an overwhelming feeling that this was the right place and the right thing." She said some prayers, "private thoughts and goodbyes." And then, "We took care of Mom."

SOME QUESTIONS TO CONSIDER ABOUT HOSPICE CARE:

Has your parent been diagnosed with a terminal disease? Will a physician certify that the disease, untreated, is likely to result in death within six months? That's what hospice eligibility requires.

Do your parent and family understand what hospice care entails? Do they know that it's an approach to the end of life, rather than a place, although a few hospice organizations do offer residences? That it aims to help patients end their lives at home?

Is your parent ready, after discussion with family members, health care providers, and hospice staff, to exchange procedures meant to cure illness for palliative care that instead provides comfort and pain management? Hospice patients need not reject all medical care, but the goals of care shift.

Would your parent prefer to die, not in a hospital, but in her own home, in a family member's home, or in the place she now calls home, an assisted living facility or nursing home?

As she nears the end of her life, would a team—including nurses, a social worker, home care aides, a chaplain—be helpful to her and to the family? Does the family want assistance with keeping the patient comfortable, understanding her status, meeting her emotional and spiritual needs? This is the hospice approach.

Are there caregivers, either family members or employees, who can be with your parent as she needs more help? Hospice patients can't live alone as they decline and can no longer care for themselves. Though hospice staffers can always be summoned in case of emergencies, they can't be with patients around the clock.

Do family members want support for themselves through this transition, as well as for their parent? Hospices regard the family, not the patient alone, as their clients.

CONCLUSION

Y OU'RE FACED WITH A SPECTRUM OF LOUSY OPTIONS," JOEL GORDON said to me as he grappled with whether and how to move his 96-year-old mother from assisted living into a nursing home.

"There's no good answer, is there?" said Sari G., pondering whether to move her ailing father out of the same nursing home, back into her own home.

Personally, I don't think all the options are lousy—but they all do have shortcomings, along with advantages. Moving a father with advancing Parkinson's disease into your home can mean excellent care for him but, as Sari G. discovered, great pressure for the caregiver who feels on duty around the clock, along with disruption and loss of privacy for the rest of the family. Assisted living can allow a mother to age in place comfortably for a while, until her health begins to fail and her increasing dementia causes her to lash out; then, as Joel Gordon learned, even with costly private aides, the facility can't provide what she needs.

There *are* good answers, for some of our parents, for periods of time—but few ideal ones, and that, of course, is what we want for our mothers and fathers. We want assistance that's always there, without delay, from skilled and saintly helpers who never have a cold, a conked-out car, or a bad day. We want places as cozy and familiar as home but with every kind of health care on tap. We want to clone ourselves so we can care for our parents and our own families and ourselves. And then we want a winning lottery ticket, to pay for it all.

Small wonder adult children get frustrated and anxious.

I rarely heard the sons and daughters I spent time with say they wanted good-enough eldercare—imperfect, sometimes exasperating, but able to meet a parent's most important needs, especially when a family is watchful. Who would admit to the merely acceptable as a goal? Yet finding good-enough care you can afford, given our system's current limitations, is actually a considerable accomplishment, something a family should be able to take pride in.

I often suspect that what we most yearn for is to restore health and vigor to a parent in decline—and that's not possible. Being baby boomers, we look to the horizon, hoping the future will bring better options for our elders and, ultimately, for ourselves. And it may.

Looking Forward

Consider, for instance, what technology may mean for both seniors and their caregivers. In the United States, faith in technology is practically a religious conviction. In the form of more effective medical interventions, technology is one of the major reasons for our graying population and the resulting strains on government, health care, and families. It can be part of the solution to those problems, too.

"We believe it will potentially reduce early, unnecessary institutionalization, which sometimes arises from the anxiety of family caregivers, especially when they're distant and concerned about the well-being of their loved ones," Majd Alwan, director of the Center for Aging Services Technologies, told me.

That could mean "not only improving the quality of life for those who prefer to remain at home but reducing the overall financial burden . . . It is an ambitious goal, but we're starting to see promising preliminary results from pilot and demonstration projects."

He was talking about such innovations as "telemedicine,"

in which wireless monitors, implanted in the body or linked to phones, computers, even beds, can track seniors' heart rates, blood pressure, blood glucose levels, respiration, and weight. As the data is transmitted, nurses and doctors can spot potential health problems, see how well drugs or other therapies are working, change approaches or prescriptions, advise patients on when to come in for office visits or to seek emergency care. "They've been proven effective for a variety of conditions," Alwan said, "including congestive heart failure, pulmonary disease, hypertension, and diabetes."

Other kinds of sensors can show caregivers how an elderly person is moving around his home, and send alerts when he hasn't left his bed or opened the refrigerator. They can even turn off a stove burner and adjust the room temperature. Games of solitaire or Scrabble via computer not only provide entertainment for seniors but also help professionals assess their cognitive functioning. Various medication reminders already on the market include talking pillboxes that remind their owners to take medications and signal caregivers when they don't. The early experience indicates that such remote health and safety monitoring can reduce the number of doctor and hospital visits and perhaps keep seniors at home longer.

Or keep them in assisted living longer. Alwan and a University of Virginia team recently installed sophisticated passive monitoring systems in the rooms of 21 assisted living residents in Minneapolis; the sensors measured not only breathing and heart rate at night but detected when residents left the bed, used the bathroom or shower, turned on the stove. After three months, the researchers found, the monitored residents required fewer medical interventions—doctor visits, lab tests, ER visits—than a control group and spent many fewer days in the hospital. And the monitoring brought "a savings of 75 percent in the cost of care," Alwan said.

Will older people accept such devices? Families worry that they'll resist or feel spied upon, but in an AARP survey in 2007, the elderly expressed willingness to use a variety of devices aimed at improving their health and safety at home. Caregivers were generally in favor, too, and felt the devices could help provide peace of mind.

As exciting a development, to my mind, is the intense interest in forming "intentional communities." Fewer than a dozen of these grassroots organizations were operational in 2008—including the trailblazer, Boston's eight-year-old Beacon Hill Village, and newer ones in Cambridge, Massachusetts; Palo Alto, California; New Canaan, Connecticut; and Washington, D.C. But in living rooms across the country, baby boomers and elders were planning hundreds more. "If we give a program on senior housing options, we'll get some people to come," said Susan Fienberg of HouseWorks, the Boston company that's the designated home care agency for Beacon Hill Village. "If we give a program about intentional communities, the room is *full*. A completely different energy."

They will all be different, these "villages," with urban and small city and suburban settings, and lists of services that reflect what each group decides it most needs. But the basic idea is, households in a neighborhood form a nonprofit organization to provide the services and referrals that will allow aging seniors to stay in their homes. Members pay annual fees of several hundred dollars, allowing the group to hire a director and perhaps other staff. Membership buys access to social and cultural events and transportation; villages may also contract, at discount rates, with home health care agencies and sometimes with medical practices. The staff will vet and recommend all kinds of helpers—handymen to change lightbulbs or make a bathroom safer, technicians to help a parent set up a computer, errand runners, and homemakers. Instead of uprooting seniors who need assistance, these organizations aim to help them—that favorite phrase, more invoked than achieved—age in place.

"Adult children do not want to repeat their parents' experience," says Andrea Cohen, HouseWorks' cofounder. "They want a lot more choice and control."

Life in Beacon Hill Village sounds far more inviting than even posh assisted living. Its 430 members, aged 53 to 99, live in two of Boston's most charming old neighborhoods. Their annual fees,

$580 for an individual or $850 for a household, help support an office, seven full- and part-time staffers, arrangements with local gyms and Mass General's geriatric practice, discounted blocks of tickets to concerts and plays.

In one recent spring month, villagers could go to exercise classes daily (walking, tai chi, and yoga included), take advantage of twice-weekly individual grocery shopping days, attend film screenings. Or tour the new exhibit at the Museum of Fine Arts and have lunch thereafter. Or join the "supper club" trying out that new French restaurant on Newbury Street. On days a villager doesn't feel up to a political lecture or a trip to Martha's Vineyard, she can have meals delivered, can ask the staff to arrange errand services, housecleaning, or home repair.

This is still a fairly active and independent group: only 5 percent use the home care aides that HouseWorks stands ready to provide. "But they want to know our services are there for them when they need it, that they can rely on that," says Fienberg.

☙

I can hear an echo in this effort, an updated chant: "Hell no, we won't go—to a nursing home."

But even nursing homes, which seem to have resisted so many years of reform efforts, are changing. Consider the Green Houses in Tupelo, Mississippi, ten new ranch houses built on a campus, each home to no more than ten residents and two aides. Designed to feel more like an actual home, the Green Houses offer private rooms and baths, with shared communal kitchens and dining rooms. Smaller, homier, far less institutional-feeling than most facilities, the Green Houses are in the vanguard of a nascent, but much-noticed movement to transform the nursing home.

"We want to create living communities, places where people can still grow and thrive and have choice and self-determination, no matter how old or sick or frail a person becomes," says Rose Marie Fagan of the Pioneer Network, the national clearinghouse for this crusade, with coalitions in 34 states.

Small-scale approaches like Tupelo's Green Houses have gotten a lot of media attention, but operators of larger nursing homes—in places like Perham, Minnesota; Seattle; and Manhattan, Kansas—have also adopted the new attitudes and strategies, tearing out walls to create "households" for 8 to 12 people with their own staff teams, so that rigid schedules can yield to individual inclinations. "People get up when they want to," Fagan explains. "They eat when they want to. They get out and about." To counteract the isolation of seniors living segregated from the rest of the population, pioneering facilities often build day care centers onsite and offer intergenerational activities.

An early study of 40 residents in Green Houses, compared to seniors in nearby traditional nursing homes, found little difference in health or functional ability, but significant differences on measures of emotional well-being—happiness, contentment, optimism. The Green Houses residents were less depressed, more satisfied with their facility. It was a small sample, but the authors concluded that the Green Houses was "a promising model" for improving the quality of life for elders in need of nursing care.

※

We'd all like to applaud these attempts to reinvent eldercare, and feel optimistic about the impact they could have. The inadequacies of the current choices are evident to us all; that knowledgeable, thoughtful innovators are doing things differently is reassuring.

But these efforts have clear limitations as well, at least for now.

Over the next few years, monitoring and communications technology can be a great help for a son or daughter who wants to keep watch over a parent who lives across town, or across the state. We'll have less of that fear about a parent who's fallen and can't summon help, or who has trouble keeping track of medications. We may have to do less driving to doctors' offices as telemedicine takes hold, and less scrambling if electronic health records link all the doctors and pharmacists our parent sees.

But when an older person is too frail or immobile to function well alone, when cognitive losses mean that even a talking pillbox may not help him remember his medications, what then? Sensors and monitors may extend the period of time when a senior can live alone, may set his mind and his family's at rest—for a while. But the technology has yet to be developed that can do hands-on care, like helping an 85-year-old with balance problems to take a shower or get dressed in the morning or use the toilet. (And would we want to use machines for such tasks even if they existed?)

"I don't think technology will ever eliminate the need for the human touch, and it shouldn't," Alwan said. Eventually, most long-lived elders will need real live helpers, paid or unpaid, either at home or in a facility.

If that facility could be as deinstitutionalized as Green Houses, we'd all be delighted. Few families will pine for the 200-bed nursing home with long corridors of "semiprivate" rooms, with staffers so eager to leave their jobs that residents barely get to know them. But there are still vastly more of those than there are alternatives.

Those aiming to reimagine the nursing home often call their mission "culture change." How widespread has it become? Of the nation's nursing homes, "probably around 1 to 2 percent are doing this in such a substantial way that when you visit you say, 'Wow, this is something different,'" Fagan says. In 2007, the Pioneer Network set a goal: It wanted to see 10 percent of facilities adopt culture change within five years. Fagan thinks it can happen. But even if it does, parents who need a nursing home in the next decade or so are still likely to enter a more traditional facility.

As for intentional communities, they're more likely to be an option for us than for our parents. They're not simple to put together; they require active board members and savvy organizers with energy, skills, and money. Even as more take root and flourish, they will be unavailable in most of the country for years.

Besides, they sound perfect for the healthier senior, someone who manages reasonably well in her own environment but needs people to retrofit her house, drive her to the supermarket each week, or go to the movies with her twice a month. But when she needs personal care, though it may be much simpler to have Beacon Hill Village summon aides from HouseWorks than to find, hire, and supervise aides herself, she still faces the issue of how to pay for them, even at reduced cost. The intentional community may prove hard to adapt to cities and towns without an upper-middle class, or to rural areas.

I asked Andrea Cohen and Susan Fienberg about these constraints. Might intentional communities wind up being something like organic food co-ops? Great assets, possible in communities full of retired academics and professionals like Cambridge and Palo Alto, but out of reach for most people and unlikely to supplant supermarkets anytime soon?

"If I were looking into a crystal ball, I'd say this is here to stay," Cohen responded. "This will be as big or bigger than senior housing"—by which she meant independent and assisted living complexes.

Fienberg added that she didn't expect a majority of the older population to become involved in a village. "But I think the movement will transform the way everybody *outside* of villages accesses services and the kinds of services that will be available."

Still, as I contemplate what my father may need over the next few years, as other adult children grapple with their responsibilities, I don't anticipate a transformed landscape, not yet. Even if my dad remains fit and independent into his 90s, I think he and I will be working with the same options we have now, pretty much—the same ones available to the families whose stories are collected here.

Looking Back

Their experiences point up the highly individual ways families respond to their parents' needs. Among the sons and daughters I came to know were those who, for quite legitimate reasons, found it unthinkable to move an ailing parent into their own homes—and those who found it unthinkable to do anything else. I saw children who were willing to tangle with their elders, to try to persuade them to make changes, and those who weren't.

I didn't encounter a lot of criticism of other people's decisions, though. Coping with the hard work of eldercare seems to make children unwilling to condemn what anyone else does. These families made what seemed the wisest, most workable decisions for themselves and their parents—and then hoped like hell that they were right.

What they shared was a deep desire to, as the commandment says, honor their fathers and mothers, carefully considering not only what the children thought best but how to respect their parents' wishes, even when they disagreed with them. They worked overtime to try to preserve their elders' dignity and independence, and sometimes came to think those values even more important than safety or longevity. I heard the phrase *quality of life* a lot.

Their stories also demonstrate, however, the way even our most careful plans can come apart. In the two and a half years I worked on *When the Time Comes*, I saw how a sudden crisis could scramble everything. People I expected to go visit in a couple of weeks were suddenly in intensive care; people whose voices I hadn't expected to hear again picked up the phone and said they were doing well. The unpredictable became predictable.

Doris Levy, the youngest of these seniors, was doing well in her specialized assisted living facility for people with dementia—until she fell and shattered her ankle in April 2008, and was no longer mobile enough to stay there. Her daughter, Marla Shachtman, moved her into the pleasantest, most highly rated nursing home she could find, and continued to visit several times a week. Mrs. Levy remained funny and good-natured as always, happy to see Marla and the family. But she couldn't remember having broken her ankle.

In the Bronx, Dora Appel still lived in her brick house around the corner from her cousin. With the help of Tekla, the live-in aide she'd grown fond of, Mrs. Appel did a little cooking, watched the news, and read the *New York Post* daily and the *Forward* (in Yiddish) on weekends. Her daughters, Anita Appel and Shirley Grill, thinking she needed more stimulation, persuaded her to try an adult day program; the jury was still out. Meanwhile, they visited and worried and still talked longingly about assisted living.

Milda Betins remained in the cottage adjoining her daughter's house in Claverack, New York, walked outside in pleasant weather, wrote letters, read novels. When the family returned from Latvia with little Kristina—a stressful ordeal that, thanks to changes in international adoption law and bureaucratic intransigence, took weeks longer than planned—Ilze Earner hired a part-time nanny and housekeeper. The idea was that she'd care for the children when Ilze and Laurence were away, create order from chaos, and not incidentally keep an eye on Milda Betins. Ilze and her mother continued their weekly visits to Mr. Betins in his nursing home.

Some of the other families suffered greater losses.

Margaret Wunderlich got her wish, in a way: She never moved into assisted living. Just after Labor Day she suffered a heart attack in her apartment in Arlington, spent a couple of weeks in a hospital, had another coronary. Her daughter, Peg Sprague, moved her to a residential hospice in Reading, Massachusetts, where, weak but clear-minded as always, she held court, receiving her children and grandchildren and friends, including the guests at her 95th birthday gathering. Peg was with her when she died in October 2007.

Five months after moving into Goddard House in Brookline, Massachusetts, John Dutton's health suddenly failed. He was hospitalized twice, and during his second stay went into cardiac arrest. He said goodbye to his sons Steve and Paul and thanked them for their care. He had told them the previous Christmas that it was the last time they would celebrate the holiday together again, and he was right. His sons were with him as the ventilator was removed and he died in early December 2007. He had already planned his own memorial service at Boston's Old South Church.

Henry B. died in November 2006, two months after leaving Greenwood House and returning to his daughter Sari's home in Bucks County, Pennsylvania. A few days before his death, the family moved him to a local hospice. Sari and her family—and a number of the home aides who had cared for him—were with him in the last days of his life.

Pauline Gordon developed pneumonia and, after two hospitalizations, returned to Greenwood House for "comfort care." She died in her room there in April 2006, at 96. At her graveside funeral, her son Joel recalled her devotion to family, her social awareness, her love of education and the arts. The following month, his daughter wore her grandmother's wedding band at her own wedding ceremony.

When they looked back at their parents' final months and years, the children were sorrowful, but they didn't reproach themselves. Much about the way our country treats our seniors should be very different; agreement on that was universal. We should have more choices and better ones; we need more help. But the children could honestly say that they had kept faith with their parents, cared for them as well as they could, and along with their sadness they could find some satisfaction in that. It sometimes occurred to them that they were showing their own children something about responsibility and compassion.

⁂

As I write, my caregiving duties are still largely before me. I've just returned from a pleasant Father's Day weekend with my dad. I know better than to buy him a present now; in his apartment, I've found an assortment of shirts, sweaters, and bathrobes my sister and I have sent for birthdays and Chanukah, not only unworn but still in their gift boxes. So I took Dad to dinner at the Greek restaurant we like, and we visited with neighbors in his NORC, and went out for breakfast the next morning at a diner where the waitress knew how he took his decaf. (And then, as is our cockeyed tradition, he slipped me a check that repaid me for everything I'd just spent. Resistance is futile.)

I think I have finally persuaded him that his cleaning lady needs to come every two weeks, not every three, but I'm waiting to see.

We talked, too, about assisted living, and I gently tried to reassure him that he has enough money to live for years in the facility he has selected. What he has to fear isn't poverty, but the toll that time will take, and none of us is immune to that. I hope I can be as steadfast and loving as the people I've written about, when the time comes.

Paula Span
Montclair, New Jersey
June 2008

SOURCE NOTES

Introduction

AARP Knowledge Management, "Aging Then and Now: Comparing the Older Population of Today with That of Previous Decades," provided to the author October 2004.

National Center for Health Statistics, "Health, United States, 2006," Table 27.

Merck Institute of Aging and Health and the Gerontological Society of America, "The State of Aging and Health in America."

Brenda C. Spillman, "Changes in Elderly Disability Rates and the Implications for Health Care Utilization and Cost," *The Milbank Quarterly* 82, no. 1 (2004).

Centers for Disease Control and Prevention and the Merck Company Foundation, "The State of Aging and Health in America 2007" (2007).

AARP, "The State of 50+ America" (2007).

Joshua M. Wiener, "You Can Run, but You Can't Hide: Long-Term Care for Older People and Younger Persons with Disabilities," testimony before the House Committee on Energy and Commerce (May 17, 2006).

Brenda C. Spillman and Liliana E. Pezzin, "Potential and Active Family Caregivers: Changing Networks and the 'Sandwich Generation,'" *The Milbank Quarterly* 78, no. 3 (2000).

Lisa Alecxih, "Nursing Home Use by 'Oldest Old' Sharply Declines," report by the Lewin Group (November 2006).

Richard W. Johnson and Joshua M. Wiener, "A Profile of Frail Older

Americans and Their Caregivers," The Urban Institute (February 2006).

Douglas A. Wolf and Charles F. Longino, "Our 'Increasingly Mobile Society'? The Curious Persistence of a False Belief," *The Gerontologist* 45, no. 1 (February 2005).

Linda L. Barrett, "The Costs of Long-Term Care: Public Perceptions Versus Reality in 2006—AARP Fact Sheet" (December 2006).

"Keys to Quality Care," National Hospice and Palliative Care Organization, www.nhpco.org.

Barbara L. Kass-Bartelmes and Ronda Hughes, "Advance Care Planning: Preferences for Care at the End of Life," *Research in Action* 12 (March 2003), www.ahrq.gov/research/endliferia/endria.htm.

Rosemary L. Hoffman and Ann M. Mitchell, "Caregiver Burden: Historical Development," *Nursing Forum* 33, no. 4 (October–December 1998).

Lynn Friss Feinberg, Kari Wolkwitz, and Cara Goldstein, "Ahead of the Curve: Emerging Trends and Practices in Family Caregiving Support," AARP Public Policy Institute (March 2006).

Carol Levine, Susan C. Reinhard, and others, "Family Caregivers on the Job: Moving Beyond ADLs and IADLs," *Generations: Journal of the American Society on Aging* 35, no. 4 (Winter 2003–2004).

Mary Jo Gibson and Ari Houser, "Valuing the Invaluable: A New Look at the Economic Value of Family Caregiving," AARP Public Policy Institute (June 2007).

Mary Ann Parris Stephens and Aloen L. Townsend, "Stress of Parent Care: Positive and Negative Effects of Women's Other Roles," *Psychology and Aging* 12, no. 2 (1997).

National Alliance for Caregiving and AARP, "Caregiving in the U.S." (2004).

MetLife Mature Market Institute, "MetLife Juggling Act Study: Balancing Caregiving with Work and the Costs Involved" (November 1999).

Evercare and the National Alliance for Caregiving, "Family Caregivers: What They Spend, What They Sacrifice" (November 2007).

USA Today/ABC News elderly care poll, June 24, 2007.

David Leonhardt, "A Reversal in the Index of Happy," *New York Times*, September 26, 2007.

Alan B. Krueger, "Are We Having More Fun Yet? Categorizing and Evaluating Changes in Time Allocation," prepared for the Brookings Panel on Economic Activity, Fall 2007.

Alice Ho, Sara R. Collins, and others, "A Look at Working-Age Caregivers' Roles, Health Concerns, and Need for Support," Issue Brief: The Commonwealth Fund (August 2005).

Martin Piquart and Silvia Sorenson, "Differences Between Caregivers and Noncaregivers in Psychological Health and Physical Health: A Meta-Analysis," *Psychology and Aging* 18, no. 2 (2003).

Jennifer L. Yee and Richard Schulz, "Gender Differences in Psychiatric Morbidity Among Family Caregivers: A Review and Analysis," *The Gerontologist* 40, no. 2 (April 2000).

Richard Schulz, "Chronic Stress Exposure and Health Effects in Family Caregiving," Conference Proceedings, Family Caregiving: State of the Art, Future Trends (March 6, 2007).

Betty J. Kramer, "Gain in the Caregiving Experience: Where Are We? What Next?" *The Gerontologist* 37, no. 2 (April 1997).

Marla Berg-Weger, Doris McGartland Rubio, and Susan S. Tebb, "Strengths-Based Practice with Family Caregivers of the Chronically Ill: Qualitative Insights," *Families in Society* 82, no. 3 (May–June 2001).

Kenneth J. Doka, "The Spiritual Gifts—and Burdens—of Family Caregiving," *Generations* 27, no. 4 (Winter 2003–2004).

Tamara L. Smith and Ronald W. Toseland, "The Effectiveness of a Telephone Support Program for Caregivers of Frail Older Adults," *The Gerontologist* 46, no. 5 (October 2006).

Karl Pillemer and J. Jill Suitor, " 'It Takes One to Help One': Effects of Similar Others on the Well-Being of Caregivers," *Journal of Gerontology Series B: Psychological Sciences and Social Sciences* 51, no. 5 (September 1996).

Interviews with Elinor Ginzler of AARP, Joshua Wiener of RTI International, Richard Johnson and Brenda Spillman of the Urban Institute, Barbara Moscowitz of the Massachusetts General Hospital Geriatric Medicine Unit, Lynn Feinberg of the Family Caregiver Alliance, David Ekerdt of the University of Kansas, and Suzanne Mintz of the National Family Caregivers Association.

Chapter One

Administration on Aging, U.S. Department of Health and Human Services, "A Profile of Older Americans: 2005."

AARP, "The State of 50+ America" (2006).

Leslie Gray and Lynn Friss Feinberg, "Survey of Californians About In-Home Care Services," Family Caregiver Alliance.

Hospital and Healthcare Compensation Service, "Hospital CNAs Receive Higher Pay than Nursing Home and Home Health CNAs" (November 28, 2007).

Ingrid J. McDonald, "Respectful Relationships: The Heart of Better Jobs Better Care," *Better Jobs Better Care* Issue Brief, no. 7 (April 2007).

Yoshiko Yamada, "Profile of Home Care Aides, Nursing Home Aides, and Hospital Aides: Historical Changes and Data Recommendations," *The Gerontologist* 45, no. 5 (October 2005).

Hospital and Healthcare Compensation Service, "2007 Homecare Salary and Benefits Report."

Carol Regan, "The Invisible Gap: Caregivers without Health Coverage," Health Care for Health Care Workers (May 2008).

Debra Lipson, "Health Insurance Coverage for Direct Care Workers: Riding Out the Storm," *Better Jobs Better Care* Issue Brief, no. 3 (March 2004).

MetLife Mature Market Institute, "The MetLife Market Survey of Adult Day Services and Home Care Costs" (September 2008).

MetLife Mature Market Institute, "The MetLife Market Survey of Nursing Home and Assisted Living Costs" (October 2008).

Wendy Fox-Grage, Barbara Coleman, and Marc Freiman, "Rebalancing: Ensuring Greater Access to Home and Community-Based Services," AARP Public Policy Institute (September 2006).

Jane Gross, "Its Appeal Slipping, the Senior Center Steps Livelier," *New York Times*, March 25, 2008.

Wake Forest University School of Medicine, "National Study of Adult Day Services" (2002).

Erin L. Woodhead, Stephen H. Zarit, and others, "Behavioral and Psychological Symptoms of Dementia: The Effects of Physical Activity at Adult Day Service Centers," *American Journal of Alzheimer's Disease and Other Dementias* 20, no. 3 (May–June 2005).

E. E. Femia, S. H. Zarit, and others, "Impact of Adult Day Services on Behavioral and Psychological Symptoms of Dementia," *The Gerontologist* 46, no. 6 (December 2007).

Joseph E. Gaugler, Shannon E. Jarrott, and others, "Adult Day Service Use and Reductions in Caregiving Hours: Effects on Stress and Psychological Well-Being for Dementia Caregivers," *International Journal of Geriatric Psychiatry* 18, no. 1 (2003).

S. H. Zarit, M. A. Stephens, and others, "Stress Reduction for Family Caregivers: Effects of Adult Day Care Use," *Journals of Gerontology Series B: Psychological Sciences and Social Sciences* 53, no. 5 (September 1998).

Laura N. Gitlin, Karen Reever, and others, "Enhancing Quality of Life of Families Who Use Adult Day Services: Short- and Long-Term Effects of the Adult Day Services Plus Program," *The Gerontologist* 46, no. 5 (October 2006).

Shannon E. Jarrott, Steven H. Zarit, and others, "Instrumental Help and Caregivers' Distress: Effects of Change in Informal and Formal Help," *American Journal of Alzheimer's Disease and Other Dementias* 20, no. 3 (May–June 2005).

Kathleen W. Piercy and Gregory J. Dunkley, "What Quality Paid Home Care Means to Family Caregivers," *The Journal of Applied Gerontology* 23, no. 3 (September 2004).

Nicholas Confessore, "Two Trainers of Home Aides Admit Fraud in Certification," *New York Times*, August 24, 2007.

Nicholas Confessore, "2 in Brooklyn Plead Guilty to Fraud in Home Care," *New York Times*, August 28, 2007.

Nicholas Confessore and Sarah Kershaw, "As Home Health Industry Booms, Little Oversight to Counter Fraud," *New York Times*, September 2, 2007.

Sarah Kershaw, "11 Accused of Grand Larceny in Home Health Aide Inquiry," *New York Times*, September 27, 2007.

United States General Accounting Office, "Medicare Home Health Agencies: Weaknesses in Federal and State Oversight Mask Potential Quality Issues" (July 2002).

United States General Accounting Office, "Long-Term Care: Federal Oversight of Growing Medicaid Home and Community-Based Waivers Should Be Strengthened" (June 2003).

Donna Folkemer and Barbara Coleman, "Home Care Quality: Emerging State Strategies to Deliver Person-Centered Care," AARP Public Policy Institute (February 2006).

Pamela Doty, "Consumer-Directed Home Care: Effects on Family Caregivers," Family Caregiver Alliance Policy Brief (October 2004).

Barbara Phillips, Kevin Mahoney, and others, "Lessons from the Implementations of Cash and Counseling in Arkansas, Florida, and New Jersey," Mathematica Policy Research Inc. (June 2003).

Ruth E. Matthias, "Abuse and Neglect of Clients in Agency-Based and Consumer-Directed Home Care," *Health and Social Work* (August 1, 2003).

National Alliance for Caregiving and AARP, "Caregiving in the U.S." (2004).

Pamela B. Teaster, "A Response to the Abuse of Vulnerable Adults: The 2000 Survey of State Adult Protective Services," National Center on Elder Abuse.

"Fact Sheet: Elder Abuse Prevalence and Incidence," National Center on Elder Abuse.

Richard J. Bonnie and Robert B. Wallace, editors, "Elder Mistreatment: Abuse, Neglect, and Exploitation in an Aging America," National Academies Press (2002).

Kathleen W. Piercy, "When It Is More Than a Job: Close Relationships Between Home Health Aides and Older Clients," *Journal of Aging and Health* 12, no. 3 (August 2000).

Interviews with Elinor Ginzler and other long-term care experts at AARP, Gail Hunt of the National Alliance for Caregiving, Lynn Feinberg and Donna Schempp of the Family Caregiver Alliance, Barbara Moscowitz of the Massachusetts General Hospital Geriatric Medicine Unit, Suzanne Mintz of the National Family Caregivers Association, Peter Notarstefano of the American Association of Homes and Services for the Aging, Mary St. Pierre of the National Association for Home Care and Hospice, Gene Coffey of the National Senior Citizens Law Center, and Jessica Cantor of SAGE Eldercare in Summit, New Jersey.

Chapter Two

"Households and Families: 2000," U.S. Census Bureau (September 2001).

Sheel Pandya, "Racial and Ethnic Differences Among Older Adults in Long-Term Care Service Use," AARP Public Policy Institute (June 2005).

AARP, "In the Middle: A Report on Multicultural Boomers Coping with Family and Aging Issues" (July 2001).

Laura Skufca, "Are Americans Talking with Their Parents About Independent Living: A 2007 Study Among Boomer Women," AARP Knowledge Management (2007).

Kathleen McGarry and Robert F. Schoeni, "Social Security, Economic Growth, and the Rise in Elderly Widows' Independence in the Twentieth Century," *Demography* 37, no. 2 (May 2000).

Gary V. Englehardt, Jonathan Gruber, and Cynthia D. Perry, "Social Security and Elderly Living Arrangements," National Bureau of Economic Research (April 2002), www.nber.org/papers/w8911.

Gary V. Englehardt, Jonathan Gruber, and others, "Households and Families: 2000," National Bureau of Economic Research, www.nber.org.

National Alliance for Caregiving and AARP, "Caregiving in the U.S." (2004).

Lynn Friss Feinberg, Kari Wolkwitz, and Cara Goldstein, "Ahead of the Curve: Emerging Trends and Practices in Family Caregiving Support," AARP Public Policy Institute (March 2006).

Alice Ho, Sara R. Collins, and others, "A Look at Working-Age Caregivers' Roles, Health Concerns, and Need for Support," Issue Brief: The Commonwealth Fund (August 2005).

Martin Piquart and Silvia Sorenson, "Differences Between Caregivers and Noncaregivers in Psychological Health and Physical Health: A Meta-Analysis," *Psychology and Aging* 18, no. 2 (2003).

Jennifer L. Yee and Richard Schulz, "Gender Differences in Psychiatric Morbidity Among Family Caregivers: A Review and Analysis," *The Gerontologist* 40, no. 2 (April 2000).

Richard Schulz, "Chronic Stress Exposure and Health Effects in Family Caregiving," Conference Proceedings, Family Caregiving: State of the Art, Future Trends (March 6, 2007).

Karl Pillemer and J. Jill Suitor, " 'It Takes One to Help One': Effects of Similar Others on the Well-Being of Caregivers," *Journal of Gerontology Series B: Psychological Sciences and Social Sciences* 51, no. 5 (September 1996).

AARP, "In the Middle: A Report on Multicultural Boomers Coping with Family and Aging Issues" (July 2001).

Namkee G. Choi, "Nonmarried Aging Parents' and Their Adult Children's Characteristics Associated with Transitions Into and Out of Intergenerational Coresidence," *Journal of Gerontological Social Work* 40, no. 3 (2003).

Interviews with Robert F. Schoeni of the University of Michigan, Gail Hunt of the National Alliance for Caregiving, Barbara Moscowitz of the Massachusetts General Hospital Geriatric Medicine Unit, and authors Sharon Graham Niederhaus and John L. Graham.

Chapter Three

Genworth Financial, "2008 Cost of Care Survey: Home Care Providers, Adult Day Health Care Facilities, Assisted Living Facilities and Nursing Homes" (April 2008).

"2006 Overview of Assisted Living," American Association of Homes and Services for the Aging, American Seniors Housing Association, Assisted Living Federation of America, National Center for Assisted Living, and the National Investment Center for the Seniors Housing and Care Industry.

Catherine Hawes, Charles D. Phillips, and Miriam Rose, "A National Study of Assisted Living Facilities," *The Gerontologist* 43, no. 6 (December 2003).

Lea C. Watson, Susan Lehmann, and others, "Depression in Assisted Living Is Common and Related to Physical Burden," *American Journal of Geriatric Psychiatry* 14, no. 10 (October 2006).

Sheryl Zimmerman, Philip D. Sloane, and J. Kevin Eckert, editors, *Assisted Living: Needs, Practices, and Policies in Residential Care for the Elderly* (Baltimore: Johns Hopkins University Press, 2001).

Mary M. Ball, Frank J. Whittington, and others, "Quality of Life in Assisted Living Facilities: Viewpoints of Residents," *Journal of Applied Gerontology* 19, no. 3 (September 2000).

Catherine Hawes, Charles D. Phillips, and Miriam Rose, "A National Study of Assisted Living for the Frail Elderly: Final Summary Report," Office of Disability, Aging, and Long-Term Care Policy, U.S. Department of Health and Human Services (November 2000).

Larry Polivka, "Community-Residential Care for the Frail Elderly: What Do We Know; What Should We Do?" (July 2004).

Debra Street, Stephanie Burge, and others, "The Salience of Social Relationships for Resident Well-Being in Assisted Living," *Journal of Gerontology Series B: Psychological Sciences and Social Sciences* 62, no. 2 (2007).

Charles D. Phillips, Yolanda Munoz, and others, "Effects of Facility Characteristics on Departures from Assisted Living: Results from a National Study," *The Gerontologist* 43, no. 5 (October 2003).

Sheryl Zimmerman, Philip D. Sloane, and others, "How Good Is Assisted Living? Findings and Implications from an Outcomes Study," *Journal of Gerontology Series B: Psychological Sciences and Social Sciences* 60, no. 4 (July 2005).

Sheryl Zimmerman, Anne C. Scott, and others, "Social Engagement and Its Relationship to Service Provision in Residential Care and Assisted Living," *Social Work Research* 27, no. 1 (March 2003).

Sherry M. Cummings, "Predictors of Psychological Well-Being Among Assisted-Living Residents," *Health and Social Work* 27, no. 4 (November 2002).

Robert Jenkens, Janet O'Keeffe, and others, "Study of Negotiated Risk Agreements in Assisted Living: Final Report," U.S. Department of Health and Human Services (February 13, 2006).

Debra Dobbs, Jean Munn, and others, "Characteristics Associated with Lower Activity Involvement in Long-Term Care Residents With Dementia," *The Gerontologist* 45, Special Issue I (October 2005).

Cynthia L. Port, Sheryl Zimmerman, and others, "Families Filling the Gap: Comparing Family Involvement for Assisted Living and Nursing Home Residents with Dementia," *The Gerontologist* 45, Special Issue I (October 2005).

Louise Crawford Mead, J. Kevin Eckert, and others, "Sociocultural Aspects of Transitions from Assisted Living for Residents with Dementia," *The Gerontologist* 45, Special Issue I (October 2005).

Joseph E. Gaugler and Robert L. Kane, "Families and Assisted Living," *The Gerontologist* 47, Special Issue III (December 2007).

Interviews with Karen Love of the Center for Excellence in Assisted Living; Sheryl Zimmerman and Philip Sloane of the University of North Carolina; Catherine Hawes of Texas A&M University; Barbara Moscowitz of the Massachusetts General Hospital Geriatric Medicine Unit; Robyn Stone of American Association of Homes and Services for the Aging; Elinor Ginzler and Susan Reinhard of AARP; geriatric care manager Suzanne Modigliani in Brookline, Massachusetts; David Kyllo of the National Center for Assisted Living; Louise Rachin of Providence House in Brighton, Massachusetts; and Nancy Shapiro of Goddard House in Brookline, Massachusetts.

Chapter Four

Genworth Financial, "2008 Cost of Care Survey: Home Care Providers, Adult Day Health Care Facilities, Assisted Living Facilities and Nursing Homes" (April 2008).

Lisa Alecxih, "Nursing Home Use by 'Oldest Old' Sharply Declines," report by the Lewin Group (November 2006).

Anthony T. Lo Sasso and Richard W. Johnson, "Does Informal Care from Adult Children Reduce Nursing Home Admissions for the Elderly?" *Inquiry* 39 (Fall 2002).

Charlene Harrington, Helen Carrillo, and others, "Nursing Facilities, Staffing, Residents, and Facility Deficiencies, 2000 through 2006," Department of Social and Behavioral Sciences, University of California, San Francisco (September 2007).

"Trends in Nursing Facility Characteristics," American Health Care Association (June 2007).

Gwendolen T. Buhr, Maragatha Kuchibhatla, and Elizabeth C. Clipp, "Caregivers' Reasons for Nursing Home Placement: Clues for Improving Discussions with Families Prior to the Transition," *The Gerontologist* 46, no. 1 (February 2006).

Brenda C. Spillman and Sharon K. Long, "Does High Caregiver Stress Lead to Nursing Home Entry?" Office of Disability, Aging, and Long-Term Care Policy, U.S. Department of Health and Human Services (January 26, 2007).

Joseph E. Gaugler, Stephen H. Zarit, and Leonard I. Pearlin, "Caregiving and Institutionalization: Perceptions of Family Conflict and Socioemotional Support," *International Journal of Aging and Human Development* 49, no. 1 (1999).

Kathryn G. Allen, "Nursing Home Reform: Continued Attention Is Needed to Improve Quality of Care in Small but Significant

Share of Homes," testimony before the Senate Special Committee on Aging (May 2, 2007).

My Innerview, 2007 National Survey of Consumer and Workforce Satisfaction in Nursing Homes (May 2008), www.myinnerview .com.

Y. Danielli, "Treating Survivors and Children of Survivors of the Nazi Holocaust," cited in Jodeme Goldhar and Paula David, "The Effects of a Support Group Intervention on Adult Children of Holocaust Survivor's Self-Reports of Feelings of Isolation," Baycrest Center for Geriatric Care (September 2000).

Rachel Yehuda, James Schmeidler, and others, "Vulnerability to Posttraumatic Stress Disorder in Adult Offspring of Holocaust Survivors," *American Journal of Psychiatry* 155 (September 1998).

Catherine Hawes, "Nursing Home Quality: Problems, Causes, and Cures," testimony before the U.S. Senate Committee on Finance (July 17, 2003).

United States Government Accountability Office, "Nursing Homes: Federal Monitoring Surveys Demonstrate Continued Understatement of Serious Care Problems and CMS Oversight Weaknesses" (May 2008).

Jerry H. Gurwitz, Terry S. Field, and others, "Incidence and Preventability of Adverse Drug Events in Nursing Homes," *The American Journal of Medicine* 109, no. 2 (August 1, 2000).

Jeanie Kayser-Jones, Ellen S. Schell, and others, "Factors Contributing to Dehydration in Nursing Homes: Inadequate Staffing and Lack of Professional Supervision," *Journal of the American Geriatrics Society* 47, no. 10 (1999).

Catherine Hawes, "Elder Abuse in Residential Long-Term Care Facilities: What Is Known About Prevalence, Causes and Prevention," testimony before the U.S. Senate Committee on Finance (June 18, 2002).

Bernadette Wright, "Direct Care Workers in Long-Term Care," AARP Public Policy Institute (May 2005).

My Innerview, 2006 National Survey of Consumer and Workforce

Satisfaction in Nursing Homes (June 2007), www.myinnerview .com.

Charlene Harrington, Christine Kovner, and others, "Experts Recommend Minimum Nurse Staffing Standards for Nursing Facilities in the United States," *The Gerontologist* 40, no. 1 (February 2000).

Joshua M. Wiener, "An Assessment of Strategies for Improving Quality of Care in Nursing Homes," *The Gerontologist* 43, Special Issue II (April 2003).

Charlene Harrington, Steffie Wollhandler, and others, "Does Investor Ownership of Nursing Homes Compromise the Quality of Care?" *American Journal of Public Health* 91, no. 9 (September 2001).

Vincent Mor, Jacqueline Zinn, and others, "Driven to Tiers: Socioeconomic and Racial Disparities in the Quality of Nursing Home Care," *The Milbank Quarterly* 82, no. 2 (2004).

Charlene Harrington, David Zimmerman, and others, "Nursing Home Staffing and Its Relationship to Deficiencies," *Journal of Gerontology Series B: Psychological Sciences and Social Sciences* 55, no. 5 (2000).

Terry Peak, "Families and the Nursing Home Environment: Adaptation in a Group Context," *Journal of Gerontological Social Work* 33, no. 1 (2000).

Marie T. Duncan and David L. Morgan, "Sharing the Caring: Family Caregivers' Views of Their Relationships with Nursing Home Staff," *The Gerontologist* 34, no. 2 (April 1994).

Karl Pillemer, J. Jill Suitor, and others, "A Cooperative Communication Intervention for Nursing Home Staff and Family Members of Residents," *The Gerontologist* 43, Special Issue II (April 2003).

Linda Vinton and Nicholas Mazza, "Aggressive Behavior Directed at Nursing Home Personnel by Residents' Family Members," *The Gerontologist* 34, no. 4 (August 1994).

Interviews with Susan Reinhard and Elinor Ginzler at AARP; Richard Johnson and Brenda Spillman at the Urban Institute; Janet

Wells and Alice Hedt at NCCNHR; Robyn Stone at American Association of Homes and Services for the Aging; Charlene Harrington at the University of California, San Francisco; Catherine Hawes at Texas A&M University; Joshua Wiener at RTI International; and Rick Goldstein, Carol Geraci, and Joan Rubin-Kritz at Greenwood House for the Jewish Aged in Ewing, New Jersey.

Chapter Five

Susan C. Miller and True Ryndes, "Quality of Life at the End of Life: The Public Health Perspective," *Public Health and Aging* (Summer 2005).

Stephen R. Connor, Kathryn Fitch, and others, "Comparing Hospice and Nonhospice Patient Survival Among Patients Who Die Within a Three-Year Window," *Journal of Pain and Symptom Management* 33, no. 3 (March 2007).

Linda K. George, "Research Design in End-of-Life Research: State of Science," *The Gerontologist* 42, Special Issue III (October 2002).

Theresa S. Drought and Barbara A. Koenig, "'Choice' in End-of-Life Decision Making: Researching Fact or Fiction," *The Gerontologist* 42, Special Issue III (October 2002).

Barbara L. Kass-Bartelmes and Ronda Hughes, "Advance Care Planning: Preferences for Care at the End of Life," *Research in Action* 12 (March 2003).

Jeanie Kayser-Jones, "The Experience of Dying: An Ethnographic Nursing Home Study," *The Gerontologist* 42, Special Issue III (October 2002).

Ann Berger, Donna Pereira, and others, "A Commentary: Social and Cultural Determinants of End-of-Life Care for Elderly Persons," *The Gerontologist* 42, Special Issue III (October 2002).

Renee Shield, Joan Teno, and others, "End of Life in Nursing Homes: Experiences and Policy Recommendations," AARP Public Policy Institute (November 2004).

Mathy Mezey, Nancy Neveloff Dubler, and others, "What Impact

Do Setting and Transitions Have on the Quality of Life at the End of Life and the Quality of the Dying Process?" *The Gerontologist* 42, Special Issue III (October 2002).

Elizabeth H. Bradley, Melissa D. A. Carlson, and others, "Depression Among Surviving Caregivers: Does Length of Hospice Enrollment Matter?" *American Journal of Psychiatry* 161 (December 2004).

Susan Miller, "Nursing Home/Hospice Partnerships," Center for Gerontology and Health Care Research, Brown University Medical School (February 2007).

Annotated Bibliography, National Hospice and Palliative Care Organization.

Bruce Jennings, True Ryndes, and others, "Access to Hospice Care: Expanding Boundaries, Overcoming Barriers," supplement to the *Hastings Center Report* (March–April 2003).

National Hospice and Palliative Care Organization, "NHPCO Facts and Figures: Hospice Care in America" (October 2008).

F. P. Hopp and S. A. Duffy, "Racial Variations in End-of-Life Care," *Journal of the American Geriatrics Society* 48, no. 6 (June 2000).

Leslie J. Blackhall, Gelya Frank, and others, "Ethnicity and Attitudes Towards Life-Sustaining Technology," *Social Science and Medicine* 48, no. 12 (June 1999).

Nicholas A. Christakis, "The Bad News First," *New York Times*, August 24, 2007.

Joan M. Teno, Janet E. Shu, and others, "Timing of Referral to Hospice and Quality of Care: Length of Stay and Bereaved Family Members' Perceptions of the Timing of Hospice Referral," *Journal of Pain and Symptom Management* (2007).

Alison E. Kris, Emily J. Cherlin, and others, "Length of Hospice Enrollment and Subsequent Depression in Family Caregivers: 13-Month Follow-Up Study," *American Journal of Geriatric Psychiatry* 14 (March 2006).

Melissa Carlson, William T. Gallo, and others, "Ownership Status and Patterns of Care in Hospice: Results from the National Home and Hospice Care Survey," *Medical Care* 42, no. 5 (May 2004).

Interviews with Stephen R. Connor and Don Schumacher, National Hospice and Palliative Care Organization, and with Regina Bodnar and the staff of Hospice of Baltimore, now Gilchrist Hospice Care.

Conclusion

Majd Alwan, Elene Brito Sifferlin, and others, "Impact of Passive Health Status Monitoring to Care Providers and Payers in Assisted Living," *Telemedicine and e-Health* 13, no. 3 (June 1, 2007).

Majd Alwan and Jeremy Nobel, "State of Technology in Aging Services: Summary," Center for Aging Services Technologies (March 2008)

Linda L. Barrett, "Healthy@Home," AARP Knowledge Management (March 2008).

Rosalie A. Kane, Terry Y. Lum, and others, "Resident Outcomes in Small-House Nursing Homes: A Longitudinal Evaluation of the Initial Green House Program," *Journal of the American Geriatrics Society* 55, no. 6 (June 2007).

Interviews with Majd Alwan of the Center for Aging Services Technologies at the American Association of Homes and Services for the Aging; Susan Fienberg and Andrea Cohen of HouseWorks in Newton, Massachusetts; Gail Kohn of Capitol Hill Village in Washington, D.C.; and Rose Marie Fagan of the Pioneer Network.

FOR MORE INFORMATION:

Selected Resources

General Eldercare

These books and Websites provide valuable overviews of many aspects of caregiving and useful starting points for planning. Resources that address particular needs and options follow in separate sections.

Books

Hugh Delehanty and Elinor Ginzler, *Caring for Your Parents: The Complete AARP Guide*, Sterling, 2005.

Claire Berman, *Caring for Yourself While Caring for Your Aging Parents: How to Help, How to Survive*, Owl Books, 2005.

Dennis McCullough, M.D., *My Mother, Your Mother: Embracing "Slow Medicine," the Compassionate Approach to Caring for Your Aging Loved Ones*, HarperCollins, 2008.

Virginia Morris, *How to Care for Aging Parents*, Workman, 2004.

Web Resources

Helpful information from consumer advocacy groups, from other nonprofit organizations, and from caregiving projects underwritten by corporations, plus downloadable publications. Some sites include online support groups and forums.

AARP
601 E Street NW
Washington, DC 20049
888-OUR-AARP
www.aarp.org/caregiving

Family Caregiver Alliance
180 Montgomery Street, Suite 1100
San Francisco, CA 94104
800-445-8106
www.caregiver.org

National Alliance for Caregiving (with online Family Care Resource
    Clearinghouse)
4720 Montgomery Lane, 5th Floor
Bethesda, MD 20814
301-718-8444
www.caregiving.org

National Family Caregivers Association
10400 Connecticut Avenue, Suite 500
Kensington, MD 20895
800-896-3650
www.nfcacares.org

American Association of Homes and Services for the Aging
2519 Connecticut Avenue NW
Washington, DC 20008-1520
202-783-2242
www.aahsa.org

Strength for Caring (from Johnson & Johnson)
www.strengthforcaring.com

Caring for Your Parents Handbook (from PBS and the MIT Work-
    place Center)
www.pbs.org/wgbh/caringforyourparents/handbook

Since You Care Guides
Metlife Mature Market Institute
www.maturemarketinstitute.com

Federal Agencies Providing Consumer Information

U.S. Administration on Aging
Washington, DC 20201
202-619-0724
www.aoa.gov

The Eldercare Locator (from the U.S. Administration on Aging)
800-677-1116
www.eldercare.gov

National Institutes of Health
www.NIHSeniorHealth.gov

About Dementia

Books

Joanne Koenig Coste, *Learning to Speak Alzheimer's: A Ground-breaking Approach for Everyone Dealing with the Disease*, Houghton Mifflin, 2004.

Nancy L. Mace and Peter V. Rabins, *The 36-Hour Day: A Family Guide to Caring for People with Alzheimer Disease, Other Dementias, and Memory Loss in Later Life*, Johns Hopkins University Press, 2006.

DVD and Resource Journal

Family Matters: Coming Together for Alzheimer's, Massachusetts General Hospital, 2006. (For organizations)
www.massgeneral.org/familymatters

Organizations, Helplines, Websites

Alzheimer's Association
225 N. Michigan Avenue, 17th Floor
Chicago, IL 60601-7633
800-272-3900
www.alz.org

See also these resources listed under General Eldercare on pages
  262–263:
AARP
National Alliance for Caregiving
Family Caregiver Alliance
National Family Caregivers Association
The Eldercare Locator
Caring for Your Parents Handbook
Strength for Caring
Since You Care Guides

Home Care

Books

Robert F. Bornstein and Mary A. Languirand, *When Someone You
  Love Needs Nursing Home, Assisted Living, or In-Home Care: The
  Complete Guide*, 2nd ed., Newmarket Press, 2009.
Maria M. Meyer and Paula Derr, *The Comfort of Home: A Complete
  Guide for Caregivers*, 3rd ed., CareTrust Publications, 2007.

Organizations and Websites

National Association for Home Care and Hospice
228 7th Street SE
Washington, DC 20003
202-547-7424
www.nahc.org

Visiting Nurse Asssociations of America
900 19th Street NW, Suite 200
Washington, DC 20006
202-384-1420
www.vnaa.org

To compare Medicare-certified home health agencies in your area:
www.medicare.gov

For home modifications:
CAPS (Certified Aging-in-Place Specialists) Directory
National Association of Home Builders
1202 15th Street NW
Washington, DC 20005
800-368-5242
www.nahb.org

For meal delivery:
Meals on Wheels Association of America
203 S. Union Street
Alexandria, VA 22314
703-548-5558
www.mowaa.org

For adult day programs:
National Adult Day Services Association
85 S. Washington, Suite 316
Seattle, WA 98104
877-745-1440
www.nadsa.org

For transportation:
National Center on Senior Transportation
866-528-NCST
seniortransportation.easterseals.com

See also these resources listed under General Eldercare on pages
   262–263:
AARP
National Alliance for Caregiving
Family Caregiver Alliance
National Family Caregivers Association
The Eldercare Locator
Strength for Caring
Caring for Your Parents Handbook
Since You Care Guides

Downsizing and Moving

Books

Linda Hetzer and Janet Hulstrand, *Moving On: A Practical Guide to
   Downsizing the Family Home,"* Stewart, Tabori & Chang, 2004.
Vickie Dellaquila, *Don't Toss My Memories in the Trash: A Step-by-
   Step Guide to Helping Seniors Downsize, Organize, and Move,"*
   Mountain Publishing, 2007.

Finding Professionals

National Association of Professional Organizers
15000 Commerce Parkway, Suite C
Mount Laurel, NJ 08054
856-380-6828
www.napo.net

National Association of Senior Move Managers
PO Box 209
Hinsdale, IL 60522
877-606-2766
www.nasmm.org

Shared Households

Books

Sharon Graham Niederhaus and John L. Graham, *Together Again: A Creative Guide for Successful Multigenerational Living*, M. Evans, 2007. (Focuses on healthier seniors)

Organizations and Websites

Family Caregiver Alliance
180 Montgomery Street, Suite 1100
San Francisco, CA 94104
800-445-8106
www.caregiver.org

See also these resources listed under Home Care on pages 264–265:
National Association for Home Care and Hospice
Visiting Nurse Asssociations of America
The Eldercare Locator
CAPS Directory, National Association of Home Builders
Meals on Wheels Association of America
National Adult Day Services Association
National Center on Senior Transportation

Assisted Living

Books, Handbooks, and Video

Robert F. Bornstein and Mary A. Languirand, *When Someone You Love Needs Nursing Home, Assisted Living, or In-Home Care: The Complete Guide*, 2nd ed., Newmarket Press, 2009.
Choosing an Assisted Living Facility: Considerations for Making the Right Decision, 2nd ed., Consumer Consortium on Assisted Living (see listing on page 268).
Choosing Assisted Living . . . What You Need to Know (video), Consumer Consortium on Assisted Living.

Consumer-Oriented Organizations and Websites

Consumer Consortium on Assisted Living
2342 Oak Street
Falls Church, VA 22046
703-533-8121
www.ccal.org

The CEAL Clearinghouse
Center for Excellence in Assisted Living
www.theceal.org/clearinghouse.php

Industry Groups

Assisted Living Federation of America
1650 King Street, Suite 602
Alexandria, VA 22314-2747
703-894-1805
www.alfa.org

National Center for Assisted Living
1201 L Street NW
Washington, DC 20005
202-842-4444
www.ncal.org

See also these resources listed under General Eldercare on pages
    262–263:
AARP
National Alliance for Caregiving
Family Caregiver Alliance
National Family Caregivers Association
American Association of Homes and Services for the Aging
The Eldercare Locator
Strength for Caring
Since You Care Guides

Nursing Homes

Books

Robert F. Bornstein and Mary A. Languirand, *When Someone You Love Needs Nursing Home, Assisted Living, or In-Home Care: The Complete Guide*, 2nd ed., Newmarket Press, 2009.

Sarah Green Burger, Virginia Fraser, Sara Hunt, and Barbara Frank, *Nursing Homes: Getting Good Care There (Second Edition)—A Consumer Action Manual Prepared by the National Citizens' Co-alition for Nursing Home Reform*, Impact Publishers, 2002.

Consumer Reports Nursing Home Guide 2006, www.consumer reports.org/nursinghomes.

National Senior Citizens Law Center, Eric M. Carlson, and Katha-rine Bau Hsiao, *The Baby Boomer's Guide to Nursing Home Care*, Taylor Trade Publishing, 2006.

Eric Carlson *20 Common Nursing Home Problems—and How to Re-solve Them*, National Senior Citizens Law Center, 2005.

Order from the National Senior Citizens Law Center
1444 I Street NW, Suite 1100
Washington, DC 20005
202-289-6976
www.nsclc.org

Organizations and Web Resources

NCCNHR
National Citizens' Coalition for Nursing Home Reform
1828 L Street NW, Suite 801
Washington, DC 20036
202-332-2275
www.nccnhr.org

The Pioneer Network
PO Box 18648
Rochester, NY 14618
585-271-7570
www.pioneernetwork.net

To compare nursing homes in your area:
www.medicare.gov

See also these resources listed under General Eldercare on pages
    262–263:
AARP
National Alliance for Caregiving
Family Caregiver Alliance
National Family Caregivers Association
American Association of Homes and Services for the Aging
The Eldercare Locator
Strength for Caring
Since You Care Guides

Hospice and End-of-Life Care

Books

Maggie Callanan, *Final Journeys: A Practical Guide for Bringing
    Care and Comfort at the End of Life*, Bantam, 2008.
Stephen P. Kiernan, *Last Rights: Rescuing the End of Life from the
    Medical System*, St. Martin's, 2007.

Organizations and Web Resources

National Hospice and Palliative Care Organization
1731 King Street, Suite 100
Alexandria, VA 22314
800-658-8898
877-658-8898 (Spanish)
www.nhpco.org

Caring Connections (from the National Hospice and Palliative
    Care Organization)
www.caringinfo.org

Hospice
www.hospicenet.org

See also these resources listed in General Eldercare on pages
262–263:
AARP
National Alliance for Caregiving
Family Caregiver Alliance
Strength for Caring
Since You Care Guides

Services and Professionals

To find a geriatric care manager:
National Association of Professional Geriatric Care Managers
1604 N. Country Club Road
Tucson, AZ 85716-3102
520-881-8008
www.caremanager.org

For legal matters:
National Senior Citizens Law Center
85 S. Washington, Suite 316
Seattle, WA 98104
877-745-1440
www.nsclc.org

National Academy of Elder Law Attorneys
1604 N. Country Club Road
Tucson, AZ 85716
520-881-4005
www.naela.org

A nonprofit that advises on Medicare and health care access:
Center for Medicare Advocacy
PO Box 350

Willimantic, CT 06226
800-262-4414
www.medicareadvocacy.org

For information on abuse and ways to report suspected abuse:
National Center on Elder Abuse
Center for Community Research and Services
University of Delaware
297 Graham Hall
Newark, DE 19716
302-831-3525
Helpline: The Eldercare Locator 800-677-1116
www.ncea.aoa.gov

See also these resources listed under Home Care on page 265:
National Adult Day Services Association
CAPS Directory, National Association of Home Builders
Meals on Wheels Association of America
National Center on Senior Transportation

ACKNOWLEDGMENTS

A host of scholars, leaders, and authorities—gerontologists, social workers, economists, sociologists, public policy analysts, industry executives, directors of advocacy organizations and senior service agencies—shared their knowledge with me in extensive interviews. I am grateful to Richard Johnson and Brenda Spillman of the Urban Institute, Lynn Feinberg and Donna Schempp of the Family Caregiver Alliance, Gail Hunt of the National Alliance for Caregiving, Suzanne Mintz of the National Family Caregivers Association, and Elizabeth Clemmer.

At AARP, I appreciated the help and wisdom of Susan Reinhard, Elinor Ginzler, Rhonda Richards, Susan Lutz, and Nancy Wood. At the American Association of Homes and Services for the Aging, I relied on Robyn Stone and Peter Notarstefano, Majd Alwan of AAHSA's Center for Aging Services Technologies, and Sarah Mashburn. Thanks to Janet Wells and Alice Hedt of NCCNHR, the National Citizens' Coalition for Nursing Home Reform; Joshua Wiener of RTI International; David Ekerdt at the University of Kansas Gerontology Center; Catherine Hawes of Texas A&M University; Charlene Harrington at the University of California, San Francisco; Karen Love at the Center for Excellence in Assisted Living; Rose Marie Fagan of the Pioneer Network; and Barbara Moscowitz at the Massachusetts General Hospital Geriatric Medicine Unit.

And Sheryl Zimmerman and Philip Sloane at the University of North Carolina, Chapel Hill; Mary St. Pierre at the National Association for Home Care and Hospice; Robert Schoeni at the University of Michigan; geriatric care manager Suzanne Modigliani in Brookline, Massachusetts; Donald Schumacher and Stephen Connor of the National Hospice and Palliative Care Organization; Andrea Cohen and Susan Fienberg of HouseWorks in Newton, Massachusetts; and authors Sharon Graham Niederhaus and John L. Graham.

For favors and assistance, thanks to Rosanne Zabka of the Hospital and Healthcare Compensation Service, Paul Williams of the Assisted Living Federation of America, Patricia Walker of the Gerontological Society of America, Gene Coffey of the National Senior Citizens Law Center, Ann Krauss of the National Association of Professional Geriatric Care Managers. And to Joan Butler at Minuteman Senior Services in Burlington, Massachusetts; and David Kyllo, Lisa Gelhaus, and Donna Doneski at the National Center for Assisted Living.

I'm particularly grateful to Barbara Moscowitz, Donna Schempp, Karen Love, Robyn Stone, Stephen Connor, and Regina Bodnar for taking the considerable time to review—or, more accurately, listen to—sections of the manuscript and offering their insight, corrections, and perspective.

As I researched and reported each chapter, people who led organizations and programs for the elderly were open, cooperative, and generous with their time. I'm indebted to Bill Millanes and the staff of Arden Courts in West Orange, New Jersey; to Joe Romano of the Veterans Memorial Home in Vineland, New Jersey; to Jessica Cantor at SAGE Eldercare in Summit, New Jersey; and to Richard Rothstein and Lainie Messina of the Visiting Nurse Service of New York. Geriatric care manager Laura Murray of Ghent, New York, was extremely helpful.

In Massachusetts, thanks to Nancy Shapiro and the staff and residents of Goddard House in Brookline, Louise Rachin at Providence House in Brighton, and ace organizer Judy Hersh of All Together Now in Newton.

In New Jersey, I'm very obliged to Joan Rubin-Kritz, Carol Geraci, and Rick Goldstein, and the staff and residents of Greenwood House, an excellent nursing home in Ewing. And to former residents Evelyn Nade and Perry Albert and their children, Karen Cohen and Toni Albert. And to my old Millville friend Eileen Abrams Wolf for making the introductions.

In Maryland, my thanks to Regina Bodnar and the extraordinary staff at the former Hospice of Baltimore, now called Gilchrist Hospice Care, affiliated with the Greater Baltimore Medical Center.

A cadre of friends listened to me muse, moan, curse, and exult over the two and a half years I worked on this project. Peg Rosen, Dale Russakoff, and Betsy Schwartz helped me locate families to interview. Emily Thayer Campbell, Judith Goleman and Neal Bruss, and Bob Thompson and Deborah Johnson lent me their guest rooms—multiple times—and were openhanded with support and companionship.

Glenn Frankel, my favorite former boss and a consummate journalist, read the entire manuscript and made his usual gentle and invaluable suggestions.

My supersearcher friend Mary Ellen Bates, of Bates Information Services in Longmont, Colorado, dug up the reams of research that inform this book. In return, she asked only that I make a contribution to a worthy organization. The U.S. Fund for UNICEF and I are both beneficiaries of her generosity.

Agent Richard Abate took on this project with enthusiasm, editor Karen Murgolo of Springboard Press gave it a home, and agent

Andrea Barzvi of ICM shepherded it thereafter. Rachel Bennett helped with transcribing and other tasks.

Jon Katz and Emma Span have been in my corner all through this long process.

At heart, *When the Time Comes* is a series of family stories. Some children and parents are unnamed or play subsidiary roles, but the time they spent talking with me was very useful, and I appreciate it. Thanks, Robin Langer, Sheelah Ward, Linda Rosati, Nancy Gerber, Inna Shames, Louise Price, Kate Waldron, Beverly Lazar Davis, Susan Yemin and Judah Tiktin, Becky and Elizabeth Wetzel, Judith and Sally Eisenberg.

Especially, I am grateful beyond reckoning to those families who permitted me to follow them through difficult and painful transitions, who shared their thoughts and emotions, who opened their lives to a stranger with a notebook. Over many months, though strained and exhausted, they never told me to go away and leave them alone, never said that some question was none of my business. They wanted their stories told, in hopes that others would benefit from their experiences, and I hope I have done those stories justice.

Thank you, Marla Shachtman and Doris Levy. Shirley Grill, Anita Appel, and Dora Appel. Ilze Earner, Hans Betins, and Milda Betins. Peg Sprague, Fred Wunderlich, and Margaret Wunderlich. Paul, Steve, and John Dutton. Sari G. and Henry B. Joel and Marlene Gordon and Pauline Gordon. Patricia Marshall and Paul Hardaway. Debbie Mueller and Dolores Noto.

ABOUT THE AUTHOR

PAULA SPAN spent much of her career at the *Washington Post*, first as the New York–based correspondent for the Style section, then as a staff writer for the *Washington Post Magazine*. She has also written for the *Philadelphia Inquirer*, the *Boston Globe*, the *Wall Street Journal*, *USA Today*, *New York Magazine*, *Newsweek*, *Glamour*, *Good Housekeeping*, *Ms.*, *Esquire*, *Parenting*, a number of city magazines, and other publications. She is currently a contributing writer for the *Washington Post Magazine*, writes for the *New York Times*, and teaches at the Columbia University Graduate School of Journalism.